EXPLORING

THE

ALAMO
LEGENDS

EXPLORING
THE
ALAMO
LEGENDS

Wallace O. Chariton

Wordware Publishing, Inc.

 **REGIONAL DIVISION**

Library of Congress Cataloging-in-Publication Data

Chariton, Wallace O.
    Exploring the Alamo legends / by Wallace O. Chariton.
        p.   cm.
    Bibliography: p.
    Includes index.
    ISBN 1-55622-255-6
    1. Alamo (San Antonio, Tex.) — Seige, 1836.   I. Title.
F390.C48   1989
976.4'03   dc20   89-5803

All inquiries for volume purchases of this book should be addressed
to Wordware Publishing, Inc., at the above address. Telephone
inquiries may be made by calling:

(214) 423-0090

Contents

Acknowledgements

As you have probably read, any author owes much to a cast of supporting players. And generally speaking, the supporting cast does not receive enough recognition. There never has been a book produced that did not involve the efforts and talents of many people — so many in fact that it is always impossible to thank everyone.

I would especially acknowledge the kind assistance of Bernice Strong of the Daughters of the Republic of Texas library at the Alamo in San Antonio. Although I was frequently a pest, Mrs. Strong always managed a smile and always knew just where to look for the little scraps of information I needed to complete a chapter.

Michael Green, archivist for the Texas state library in Austin, is another person who always seems willing to help. And I would bet there are very few people who know more about Texas than Mr. Green.

Jean Hudon of the Texas/Dallas History division of the Dallas Public library always tried to help in any way possible even though my requests were often vague and strange. She once spent a day and a half searching old maps for something called Rovia, which probably never existed in the first place.

Once the research is complete and you have a rough draft, the editor takes over and the fun begins. Barbara Forsyth is, in my book, one of the best editors around. She quickly learned to read my mind and could handle manuscript corrections with rare and insightful professionalism. She perhaps deserves the biggest thanks of all.

When the research, writing, and editing are finally complete, it takes a talented, dedicated staff to turn the manuscript into a real book. I would especially acknowledge the cooperation, understanding, and patience of the staff of Wordware Publishing, Inc. Thanks to Russ and Dianne Stultz, and Kenni "Jet" Driver for believing in the project in the first place. Then many thanks to Alan and Martha McCuller and Jana Gardner-Koch for helping make dreams come true.

And last but certainly not least, thanks to Ricci "The Rockin' Ghost" Ware, the early rock-and-roll disc jockey in San Antonio, Texas. Ricci helped kindle a love affair between me and the Alamo that continues to this day.

Special Dedication

This book is specially dedicated to the Daughters of the Republic of Texas. The fine ladies in that organization have lovingly cared for the Alamo shrine for generations and done a masterful job without the support of tax dollars. They deserve a hearty thank-you from every Texan, but instead, some meddlesome politicians would like to take control of the shrine and place it under the jurisdiction of a state agency. It is time Texans recognized the contribution of the DRT and congratulated them for a job well done. I will be the first. Thank you, ladies, for all you have done on behalf of Texas. I am sure Travis, Bowie, Bonham, Crockett and all the rest are proud of your efforts to see to it their sacrifice will never be forgotten.

Preface

This book was an accident in that it was not specifically planned. No brilliant single story idea instigated plot development, a comprehensive outline, and numerous rewrites. Instead, this book evolved from a love affair with the Alamo saga spanning more than twenty-seven years.

The story of this book actually began in the late 1950s when I was growing up in the shadow of the Alamo in San Antonio, Texas. My Sunday school teacher (who was also an early rock-and-roll disc jockey on KTSA, by the name of Ricci "The Rockin Ghost" Ware) landed a bit part in John Wayne's movie *The Alamo*. Ware's involvement in the project inspired an interest in the Alamo that has continued unabated ever since.

Then in 1961, publication of Walter Lord's *A Time to Stand*, a well-researched, authentic account of the fall of the Alamo, enticed me for the first time in my life to spend hard-earned allowance money for a book that was not full of comic characters. I was even lucky enough to obtain Mr. Lord's signature on my copy of the book during one of his autograph sessions. That book remained a prized possession until at college when I lost it in the tornado that hit Lubbock, Texas (and my living room) in 1970.

If the truth were known, I had an ulterior motive for buying Lord's book. I was working on a term paper and the subject was, you guessed it, the Alamo. The newspaper ads promoted *A Time to Stand* as the best book ever on the Alamo, so I assumed it would be all I needed as reference for my paper. Since the libraries did not yet have the book, I bit the bullet and redirected my comic-book funds. It was a sacrifice I was willing to make if it would help me write the paper with a minimum of pain and grief. The plan worked. The teacher favored me with a B or B+, which was some kind of record.

Of course, when the paper was complete, I no longer needed the book. Familiar with the Alamo since a youngster, I suffered from a surfeit of Alamo tradition. When you live in San Antonio, the first thing visiting relatives and friends want to do is see the Alamo shrine.

We spent so much time in the chapel of the old mission that the curator called family members by name. The last thing I needed to do was to sit around the house reading about the shrine. Yet that's what I did.

For some reason, the Lord book aroused a deep, apparently inherent, infatuation with the Alamo saga. I read *A Time to Stand* a couple more times and then moved on to Lon Tinkle's *13 Days to Glory* and John Meyers *The Alamo.* By then I was hooked; I became an Alamo junkie. I have remained under the spell of the Alamo for almost three decades.

The Alamo is, without much doubt, one of the most studied and written about events in American history. It was an epic struggle of men desiring freedom from tyranny and risking their all for independence. Any time brave men make such a heroic stand, the sure product is romance. And the by-products of romance are mystery and intrigue.

As far as the Alamo is concerned, permanent intrigue seems to be the destiny of the aged shrine. After the fall of the Alamo in 1836, the remaining buildings sat vacant for a time until taken over by troops of the U. S. Army who used the structure as a quartermaster depot. When the army moved out, merchants moved in and for many years the Alamo—one of the dearest shrines in all of American history—served variously as a warehouse, clothing store, and even as a grocer's depot where beer, wine, and spirits were sold. As the twentieth century approached, the Alamo was again vacated and left to further decay. Incredibly, had it not been for the patriotic actions of Adina de Zavala and Clara Driscoll, the old church probably would have been demolished and some glass shrouded hotel would rise into the Texas sky on the very spot where so many died so long ago.

When the state of Texas finally recognized the irreplaceable value of the shrine and took control of what was left of the Alamo, state leaders had the foresight to place control of the structure in the capable hands of the Daughters of the Republic of Texas. For several generations the Daughters have done a tremendous job in maintaining the integrity and reverence of the shrine. But now, incredibly some special interest groups and meddlesome politicians are trying to launch a movement to wrestle control of the Alamo away from the Daughters. Apparently that group of grand ladies is guilty of quietly going about their business while working hard not to be caught up in the strangulation of bureaucratic red tape. Somehow the thought of the Alamo being under the jurisdiction of the Parks and Wildlife Department of Texas is disconcerting.

For the students of Texas history, the mystery and intrigue of the Alamo saga goes far beyond the matter of who should control the shrine. The fact is the Alamo saga is a hotbed of perplexing questions and intriguing, unexplained legends that cry out for investigation. Using applied logic, common sense, and some serious, unrelenting research, I have moved in and out of the Alamo shadows searching for answers to questions that may never be answered to the satisfaction of all.

In the spirit of true investigative journalism, I did my best to maintain an unbiased objectivity because, after all, my mission was to seek the truth wherever it might lie. However, as a fifth-generation Anglo-Texan, there were some issues where my almost inherent bias rose to the surface despite my best efforts to prevent it. When considering such questions as, Did Davy Crockett surrender? Did Travis draw the famous line? and Did Travis and Bowie commit suicide? I must confess to a secret desire that my research would prove the traditional Texas versions correct.

Generations of Texans have grown up believing Crockett died fighting to the end, that Travis did draw the line, and neither Travis nor Bowie would have ever considered taking his own life. Admittedly, many of the traditional beliefs about the events in the Alamo are based largely on Anglo versions of what happened. Recently, however, a new wave of research, based largely on the Mexican versions, is making its way through the literary works. Unfortunately, many of the modern researchers using the Mexicans versions are making the same mistakes that Anglos did for generations—they are not considering all the evidence and they are not attempting, as any true researcher should, to impeach their own evidence.

In an attempt to rise above such controversy, I tried to fully explore both sides on any issue. Whenever possible, I have presented all the evidence uncovered so the reader can follow the logical sequence used to derive any conclusion. It must be pointed out that all conclusions are my own and all are based solely on the evidence presented. When my natural bias showed through, I took special care to present as much evidence as possible to allow you to make up your own mind.

In addition to the more traditional questions, I used my applied logic and common sense to address many of the lesser known but equally interesting Alamo questions such as: Did Sam Houston order James Bowie to blow up the Alamo? What's the true story of Louis Rose and his supposed escape from the fortress? What caused the fall of the Alamo? What is the truth about Susanna Dickinson, the lady who survived the Alamo massacre? How many men died in the final battle? What happened to James C. Neill, the real Alamo commander? In some cases, the absolute answers to these questions are left to conjecture but, hopefully, enough information has been provided to allow you to draw your own conclusion, whether or not your opinion agrees with mine. I have presented the results of my investigations with the hope that you will be entertained and challenged by the findings.

You are welcome to respond to any material presented, either to agree or disagree. Write to the author in care of Wordware Publishing, Inc., 1506 Capital Avenue, Plano, Texas 75074. All correspondence will be promptly answered. If you want to challenge any of my conclusions, please include specific historical references so I can check them and properly respond.

I sincerely hope you enjoy this book and I would enjoy hearing what you think of my conclusions. If you have ever enjoyed the work the Daughters of the Republic of Texas have done in maintaining the Alamo, please tell your congressman today. Don't ever forget to Remember the Alamo!

Wallace O. Chariton
Plano, Texas

Unless we could be united, had we not better be quiet, and settle down for awhile? There is now no doubt but that a central government will be established. What will Texas do in that case? . . . I do not know the minds of the people upon the subject; but if they had a bold and determined leader, I am inclined to think they would kick against it . . . General Cos writes that he wants to be at peace with us; and he appears to be disposed to cajole and soothe us. Ugartechea does the same . . . God knows what we are to do! I am determined, for one, to go with my countrymen; *right or wrong, sink or swim, live or die, survive or perish,* I am with them!

William B. Travis to James Bowie,
San Felipe de Austin, July 30, 1835

Sam Houston
and the Alamo Conspiracy

It appears the Alamo saga had its own little "Watergate" type intrigue involving no less a figure than General Sam Houston. The central question in this possible intrigue is: Did Sam "Jacinto" Houston really order James Bowie to blow up the Alamo, or did Sam Houston offer that to preclude the finger of blame for the disaster from being pointed his way?

Houston certainly said he ordered the Alamo destroyed and the garrison abandoned. In a speech before the United States Congress in 1859, Houston said in part:

> While at Goliad, he [referring to himself as then commander-in-chief of the Texas Army] sent an order to Colonel Neill, who was in command of the Alamo, to blow up that place and fall back to Gonzales, making that a defensive position, which was supposed to be the furthest boundary the enemy would ever reach.
>
> This was on the 17th of January. That order was secretly superseded by the Council; and Col. Travis, having relieved Col. Neill, did not blow up the Alamo. . . .[1]

Sam Houston, shown in a rather sinister pose. The flowing style he used for his signature has led some to believe he actually wrote "I am Houston." (*Courtesy of the Archives Division of the Texas State Library in Austin.*)

Houston also wrote that he gave the order. On January 30, 1860, in a letter answering a lady about whether or not her brother had died in the Alamo, Houston said, "I sent him with Bowie and Bonham from Goliad to the Alamo, with an express to blow up the Alamo, on the 17th of Jany. 1836."[2]

Nonetheless, the evidence seems to indicate there might be more to the story, and therein lies the mystery. Call it Alamogate.

Even though Sam Houston was commander in chief of the meager Texas army at the time the Alamo fell, he was not accused of complicity in the loss of the men and the garrison. Instead, he went on to become a legendary hero known as the man who saved Texas from the Mexicans. His heroics and contributions to the state live on in the pages of Texas history and there is no intent here to change that. But in a more modern context, were all the evidence considered, Houston might be called before a court martial to answer for various inconsistencies in his part of the Alamo saga.

Since Sam has long since taken refuge in the history books, we can examine only what evidence remains. Based on that evidence, it appears the general ought to face charges on two counts. Count one is the charge of lying as to his specific orders concerning the Alamo, and count two is the charge of conspiring to cover-up his involvement. The evidence follows; you be the jury.

Any jury asked to make a decision needs to know the whole story, and this one actually begins in early December, 1835. A small rag-tag army of Texas sympathizers under General Edward Burleson succeeded in storming San Antonio and forcing Santa Anna's brother-in-law, General Martin Perfecto de Cos, to surrender. To save his hide, Cos agreed to vacate the Alamo, the village, and supposedly, the entire province of Texas. History shows he did not quite carry through with that last part as he returned to help Santa Anna retake the Alamo three months later.

The winning of the first battle of the Alamo was preceded by small victories at Mission Concepcion and at Gonzales where the Mexicans were challenged to "Come And Take It" when they demanded the town's people relinquish their one little pitiful cannon. So, by early

December of 1836, the army of Texans was on an undefeated roll and feeling frisky, perhaps unbeatable.

Even before the taking of the Alamo, a wild-eyed
scheme had been circulating about the Texas army's taking
the war onto Mexican soil by attacking Matamoros, just
across the Rio Grande. Once Cos had been soundly
defeated, the prospects of a Matamoros expedition seemed
even more favorable. The idea was to launch an offensive
and catch the Mexicans off guard. It was reasoned, perhaps correctly, that any reprisal would then come against
Matamoros, and while Santa Anna was busy with that
chore, the rest of Texas would have more time to prepare a
proper welcome should the dictator ever decide to invade
Texas proper. It was a plan that might have worked and
could have changed the course of history. But it never
happened.

Sam Houston did not necessarily favor the expedition.
He felt the success of the Texas revolt might hinge on the
cooperation of friendly Mexican liberals who disliked the
prospects of a dictator as much as the Anglos, and he felt
an unprovoked raid into Mexico might cost Texas that
cooperation. But Sam was a man who could take orders.
When Henry Smith, the governor, ordered Houston to
proceed with the Matamoros expedition, the general
turned to his old friend James Bowie.

On December 17, 1835, Houston wrote to Bowie, "I
have the honor to direct that, in the event you can obtain
the services of a sufficient number of men for the purpose,
you will forthwith proceed on the route to Matamoros,
and, if possible, reduce the place and retain possession
until further orders."[3] No way Bowie could have mis-
understood those orders if he had gotten them. The
problem was, he was in transit between posts and did not
get word of his assignment for almost two weeks. Consequently, nothing was done. That is, nothing was done
by Bowie.

At that particular time, the governing body of Texas was
a general council comprised of elected delegates from
around the province. The council was certainly in favor of
the expedition, and when nothing much was getting done,
they decided to take matters into their own hands.
Accordingly, they suggested Francis W. Johnson, then

James Bowie, from an original oil painting. Benjamin West, the artist often credited for the portrait, died in England in 1820 after a sixty-six year absence from the United States. The painting was probably done by George P. A. Healy for an early book illustration. *(Photo courtesy of the Archives Division of the Texas State Library in Austin.)*

commander of the volunteer force at San Antonio de Bexar, organize and lead the expedition.

Johnson took the suggestion as gospel and set the wheels in motion. He looted the Alamo of much needed supplies and ordered two hundred men to march toward Goliad with Mexico as their ultimate destination. Johnson then left James C. Neill in command of the hundred or so men who remained in the Alamo and headed for San Felipe de Austin to parley with the council.

The first week in January 1836 was an exciting time in San Felipe. Johnson, the council's man, arrived to inform all that the expedition was underway. This presumptuous action angered the governor who felt Johnson acted too independently. Then Bowie showed up to get his long overdue orders, and he quickly informed the council he intended to follow through as Sam Houston had directed. So, while the council, the governor, and Johnson argued the issue, Bowie slipped out of town and headed for Goliad to see if he could find the means to carry out his orders. Eventually, the governor tried to dismiss the council, who, in turn, impeached the governor; and for all practical purposes, by January 17, 1836, there was no government in Texas.

Sam Houston re-enters the story when he joined Bowie in Goliad in mid-January. By that time, he was certain he wanted no part of the Matamoros expedition. To make matters worse, an urgent dispatch arrived from Bexar informing the general of the appalling conditions left behind by Johnson when he beat a hasty exit and took two-thirds of the men with him. Houston was dismayed, to say the least, but he felt something had to be done for Bexar. Since the general had no money or provisions for the post, he sent the next best thing, the famous James Bowie.

On January 17, Houston wrote Governor Smith to explain the action. He said, "I have ordered the fortifications in the town of Bexar to be demolished, and if you should think well of it, I will remove all the cannon and other munitions of war to Gonzales and Copano, blow up the Alamo, and abandon the place, as it will be impossible to keep up the Station with volunteers, the sooner I can be authorized the better it will be for the country."[4] With those instructions, Bowie marched to the Alamo. As history shows, the garrison was not abandoned, the Alamo was not blown up, and Bowie died with the rest when the fortress was overrun on Sunday, March 6, 1836.

One point about Houston's letter of January 17 cries out to be examined. The general clearly says *he* has ordered the fortifications of the town of Bexar to be demolished, but evidence exists to suggest he might have taken this idea from none other than F. W. Johnson, the architect of the Matamoros expedition and former commander of the volunteers in the Alamo. On January 3, fourteen days before Houston wrote his letter, Johnson himself wrote to the general council. In part he said,

> I have ordered all the guns from the town into the Alamo and the fortifications in the town to be destroyed.[5]

When Houston wrote his letter, he was in Goliad where many of Johnson's men were located. Because of the similarities of the words and the intent, it seems very suspicious that Houston would duplicate exactly the order given by Johnson. Is it not possible someone told the general of Johnson's orders and Houston then jumped on the band wagon to make himself look better as a commander in chief?

General Sam quickly found himself in a Texas-sized squabble with the council. Johnson was acting like a commander and proceeded with the Matamoros plans although Houston felt strongly that the expedition should be abandoned. By the end of the month, the general had been relieved of command and strongly censured by the advisory committee that was acting in place of the full council. Houston subsequently received a furlough; he issued a scalding rebuttal in his own defense and departed for a month-long sojourn among the Indians to treat for peace. James Bowie and the men of the Alamo were left in the breach of history waiting for orders from a governor no longer in power and a deposed commander who was long gone.

Houston returned to the white man's world on February 29, six days after Santa Anna laid siege to the Alamo, and just in time for the constitutional convention which convened on March 1, 1836. On March 2, independence was declared; on March 4, Houston was confirmed as major general in command of the army;[6] on March 6, Travis' last plea for help arrived, and Houston was ordered to depart at once to organize an army and go to the aid of the men in the Alamo. As Houston rode out of Washington on March 6, Santa Anna's funeral pyres were heating up in San Antonio, and the bodies of more than 180 brave men, including Bowie, were unceremoniously cremated.

It took Houston an incredible five days to reach Gonzales, a length of time that seems to indicate he was in no particular hurry, even though time was precious. Shortly after his arrival, two Mexicans arrived with dramatic news. The Alamo had fallen; all the men were gone; seven survivors had tried to surrender and were murdered; all the bodies were denied Christian burial and burned. It was horrible, disheartening news, but apparently it was true. No signal shots had been heard from the Alamo for forty-eight hours, and Travis had said he would fire three blasts per day as long as the garrison held out. Official confirmation of the fall arrived in Gonzales on March 13, with Susanna Dickinson[7] and her daughter, survivors of the carnage. They were spared by Santa Anna so that they might spread the word of his glorious victory among the Anglos. Clearly, had the Alamo been destroyed and the men moved to Goliad, they would have lived to fight another day.

Historians have long argued over whether Houston actually ordered the Alamo destroyed. If, in fact, he issued any written orders, they did not survive the massacre. The only record uncovered that suggests Houston issued written orders to James C. Neill, then commander of the Alamo, is the mention he made in the 1860 letter to the lady about her brother. Houston does say that Bowie and Bonham were sent "with an express." (In 1836, *express* was often used to mean letter or written correspondence.) However, since at that time carbon paper and copy machines were yet to be invented, it was also customary for persons issuing official letters, or expresses, to make a duplicate copy for their personal files. No such duplicate of a letter to Neill ordering him to blow up the Alamo, or anything else, can be found among Houston's papers.

More than likely, since Bowie was at hand, Houston simply gave him verbal instructions and then advised the governor of what he had done in writing. The general lived for twenty-seven years after the fall of the Alamo, and when asked about the order, it is said he invariably replied that he had ordered the Alamo blown up. It's almost surprising his dying words weren't, "I ordered the Alamo blown up."

At the heart of this issue is the discrepancy between what he wrote and what he said. In his dispatch to the governor on the day Bowie left, he clearly indicated the decision to blow up the Alamo would be the governor's. But many feel he had privately ordered Bowie to go ahead and blow it up. Fans of that possibility point to a letter Houston wrote on March 15, two days *after* he had confirmation of the disaster, in which he said, "Our forces must not be shut up in forts, where they can neither be supplied with men nor provisions. Long aware of this fact, I directed, on the 16th of January last that the artillery should be removed and the Alamo blown up. . . ."[8] The General Council apparently felt that's what he had done, for on January 30, they complained he had ordered the destruction of all defenses and the garrison abandoned. Houston had no chance to respond since he was on his way to the Indians for treaty talks.

No less an authority than Walter Lord concluded that Bowie was ordered to set the charges that would have changed history and saved his neck at the same time. Lord, who did a monstrous amount of research for his excellent work *A Time To Stand*, apparently reached his conclusion based on the letter of March 15 and the reaction of the council. He may be correct. However, taking nothing away from Lord or anyone else who has reached that same conclusion, it appears possible that Houston lied about the orders to Bowie in order to cover up any responsibility on his part for the loss of the men, the loss of the cannons, and what easily could have been the loss of the freedom of Texas.

As to charge one in this hypothetical court martial, you, the jury, are asked to consider whether or not Sam Houston lied to the people of Texas about his specific orders concerning the disposition of the Alamo. The evidence consists entirely of testimony given by actual participants in the Texas revolution.

The bell cow in the herd of evidence against Sam has to be the letter he wrote on January 17, 1836. He clearly says the fortifications in the town were ordered destroyed, a directive which makes sense since there were not enough men to protect both the town and the mission. But as for the rest of the orders, he just as clearly says to the governor, "if you think well of it." He goes on to say that he will march to Refugio Mission, "where I will await orders from your Excellency." No mistake, he was asking for orders, not giving orders.

In the same letter, Houston also advised the governor that he was ordering Captain Phillip Dimitt to, "raise 100 more men and march to Bexar forthwith." If James Bowie had been ordered to blow up the Alamo, why send in more men?

Two months, almost to the day, after he sent Bowie to San Antonio, Houston claimed he had long been aware that men in forts could not be supplied, which is why Bowie was to blow up the fort and hightail it. If indeed he thought that at the time, how is it possible he did not mention that little tidbit of information to the governor? He did ask the governor for a quick reply, and if Houston had really wanted the Alamo blown up, then surely any thoughts he had about the inadvisability of forts would have helped sway the governor to act rapidly.

If that were his position on forts in mid-January, he had certainly done an about-face since December 15, 1835. On that date, he wrote in a letter to D. C. Barrett that he wanted a field officer in San Antonio and, "I also design the employment of an Engineer, and to have the fortifications and defenses of the place improved." He went on to implore that fifty to one hundred men be stationed at La Bahia [Goliad] and that the port of Copano should have the main force and that, "Refugio Mission will probably be the best situation for a force to be stationed." He finished the letter with a postscript saying, "Engineers for the different stations will be indispensably necessary for the construction of works, as well as for the selection of sites and the designs necessary."9

About a week later, on December 21, 1836, Houston ordered James C. Neill to take command of San Antonio. In his letter to Neill, Houston spells out several things he wants accomplished, such as reports on men and munitions. He also said, ". . . you will immediately detail some capable officer to assist in fortifying the place in the best manner possible."[10]

Old Sam sure sounded sold on forts, and since no attacks of any kind occurred between December 21, 1835, and January 17, 1836, what could possibly have changed his mind? The fact is, during that time frame, very little in the way of war was going on except among the Texans themselves over the Matamoros expedition. Houston was more worried about Johnson's trying to take command than he was about forts. It is highly suspect to believe Houston was aware of the inadvisability of forts on January 17, as he later stated.

More damaging evidence against Houston's "long aware" contention can be found in his letter of January 30, 1836, to the governor. The general was preparing to leave on furlough to treat with the Indians, and he took time to write the longest, most detailed letter of the Texas Independence period. In the letter, Houston talked of his orders to Bowie but made no mention of blowing anything up. He said, "An express reached me from Lieutenant Colonel Neill, of Bexar, of an expected attack from the enemy in force. I immediately requested Colonel James Bowie to march with a detachment of volunteers to his relief."[11] What happened to "ordered him to blow up the Alamo"?

Since the letter of January 30, 1836 was to be his last for some time, perhaps a month, Houston went into great detail on many subjects, but nowhere does he mention his thoughts of abandoning the forts since they could not be supplied. What he did talk about was the sad state of affairs the government was in and what a farce the Matamoros thing had become. His mind was on many things other than strategic possibilities of forts.

The most damaging evidence comes from, of all places, James Bowie himself. On February 2, James Bowie wrote Governor Smith a most interesting letter. He acknowledges that he was sent to Bexar after Houston received Neill's call for help. He goes on to say Bexar is, "our most important post" and, "The salvation of Texas depends in great measure in keeping Bexar out of the hands of the enemy." He concludes that, "Col. Neill & Myself have come to the conclusion that we will rather die in these ditches than give it up to the enemy. These citizens deserve our protection and the public safety demands our lives rather than to evacuate this post to the enemy."[12]

If Bowie's orders had been simply to blow up the place and leave, that would not have taken two weeks. But if his orders had been exactly as Houston wrote to the governor—to remove fortifications from town and await further orders from the governor—that would explain his letter. He had come to the conclusion that Bexar must be maintained, so he wanted to convey that feeling in case the governor might decide to order the place blown up, as Houston suggested. If James Bowie had been ordered to blow up the Alamo, why didn't he specifically say he was not going to do that?

The final exhibit on the charge of lying comes from a letter James Fannin wrote on February 4, 1836. He said that a courier had arrived with news that Houston had, "recommended to Lt. Col. Neill to remove all the cannon from that post, to Victoria & Gonzales, except barely enough to protect the Alamo—but to maintain his position until further orders. . . ."[13] We do not know the source of the news and some of the facts are not correct, but the spirit of the message agrees with Houston's written version of the orders—"remove cannons from the post [the town had some cannons mounted on the roof tops] and maintain position until further orders." Most certainly, if the actual orders had been "blow up the Alamo" that would have been big news that would have spread rapidly through the rumor mill.

In fairness to Sam Houston, Fannin's letter also gives a clue as to what might have happened. After, "maintain his position until further orders," Fannin added, "or an enemy of a superior force rendered it a matter of necessity to make a retreat." Based on that flimsy evidence, some might maintain that what Houston did was order the town's fortifications removed and the cannons relocated to the Alamo and then, if the enemy drew near, to makes a retrograde movement, which in the parlance of the 1836 Texas frontier meant retreat. If those were his intentions, then Sam's ability to command should be the question in this court martial.

General Sam Houston knew very well the conditions in the Alamo. He knew they had no wagons or carts with which to remove the artillery, and he knew most of the men were on foot. Houston must have known that if an enemy of superior force made retreat necessary, there would not have been any time or way to save the artillery—there probably would not have been time to spike the cannons or drop them in the river—in which event the largest concentration of artillery in Texas would automatically fall into the hands of the enemy. He also must have known that Texans on foot would have been no match for the Mexican cavalry. Since Houston did not order an immediate retreat, the possibility that Bowie had secret orders to retreat in the face of the enemy seems remote at best.

Nowhere in any of his correspondence did Houston indicate his plans were for the garrison to be abandoned under any circumstance. If such were his plans, why did he not make them public, even after the fact? The only logical explanation is that such were not his orders, that he simply passed the entire matter into the hands of the governor and went on about his business with the Indians.

The second count in this hypothetical court martial that you, the jury, are asked to consider is the charge of obstruction of historical justice. As in charge one, the evidence consists of testimony from actual participants in the affairs of Texas in early 1836.

The evidence trail takes us back to Gonzales on March 11, 1836, the day Houston arrived and first learned the Alamo had fallen. He issued two dispatches that day, both to James Fannin in command at Goliad.[14] In one, he advised Fannin of what he felt had happened to the Alamo. In the second letter, he ordered the Goliad commander to fall back to Victoria. He also ordered, "Previous to abandoning Goliad, you will take the necessary measures to blow up that fortress; and do so before leaving the vicinity." Sure, five days after one fort has fallen, it's easy to put into writing that another fort, in harm's way, ought to be abandoned and blown up. There was little alternative.

Since Sam had no choice but to blow up Goliad (which was not done, by the way), he perhaps realized that had he actually *ordered* Bowie to blow up the Alamo, the men in the garrison would not have perished. That thought may have been the seed for the great lie.

A rather fanciful early woodcut of Sam Houston issuing orders, probably to his aide George Washington Hockley. The illustration originally appeared in *A Texas Scrap-Book,* compiled in 1875 by D. W. C. Baker. *(Author's collection.)*

By March 13, the seed was growing. In a letter to Collinsworth, he said, "The enclosed order to Colonel Fannin will indicate to you my convictions, that, with our small, unorganized force, we cannot maintain sieges in fortresses, in the country of the enemy. Troops pent up in forts are rendered useless; nor is it possible that we can ever maintain our cause by such policy."[15] What a revelation; men in forts are useless. It did, however, take the fall of the Alamo for that revelation to dawn on Houston; it was not something of which he been "long aware." If such had been the case, he most surely would not have hesitated to demand the Alamo be abandoned or at least to make his request to the governor much more detailed and convincing.

In the same letter, Houston began to spread some blame for the fall of the Alamo. His first target was the council and their ill-fated Matamoros adventure. He said, "The projected expedition to Matamoros, under the agency of the Council, has already cost us over two hundred and thirty-seven lives and where the effects are to end, none can foresee."[16]

On March 13, 1836, Sam Houston got official confirmation of the fall of the Alamo and, in a letter that day, he again attempted to place the blame. He said, "Colonel Fannin should have relieved our brave men in the Alamo. He had 430 men with artillery under his command, and had taken up the line of march with a full knowledge of the situation of those in the Alamo, and owing to the breaking down of a wagon abandoned the march, returned to Goliad and left our Spartans to their fate."[17] Now, hold on Sam, what happened to "blow up the Alamo"? Why didn't he blame Bowie for not following his *orders* instead of Fannin, who was never ordered to Bexar?

Later in the same letter, Houston spread more blame, "The conduct of the Council and that of their 'agent' [J. W. Fannin] has already cost us the lives of more than 230 brave men. Had it not been for that, we might have kept all the advantages which we had gained." Nowhere in any of his surviving correspondence does Houston ever actually blame Bowie for the fall of the Alamo. However, if he had been ordered to blow up the fort and withdraw and did not comply, then Bowie would have been at fault.

It seems certain Houston would have at least implied such blame somewhere.

We have now come full circle, from the beginning of the story back to March 15, 1836, when Sam Houston first put into writing that he had *ordered* James Bowie to blow up the Alamo. He also added a line in which he said, "but it was prevented by the expedition upon Matamoros, the author of all our misfortune." Matamoros prevented it! That may explain why he never blamed James Bowie, but the curious part is that the Matamoros expedition is the reason Bowie was sent to Bexar in the first place. Houston knew the fortress had been stripped and the men were ill-prepared to defend themselves. That was supposedly the reason Bowie was to blow the place up. Now, on March 15, that same excuse is used to explain why the fort was not blown up? Strange words, indeed, General Houston.

Of course, the fact is, the Matamoros expedition did prevent the evacuation of the cannons from the Alamo since all available wagons had been appropriated by Johnson and Grant. But Houston knew that at the time he first dispatched Bowie. It is also interesting to note that, after the fact, when Houston ordered Goliad destroyed, he also ordered the cannons sunk in the river if they could not be transported. So why not issue the same orders to Bowie since he knew there were no wagons to transport the cannons?

Perhaps the most curious part of the saga is why Houston waited until well after the fall of the Alamo to state, in writing, his supposed orders to Bowie? Could it be he was covering his backside? Bowie certainly was not around to dispute his story.

For two days, Houston was busy slinging arrows of blame at Fannin, Johnson, and the council. He also announced he did not believe forts were the preferable defense against Mexicans. Could it be that it dawned on him someone might suggest that if the Alamo and Bexar had been abandoned, as the general later ordered for Goliad, that the men of the Alamo might have been spared? Could it possibly be that the general concocted the claim about his order to Bowie to give himself a perfect alibi?

Perhaps Sam was afraid the people might point an accusing finger at him for not taking care of business in a proper military fashion. Perhaps some would say he should not have abandoned Texas to treat with the Indians at such a critical time. Perhaps some would say he should have personally gone to Bexar since he knew the governor and the council were at odds and for all practical purposes there was no government in Texas. Houston even said he would have gone to Bexar but he had to attend to the Matamoros thing. Might not someone say he was more interested in preserving his own command than in the disposition of the Alamo? As military leader on January 17, 1836, should he not have taken charge and thus been able to prevent the Alamo disaster by demanding the fortress be destroyed rather than meekly asking for orders from the governor?

These are questions that you, the jury, must decide. History does not tell of anyone openly blaming Houston for the fall of the Alamo. And why should it? Any and all possible charges against him could be answered with a simple lie, "I ordered James Bowie to blow up the Alamo."

The prosecution rests.

The Crown Jewel of Texas Legends

Texas, either as an independent republic or a member of the United States, has never had a monarch who wore a crown, if you do not count the beautiful young lady who annually serves as Miss Texas. Unlike the English or the French people, Texans do not have a secure vault full of crown jewels to marvel at and protect. However, for a lot of Texans, especially the old-time, staunch Texans, the heritage of the state is a sort of "crown" and the many legends from the pages of Texas history are the jewels in that crown. Many Texans look after those legend jewels as fiercely as if they were diamonds or rubies.

Perhaps the most shining jewel in that crown of heritage is the notion that all the men in the Alamo died fighting to the bitter end and taking as many Mexicans as possible with them to the hereafter. Some Texans have guarded that romantic notion with such a fierceness as to suggest that if the men did not die fighting, then the legend of the Alamo would be forever tarnished. In the old days, a fist fight inevitably resulted if a foreigner chanced to suggest a different ending for the Alamo saga.

In more modern times, however, discovery of new evidence and reexamination of old evidence suggests a different ending to the battle of the Alamo. There are now some among us, including some dyed-in-the-wool Texans, who would suggest that a handful of men survived the final onslaught, surrendered or were captured, and then were promptly executed by order of Santa Anna. That prospect alone goes against the Texas grain, but it gets worse. Some people now claim that perhaps a few—admittedly a precious few—Texans broke and ran as the final assault neared its bloody conclusion, and some may have actually survived the battle altogether. And worst yet, some people would have us believe that Davy Crockett himself survived the battle only to be executed. Is nothing sacred?

Unfortunately, much to detriment of the historical psyche of many Texans, it appears parts one and two of the Alamo survivor theory may have some validity. There is such a preponderance of evidence to suggest that some men did survive the battle, only to be executed, while still others broke and ran, that the possibilities cannot be totally ignored. But hold onto your patriotic heartstrings; there may be much more to the story.

One of the most curious aspects of the survivor story is that some information was known almost from the time Santa Anna's funeral pyres smoldered at the Alamo in San Antonio. General Sam Houston first got wind of the fall of the Alamo on March 11, 1836, when two suspected Mexican spies arrived in Gonzales with the dreadful news. In Houston's first written account of the event he said, "After the fort was carried, seven men surrendered, and called for Santa Anna and quarter. They were murdered by his order."[1]

In all probability the intelligence provided by those first spies is responsible for a considerable number of the "survivor" rumors that sprang up immediately. Many people almost certainly heard what the spies had to say and then passed it on. Certainly the information in Houston's letter would have been shared with any who would listen, so it is not surprising that, in the months which followed the fall, various accounts in newspapers around the nation contained some reference to the possibility that a few of the men surrendered and were then executed.

Over the years, however, as the story of the dramatic stand in the Alamo gained prominence, the part about possible survivors somehow slipped between the historical cracks. Maybe Texans chose to ignore any evidence of possible Mexican spies as being circumstantial hearsay.

Don Enrique Esparza who, with his mother and three brothers and sisters, was among the group of ten or more Mexicans who survived the siege of the Alamo. Esparza lived a long and full life in San Antonio. *(Courtesy of the Archives Division of the Texas State Library in Austin.)*

Maybe they simply preferred to believe their heroes died fighting because it had a more patriotic ring. Either way, generations of Texans have grown up believing, and cherishing, the notion that all the men died bravely fighting. Every time a teacher of Texas history taught that lesson, the crown jewel of Texas legends gained a little luster.

In a more modern context, new evidence has come under historical scrutiny which suggests that not all the men of the Alamo died fighting. This contradictory evidence appears in translated accounts of Mexican soldiers who participated in the battle for the Alamo. As many as seven of those soldiers, of various rank, left behind written accounts of the events that claim some of the Texans did survive the initial slaughter. Although the accounts vary somewhat in particulars and believability, sufficient similarities exist to make it difficult for even the staunchest of Texans to ignore the possibilities.

Among the Mexican reports generally considered most reliable, and most damaging to the Alamo mystique, is the account of Lieutenant Jose Enrique de la Pena. He said, "Some seven men who survived the general carnage, and under protection of General Castrillon, were brought before Santa Anna."[2] Ramon Martinez Caro, personal secretary to Santa Anna said Castrillon found five men hiding and brought them to El Presidente.[3] Sergeant Francisco Becerra claimed two men, Travis and Crockett, survived and were killed, although he later admitted he might have been mistaken about the names and his account of the events is so self-serving it could be, and usually is, labeled "horse feathers."[4]

Such information is, understandably, hardly palatable to many Texans. The fact that the two Mexican accounts[5] considered most reliable do not confirm the surrender theory but rather indicate the Texans were "discovered," captured, and then executed is considered of little consequence. Given a choice, many, if not most Texans, would probably prefer to cling to the fought-till-the-end theory.

Unfortunately, with so many supposed witnesses saying practically the same thing, it is difficult to dismiss the possibility that some men survived. In reality, from this distance, it seems safe to assume some of the men did manage to live through the final assault only to be slaughtered. But in many ways Texas history is like an ocean: what you see on the surface is not necessarily an indication of what lies beneath.

The Mexican accounts of the assault survivors all seem to indicate that the Texans were found or "discovered" in one of the rooms adjoining the Alamo compound. Though usually not stated specifically, the implication is generally that the men were hiding trying to save themselves, something that might reek of cowardice, an unsavory suggestion that would really irritate Texans. The central question then becomes why were the men in the rooms instead of on the field of battle?

From a military standpoint the answer to that question appears very simple. When the Mexicans began pouring over the walls in a killing frenzy, the Alamo defenders would have had no cover at all from the enemy fire except inside some of the adjoining rooms. In all probability, many, if not most, of the remaining Alamo defenders withdrew to the rooms seeking some cover from which to continue the fight. In battle logic, seeking cover in the face of a far superior enemy would seem a natural a reaction. On the other hand, the romantic theory that every man would have simply stood his ground and fought to the last is preposterous.[6]

Naturally, the complication to the scenario that the men of the Alamo withdrew to side rooms is that surely the Mexican soldiers would have promptly followed to continue their leader's war of extermination. How is it possible then that at least five and perhaps as many as seven men went undetected until the fighting was virtually over?

There is one probability, generally totally ignored by historians and researchers, that could have a profound effect on the issue of assault survivors. What if some of the Alamo defenders were not fit for combat on that fateful Sunday morning in March, 1836? What if a handful of the men, say five or six or seven, were ill or recovering from previous wounds and thus could not help in the fighting? That, as they say, might open another can of worms concerning possible survivors. And there is some evidence to suggest that might just be the case.

On January 6, 1836, James C. Neill, the commandant of the Alamo garrison, wrote to the governing council that he had 104 men.[7] On January 14, Neill wrote, "I have not more than seventy-five men fit for duty."[8] It seems clear he has other men who are not fit for duty. On January 18, Green B. Jameson, the engineer for the post, wrote in a letter to Sam Houston, "We now have 114 men counting the officers, the sick and the wounded, which leaves us about 80 efficient men. . . ."[9] If Jameson's figures are anywhere near correct, then a few weeks before the final assault, more than thirty men in the Alamo were not "efficient" due to illness or wounds. It would not require an elastic imagination to accept the possibility that some of those men still were not "efficient" on the morning of the attack.

In Lieutenant Colonel Neill's official muster roll of Alamo defenders, eight men are listed as being sick, wounded, or simply "in hospital."[10] Although this list is often thought to have been dated February 11 (the day Colonel Neill left the Alamo), it probably was written much earlier, about mid-January, since the names Bowie, Bonham, Crockett, and Travis are not on the list and yet they were known to have been in the Alamo on February 11. Still, the list is further evidence that various men in the Alamo, at one time or another, were unfit for combat.[11]

Susanna Dickinson, wife of Captain Almaron Dickinson, survived the final assault and lived to tell the story of the fall. Although much of what Susanna said was probably the product of inspired editorial prompting, she did leave behind a few clues concerning the possibility that some of the men were still incapacitated from old wounds on March 6, 1836. In 1881, after Susanna visited the Alamo for the first time in forty-five years, she gave an interview to a reporter for the *San Antonio Express*. In that report, Susanna is quoted as saying there were 160 "sound" men in the garrison. Her use of the adjective sound seems to imply that some of the troops in the fortress were not sound.[12]

In 1876, Susanna cooperated with the Texas state adjutant general, who was trying to determine exactly how many men died in the Alamo. In her statement, she said, "Among the besieged were 50 or 60 wounded ones from Cos's fight."[13] Although that number seems much too high and is probably inaccurate, the significance is that she mentioned wounded men at all. Apparently some previously wounded men were in the Alamo on the morning of the fall.[14]

Since modern miracle drugs like penicillin had not been discovered in 1836, illness and injuries often required long periods of recuperation. Bed rest of two, three, or more months was not uncommon. Thanks to the diary of Doctor J. H. Barnard,[15] we know that many of the Mexicans wounded in the assault of the Alamo were still suffering mightily several weeks later. Equally lengthy recovery periods would have been required for Texans wounded in the first siege of the Alamo in early December. It seems almost certain that some of the men were not fit for combat and thus did not participate in the defense of the mission during the final assault.

It is generally accepted that one of the defenders was indeed bedridden at the moment of truth. Almost every historian agrees that the legendary James Bowie was desperately ill—probably with typhoid pneumonia—and was unable to stand and fight with the rest of the men. Although the exact circumstances of his death are often argued about, most agree he died in bed after giving some account of himself before the enemy. Even though most of the historical press on Alamo illness deals with the great Bowie, it does not seem improbable that other defenders were also incapacitated to some degree. Perhaps, just perhaps, the Alamo defenders who were discovered and executed after the battle were sick or injured men who were unable to participate in the actual fighting.

Admittedly, there is not extensive historical evidence to support such a theory. Also, in the interest of historical accuracy, none of the Mexican accounts indicate the men who were discovered were either sick or wounded. But such a theory might help unravel the mystery of why any Texans were allowed to live long enough to be brought before Santa Anna.

We know the Mexican general was in a war of extermination, determined to rid the province of Texas of all English-speaking people. We know he flew the blood red flag and had the tune "Deguello" played, both of which indicate that no quarter would be given. Not a single Mexican soldier who attacked the Alamo had any doubt but that his commander in chief expected—demanded— that all the Texans be killed. So why were a precious few spared even for a moment?

Some of the surviving Mexican accounts seem to imply that since the attack and general carnage were basically over when the Texans were discovered, that there was no reason for the slaughter to continue. You can believe that if you like, but it does have the unmistakable ring of self-serving hogwash. We know that whatever happened, whether five or seven men were involved and whether they surrendered or were discovered, it happened very quickly after the main battle, probably even before all the fighting was over. When the surviving Texans were brought before Santa Anna, other Mexicans were surely still searching the grounds making sure all other Texans were dead. Also, a huge number of wounded Mexicans were almost certainly crying out for much needed and practically nonexistent medical attention. And yet, we are asked to believe that a sudden wave of humanity swept over a few Mexicans to inspire them to seek clemency for a handful of Texans. Hogwash does seem an applicable term.

One account of the Mexican side of the story, which is usually considered reliable, is that provided by George M. Dolson.[16] In this account, six Americans were discovered in a back room that they had defended until "defense was useless." Dolson also maintains that General Castrillon restrained his soldiers, promised the men they would be saved, and then marched them to Santa Anna.

The Dolson information is from a letter he wrote several months after the battle and is supposed to be based on his translation of an account provided by an unnamed Mexican officer captured at San Jacinto. Although there are many questions about the Dolson account, a major one is that if the Mexicans entered a back room and found the men, how did they know the Texans had defended the room until defense was useless? Perhaps that was the assumption, but if so, what possible motive could Castrillon have had for restraining his soldiers? If the Texans had put up a fight, they surely would have killed or wounded some, perhaps many, Mexicans, so why would the enemy let them live and promise they would be spared in direct contradiction to Santa Anna's orders? Such a possibility makes no logical sense at all.

The truth is, or would seem to be, that the only scenario which does make sense is that the Texans who were discovered were instantly perceived as noncombatants.

Perhaps they were found, unarmed and sick, in a hospital as suggested by Colonel Neill's muster roll. If the Mexicans deduced that the men found had not taken part in the battle and thus had not killed or wounded any of their "brothers of the heart," then possibly the Mexicans would have had a motive for seeking clemency before Santa Anna. No other possibility seems consistent with what must have been the spirit of the moment.

Naturally, such a scenario might be perceived as self-serving for the Texas side of the battle. After all, Texans who have, for generations, believed that all the men died fighting would surely be satisfied that all the able-bodied men died fighting. Under such conditions, there would be no reason for the crown jewel of Texas legends to lose its luster.

The possibility that the men who survived were non-combatants also seems to work better for the Mexican side of the affair. It would seem to be less patriotic from the Mexican point of view if one of their generals had offered to spare the lives of any Texans who had participated in the fighting. But, if that same general had humanely offered to spare noncombatants, then his actions in direct defiance of his orders would be seen as more acceptable. That possibility might also explain why some of the Mexican soldiers are said to have expressed horror that the discovered Texans were executed. Would those Mexicans have been expected to express horror at the death of a few able-bodied men after 180 others had just been killed? As for Santa Anna, the condition of the men would have been of little consequence. He probably would have ordered them killed if the Texans had been brought before him in their beds.

It appears almost certain that some Texans survived the final assault, but the legend that all men died fighting does not seem to have been unduly damaged at this point. After all, who could possibly blame sick and injured men for not fighting to the death? If, however, some able-bodied men actually abandoned the Alamo and tried to run for it, that might be a horse of a different color. Unfortunately for some devout Texans, that appears to be exactly what happened. But once again, that is not the end of the story.

Certain surviving evidence suggests that some of the able-bodied men actually broke and ran at the last moment in a desperate attempt to save their lives. Not only that, it appears some of them may have actually made their way to freedom.

In his diary entry for March 6, Colonel Juan Nepomuceno Almonte wrote that, ". . . at half past 5 the attack or assault was made, and continued until 6 A.M. when the enemy attempted in vain to fly but they were overtaken and put to the sword, and only five women, one Mexican soldier [prisoner,] and a black slave escaped instant death."[17] An unknown Mexican soldier (writing to "his brothers of the heart" while he watched the funeral pyre consume the Texans' bodies) mentioned, ". . . 257 corpses without counting those who fell in the previous thirteen days, or those who vainly sought safety in flight."[18]

Mexican Sergeant Manual Loranca provided some tantalizing details in an interview for the *Corpus Christi Free Press* in 1878. He said:

> Sixty-two Texans who sallied from the east side of the fort were received by the Lancers and all killed. Only one of these made resistance; a very active man, armed with a double barrelled gun and a single barrel pistol, with which he killed a corporal of the Lancers named Eugenio. These were all killed by the lance, except one, who enscounced himself under a bush and it was necessary to shoot him.[19]

It seems doubtful that sixty-two Texans attempted flight since that would have been a third of the entire garrison, and it is hard to imagine how that many could have broken out of the fort. Still, the fact that the sergeant mentions the incident seems to confirm that some did attempt an escape.

Santa Anna also contributes to the possibility of Texans making a break for it. In his report dictated shortly after the fall of the Alamo, the general said:

> The fortress is now in our power with its artillery stores, etc. More than six hundred corpses of foreigners were buried in the ditches and

entrenchments, and a good many, who had
escaped the bayonet of the infantry, fell in the
vicinity under the sabres of the cavalry. I can
assure your excellency that few are those who
bore to their associates the tidings of their
disaster.[20]

The general's statement is curious to the point of puz-
zlement. He clearly says six hundred foreigners were
killed, and we know that number is three times the actual
count. He also says the bodies were buried, and we know
they were burned, although he could have decided to burn
the bodies after writing the letter. He also clearly indicates
that some of the men escaped the fortress and were killed
by the cavalry patrols.

Perhaps most curious of all is the general's comment that
"few are those who bore to their associates the tidings of
their disaster." It appears Santa Anna is conceding that perhaps some of the Texans escaped. Given his penchant for
falsifying information, it is interesting and perhaps significant that the general did not boldly claim that all the
men died. It seems reasonably safe to assume if he had
even remotely thought that all the Texans had died, he
would have said so in no uncertain terms. The fact that he
did not make that assertion makes the possibility that some
Alamo defenders did survive a more believable proposition.

It is now generally accepted that Louis (or Moses) Rose
did leave the Alamo after the siege began. As shown in a
later chapter, "The Thorny Problem of Mr. Rose," there is
the very real possibility that Rose made his escape after the
fighting in the final assault began. The fact that testimony
indicates that a few of the men did break and run for their
lives supports that hypothesis. It seems extremely likely
that Rose would have been among those that ran.

Historians now believe that one man, Brigido Guerrero,
actually survived the massacre by claiming that he was a
captured Mexican soldier. In his diary entry for March 6,
1836, Almonte mentions a supposed Mexican prisoner
being spared, and Gregorio Esparza, a young boy that was
spared when the Alamo fell, tells about the same story in
his account of what happened.[21] Apparently the Bexar
county officials believed the story because Guerrero was

awarded a pension in 1878, as an Alamo survivor. It would seem that Mr. Guerreo should rank as one of the all time best Texas talkers if he first convinced the Mexicans he was a prisoner of war and then convinced the Texans he was a battle survivor.[22]

Henry Warnell is another probable Alamo survivor although he was apparently wounded making his escape and did not live long. Even though some claim Warnell died while acting as a courier for Sam Houston, strong evidence indicates that is not the case. In the General Land Office, Court of Claims Application No. 1579 dated July 30, 1858, there is a statement which reads ". . . he [Warnell] was wounded in said massacre [the Alamo] but made his escape to Port Lavaca, where he died in less than three months from the effects of said wound." Warnell apparently left no written account of his ordeal.[23]

In *A Time to Stand*, Walter Lord identifies the bare possibility that two other men might have survived. He cites an article in the *Arkansas Gazette* of March 29, 1836, as claiming two men, one severely wounded, turned up in Nacogdoches, Texas claiming "San Antonio has been retaken by the Mexicans, the garrison put to the sword—that if any others escaped the general massacre besides themselves, they were not aware of it." Lord did considerable research and concluded that the story told by these two mystery men appeared a full week before Houston's official story of the fall appeared in most other publications.[24]

The account of these two men is puzzling. If they are legitimate Alamo survivors, who were they? What happened to them? And why did they never again tell their story? Naturally, the wounded one might have died of his injuries before he could talk but what happened to the other one? Why was he so willing to talk one time and yet apparently never again opened his mouth and never bothered to write down his story?

One possible explanation is that the men may have been Alamo frauds and they may have gotten their information from none other than Louis Rose, the man who supposedly abandoned the Alamo because "he didn't want to die." The evidence that perhaps links Rose and the two men in the *Arkansas Gazette* story is very sketchy and not based on any firm foundation of fact. However, the circumstances seem to warrant giving the possibilities at least a passing glance.

When William P. Zuber first told his exotic story of Moses Rose making good his escape from the Alamo, he included a rather bizarre account of Rose encountering two men from Nacogdoches under somewhat strange circumstances. As Zuber told the story, Rose encountered the men at the first house where he stopped for aid after leaving the Alamo. Supposedly, the two men were very skeptical of Rose's story of his daring nighttime escape from San Antonio. The pair went so far as to convince the owner of the house that Rose was a total fraud since they had seen him in Nacogdoches a week earlier. The homeowner believed the two men, denounced Rose a fake, and thrust him out onto the harsh prairie without provisions. Zuber theorized the two men concocted their wild tale in an effort to get out of paying their bill of fare in the man's home. Also, according to Zuber, that experience is why Rose did not talk to anyone else about his experiences other than Zuber's parents whom he knew and trusted.[25]

It is possible that Zuber invented the story so he would have a built-in excuse to answer why Rose did not generally talk of his experiences. On the other hand, if the Zuber tale is true, the two Nacogdoches men would have had some advance information on the fall of the Alamo, thanks to Rose. If they had returned to Nacogdoches immediately, the time frame would have been about right to coincide with the newspaper article. Perhaps the men Rose encountered assumed the identity of Alamo defenders and told the Rose story as if they had lived it.

The obvious question is, Why would the men attempt such a hoax? History, of course, leaves no possible clues. There appear to be only a couple of bare possibilities. Zuber's tale of Rose's experiences makes no mention of either of the two men being wounded, and one of the men mentioned in the news item was severely wounded. If we let our imagination run wild it is not hard to conjure up the possibility that perhaps one of the men was wounded in some surreptitious manner—perhaps in the commission of a crime—and he needed an airtight alibi. Presto, the story of the fall of the Alamo came in as handy as a pocket on a shirt. Such a scenario might explain why the two never again spoke of their experiences. When dealing with unverifiable history, applying a little creative interpretation is often hard to avoid.

There is also the possibility that the two men had been on their way to the Alamo and turned back when they heard the news of the fall. Perhaps they encountered a Mexican patrol and one of the men was wounded. Perhaps the two simply did not want to admit they had never made it to the fortress, although under that interpretation, we would have to wonder why they never talked more of their experience.

It must be pointed out that there is no evidence to substantiate that the two men Rose supposedly encountered are the same two which turned up in Nacogdoches with news of the fall of the Alamo. There also is no other explanation as to who the mysterious Nacogdoches duo might have been. However, if the circumstances of the Rose story are true, it would explain the strange story in the *Gazette*. Coincidentaly, if it could ever be proved that the men were the same ones Rose met, it might prove that Rose himself did escape after the final assault began and thus would have known of the fall of the Alamo, something he would not have known about if he had left the Alamo three days before the fall as he claimed.

Based on the very slight evidence we have, it seems safe to assume that some of the Texans did take flight as the final battle drew to a close. It's a good bet that one man did escape but was wounded and soon died. Another defender, Rose, probably escaped at that time, and perhaps the Nacogdoches duo did likewise. The problem with accepting such scant evidence as fact is that one of the greatest jewels in the Texas crown of legends would be tarnished beyond polishing. Not only would Texans no longer be able to proudly proclaim that all the men died fighting, but, for goodness sake, not even all the men died. For some devout Texans such a proclamation would induce the need for smelling salts right away.

The possibility that some of the defenders took flight is not palatable to many Texans because they would assume that cowardice might have been the motive for running. Texans like to believe that their heros will stand and fight to the bitter and bloody end, and anything less is cowardice. Such a notion is, of course, pure nonsense.

The truth is, it's a miracle the men stayed as long as they did. They were tired, hungry, frustrated over the poor conditions and the lack of promised pay, and bewildered because the people of Texas did not turn out in mass to come to their aid. Their supplies and ammunition were dangerously close to being exhausted; and with the death grip the Mexicans held over the fortress, it was a certainty that no fresh supplies would be forthcoming. There was little to do but watch and wait for the end. For the besieged Texans there was no longer any doubt about what the end would be; the only question was when would it come, today, tomorrow, or the day after.

The fact that the men did not run until the final assault was underway and all hope was literally gone is testimony to their grit and gallantry. Lesser men might have tried to sneak out of the fortress like thieves in the night. But the men of the Alamo stayed and fought until fighting was no longer possible; then apparently some of them tried to save themselves. Anyone who would call such men cowards should think again. They were there in the Alamo when so many Texans were safe at home, refusing to come to the aid of the garrison. There should be very little question about who the cowards really were.

Perhaps this point could best be explained by drawing a parallel to a Texan of another age. During World War II, a young man from near Farmersville, Texas found himself in a tight spot in Germany. His platoon was pinned down by a strong force of advancing Germans. The young lieutenant ordered his squad to fall back while he held his position to direct artillery fire. He continued firing until his ammunition ran out; then he too fell back toward safety.

Instead of joining his men immediately, however, the young lieutenant jumped atop a burning tank destroyer and, using that vehicle's machine gun, continued killing Germans. When perhaps fifty of the enemy were dead or wounded, the young man again ran out of ammunition. This time he retreated all the way back to join his men and prepare for an attack. Fortunately for the Americans, the fire from the young Texan so discouraged the Germans that they broke off the attack and fell back. [26]

The story of that young Texan has a parallel with the Alamo. The lieutenant fought as long as he could and then ran for his life. Not one person has ever implied he was a

Audie Leon Murphy, the young Texan from near Farmersville
who was too small for the Marines and Navy but just right for
the Army. Heroic action during World War II earned him the
distinction of being America's most decorated hero. Audie, who
became a movie star following the war, is shown here talking to
a young admirer. *(Courtesy of the Dallas and Texas Archives of the
Dallas Public Library.)*

coward because he did not take on the Germans bare-handed and fight until he died. The men in the Alamo, by all accounts, did exactly the same thing as the young lieutenant—they fought until their ammunition was gone and all hope with it and then some made a break for it. The difference is, the young GI lived to tell his story. He even lived to star in a motion picture about his exploits. He also lived to become America's most decorated war hero, with twenty-seven medals including the Congressional Medal of Honor. His name was Audie Leon Murphy. The Texans who probably ran from the Alamo certainly found Mexican cavalry waiting and most, if not all, quickly perished. Perhaps they should each be given a medal of honor. No matter what, they should not be called cowards, and anyone doing so in the presence of a Texan ought to be prepared to duck.

It does appear that some of the popular concepts about the Alamo are based largely on legends. Perhaps the history of the Alamo should be rewritten to show that every able-bodied man fought until he could fight no more and that the disabled troops were murdered in cold blood. The scant evidence we have certainly could, and probably should, be interpreted that way, which means the crown jewel should shine on. The one question that still remains, however, is, Was Davy Crockett among the survivors of the final assault who were executed? That is a whole other story.

Crockett vs. Kilgore, Santos, et al.: Davy's Last Fight

Davy Crockett died fighting like a tiger, killing as many Mexicans as possible before he himself felt the sting of Mexican steel. For several generations of Texans (and Tennesseans), that statement is enough said on the matter. Case closed; period, paragraph. For a few people, hopefully a relatively small few, the question of how Davy died is not so simple.

At doubt here is whether Crockett was one of the Texans who survived the final assault, was captured or discovered and then executed, or as Sam Houston said, *murdered*. Surprisingly enough, it is not a new question.

Almost as soon as the smoke cleared from the battle of the Alamo, rumors sprang up as to the possibility of some of the Texans' surviving and being executed. Sam Houston heard such a report, without any reference to Crockett, in his first intelligence on the battle. Travelers arriving in New Orleans about three weeks after the fall told of Crockett's being taken alive. The *New Orleans Post Union* picked up the story and duly reported that Crockett and others had tried to surrender but were told "there was no mercy for them." The story was carried by other newspapers and eventually found its way, in various forms, into early history books.[1]

An early woodcut of David Crockett with his trusty rifle and friendly hunting dogs but without the familiar coonskin cap. The illustration originally appeared in *A Texas Scrap-Book,* complied in 1875 by D. W. C. Baker. *(Author's collection.)*

A photo taken from an early portrait of Crockett. *(Courtesy of the Daughters of the Republic of Texas Library at the Alamo.)*

As America grew and matured, however, the practice of putting the nation's hero figures on pedestals of ever increasing height became commonplace. In the case of David Crockett, his pedestal became one of the tallest. Generations came to believe that the "King of the Wild Frontier" died fighting valiantly and took as many as twenty enemy soldiers with him before he finally fell. By the early 1950s, those initial reports of Davy's death were all but totally ignored; and when Walt Disney, the Baby Boomers' best friend, told us all that Davy died bravely fighting, the proof seemed self-evident.

In 1968, a minor bleep showed up on the historical EKG connected to the Crockett legend. Respected historian Richard G. Santos published *Santa Anna's Campaign Against Texas* which was based on the general's field commands to his second in command Vicente Filisola. In the space of less than half a paragraph, Santos matter-of-factly wrote that four prominent Mexican soldiers had reported that Crockett was one of a handful of Texans that were captured after the final assault and then executed.[2]

Surprisingly, Santos' position did not cause any significant uproar among devout, Crockett-loving Texans. More than likely, most of those Texans simply paid little attention to the Santos book. Even though it was a scholarly, well-written work, Santa Anna's *Campaign Against Texas* told the Mexican side of the war, and many Texans have trouble admitting the Mexicans have a side in the Alamo saga.

Seven years later, in 1975, the Texas A&M University Press rocked and rolled the historical EKG when it published a book entitled *With Santa Anna in Texas: A Personal Narrative of the Revolution*. The book, a translation by Carmen Perry, contains the personal narrative of Jose Enrique de la Pena originally published in Mexico City in 1955.[3] De la Pena accompanied Santa Anna during the Texas campaign and participated in the storming of the Alamo. His account of the fateful events on the morning of the final assault shocked a nation, particularly the states of Texas and Tennessee. The following is Pena's account:

> *Shortly before Santa Anna's speech, an unpleasant episode had taken place, which,* since it occurred after the end of the skirmish, *was looked upon as base murder* and which contributed greatly to the

coolness that was noted. *Some seven men had survived the general carnage and, under the protection of General Castrillon, they were brought before Santa Anna. Among them* was one of great stature, well proportioned, with regular features; in whose face there was the imprint of adversity, but in whom one also noticed a degree of resignation and nobility that did him honor. He *was the naturalist David Crockett, well known in North America for his unusual adventures,* who had undertaken to explore the country and who, finding himself in Bejar at the very moment of surprise, had taken refuge in the Alamo, fearing that his status as a foreigner might not be respected. *Santa Anna answered Castrillon's intervention in Crockett's behalf with a gesture of indignation and, addressing himself to the sappers, the troops closest to him, ordered his execution. The commanders and officers were outraged at this action and did not support the order,* hoping that once the fury of the moment had blown over these men would be spared; *but several officers who were around the president and who, perhaps, had not been present during the moment of danger,* became noteworthy by an infamous deed, surpassing the soldiers in cruelty. They *thrust themselves forward,* in order to flatter their commander, *and with swords in hand, fell upon these unfortunate, defenseless men just as a tiger leaps upon his prey. Though tortured before they were killed, these unfortunates died without complaining and without humiliating themselves before their torturers.*4

Needless to say, there was an uproar in Texas over such a story. *Texas Monthly* magazine echoed the sentiments of many Texans when the translation of Pena's narrative was honored with a Bum Steer award. The consensus in Texas was something like, "Huh, Davy Crockett surrendering, the very idea! It must be a communist plot." There was talk that since Texas A&M had published the book that it might have been some kind of gigantic Aggie joke. No such luck. It was no joke.

Three years later the A&M University Press proved beyond a shadow of a doubt that it was no joke when they published *How Did Davy Die?* by Dan Kilgore. The book was actually an expanded version of a speech Kilgore gave before the Texas State Historical Society in which he purports to have proven that Davy did survive the final assault and was executed. You could almost hear a large collective gasp from Texans (and Tennesseans) at such a prospect, and the needle on the historical EKG went off the page. As the *Corpus Christi Times* reported, "Any Texan worth his lizard skin cowboy boots and Willie Nelson albums knows better than to smear the legend of Davy Crockett."[5] It was one thing for someone to publish a translation of a Mexican account, but it was something else altogether when a Texan spent his valuable time researching the subject and then pronounced it true. Clearly, Davy Crockett's last battle was still being fought.

In case you have not read *How Did Davy Die?* (and a lot of Texans haven't, you can be sure) Kilgore based his conclusions on what he called "valid documentation" consisting almost exclusively of various reports by Mexican soldiers who participated in the events of March 6, 1836. In fairness to Kilgore, he does present a convincing case, at least on the surface, and it is obvious he did considerable research. But there is other evidence that can be used to substantiate other conclusions.

In fairness to Davy Crockett, since he is not around to speak for himself, it appears appropriate that all the evidence should be considered before any historical jury is asked to pronounce a final verdict on how he died. Maybe Dan Kilgore, Richards Santos, and other modern historians are correct. Or maybe, when all the evidence is considered, the traditional view, held by most Texans, of Davy dying after fighting 'till the bitter end is correct. The evidence follows so you can decide for yourself.

The cornerstone of Kilgore's case is that no fewer than seven different accounts by Mexican soldiers seem to claim that Crockett was taken alive and executed. Kilgore included an extensive quotation from Pena (the italicized portion of the entire quotation presented previously), but he was somewhat more skimpy in his quotations from the other accounts. A point in case is the account of George M. Dolson which was in the form of a letter written on

July 19, 1836. The Dolson account is supposedly the result
of an interrogation of an unnamed Mexican officer captured at the battle of San Jacinto. The following is the
complete account of Dolson, and the parts quoted by
Kilgore are in italic:

> I am employed a considerable part of my time in
> interpreting Spanish for Colonel James Morgan,
> commander of this station. He sent for me
> yesterday [July 18, 1836] and told me there was a
> communication of importance from one of Santa
> Anna's officers, which he wished me to interpret;
> accordingly, the officer of the day was dispatched
> for the Mexican officer, who came in in a few
> minutes, and the Colonel's quarters were vacated
> of all, save us three. The Mexican was then
> requested to proceed with the statement
> according to promise; and he said he could give a
> true and correct account of the proceedings of
> Santa Anna towards the prisoners who remained
> alive at the taking of the Alamo. This shows the
> fate of colonel Crockett and his five brave
> companions — there have been many tales told,
> and many suggestions made as to the fate of
> these patriotic men; but the following may be
> relied on, being from an individual who was an
> eyewitness to the whole proceedings. The
> Colonel has taken the whole in writing, with the
> officer's name attached to it, which he observed
> to him, if he had the least delicacy, he might
> omit, but he said he had not and was willing to
> be qualified to it in the presence of his God, and
> General Santa Anna, too, if necessary. He states
> that *on the morning the Alamo was captured, between
> the hours of five and six o'clock, General Castrillon,
> who fell at the battle of San Jacinto, entered the back
> room of the Alamo, and there found Crockett and five
> other Americans, who had defended it until defense
> was useless;* they appeared very much agitated
> when the Mexican soldiers undertook to rush in
> after their General, but the humane General
> ordered his men to keep out, and, placing his
> hand on one breast, said, "here is a hand and a

heart to protect you; come with me to the General-in-Chief, and you shall be saved." Such redeeming traits, while they enoble in our estimation this worthy officer, yet serve to show in a more heinous light the damning atrocities of the chief. The brave but unfortunate men were marched to the tent of Santa Anna. *Colonel Crockett was in the rear, had his arms folded, and appeared bold as the lion as he passed my informant. Almonte, Santa Anna's interpreter, knew Colonel Crockett, and said to my informant, "The one behind is the famous Crockett."* When brought in the presence of Santa Anna, Castrillon said to him, "Santa Anna, the august, I deliver up to you six brave prisoners of war." Santa Anna replied, "Who has given you orders to take prisoners, I do not want to see them living—shoot them." As the monster uttered these words each officer turned his face the other way, and the hell-bounds of the tyrant despatched the six in his presence, and within six feet of his person. Such an act I consider murder of the blackest kind. Do you think that he can be released? No—exhaust all the mines of Mexico, but it will not release him. The one half, nor two thirds, nor even the whole of the republic, would not begin to ransom him. The combined powers of Europe cannot release him, for before they can come to his release, Texas will have released him of his existence but I coincide with the secretary of war, as to the disposal to be made of him, that is to try him as a felon. Strict justice demands it and reason sanctions it.[6]

When considered alone, the passages cited by Kilgore seem to corroborate his Crockett theory. But taken as a whole, this story is extremely suspect at best. Dolson's account is apparently the result of an interrogation of a Mexican officer by Texans who were looking for ammunition to be used against Santa Anna. As any student of Texas history should know, sentiment was high among the Texas army after San Jacinto for the execution of Santa Anna and most, unlike Dolson, saw little need for a trial. Dolson flatly states the Mexican gave his statement "according to promise" and it takes little imagination to envision the "promise" was his life for the truth, as long as the truth was what the Texans wanted to hear.

Walter Lord, the noted Alamo historian, said in *A Time to Stand* that the Mexicans had a "tendency after San Jacinto to say absolutely anything that might please a Texan."[7] If the Texans were wanting to prevent the release of Santa Anna, as Dolson implies, what better reason than he executed some of the defenders, including the famous Davy Crockett, in cold blood. Kilgore ignores this possibility. He also makes no note of the obvious error in the statement concerning the disposition of the prisoners. We know for a fact that the captives were *not* taken to Santa Anna's tent and there executed as stated by the informant.[8] If this unnamed officer really did witness whatever happened, he surely would not have made such a mistake. It appears Mr. Dolson's account should be dismissed as unreliable and yet Kilgore uses it as proof.

It also must be noted that Almonte was indeed Santa Anna's translator, but he left us no record that he knew or ever met Davy Crockett. Also, Almonte kept a careful daily record[9] of the events in the Texas campaign, but (as Dan Kilgore conveniently fails to point out) he did not mention anything of his identifying Crockett or of the executions.

Kilgore also cites the account of Lt. Col. Jose Juan Sanchez Navarro, who participated in the final assault and recorded his thoughts shortly thereafter. Navarro wrote:

> I saw actions of heroic valor I envied. I was horrified by some cruelties, among others the death of an old man named Cochran and of a boy about fourteen.[10]

Kilgore maintains that "Cochran" could easily have been mistaken for "Crockett," and he points out that there was a Robert Cochran in the Alamo but at age twenty-six he could hardly have been called an old man. Perhaps Kilgore's conjectures are correct, but he again fails to tell the whole story. It does not seem impossible that Cochran could also have been mistaken for Cottle, Courtman,

John Wayne, on the set for his 1960 movie *The Alamo*. For many Texans the thought of David Crockett surrendering at the Alamo is about as ridiculous as believing John Wayne would ever surrender anytime. *(Courtesy of Daughters of the Republic of Texas Library at the Alamo.)*

Crawford, or Crossman, all of which are names of other Alamo defenders. As to the age problem, there were twelve men in the Alamo whose ages are known to have been forty or older.[11] One defender, Robert Moore, was five years Crockett's senior. Kilgore also failed to consider that we will probably never know all the names and ages of the men who died in the Alamo. For all we know, there could have been an unknown old man named Cochran. It would be interesting to see Kilgore prove there was not.

Name also plays a part in the account of Colonel Fernando Urriza, who told his story to Dr. D. N. Labadie while the doctor was treating the colonel's wounds a few days after San Jacinto. Urriza's version is:

> I observed Castrion [sic] coming out of one of the quarters, leading a venerable looking old man by the hand; he was tall, his face was red, and he stooped forward as he walked.[12]

According to Labadie, Urriza said he heard the Mexicans call the old man Coket before Santa Anna ordered him shot. Kilgore adds, "Urriza convinced Labadie he was telling the truth about Crockett's fate." Well, a lot of Texans are not so convinced.

Urriza's account is so full of holes that it wouldn't hold hay if it were a bucket. It is another tale told after San Jacinto, the story has the name wrong, only one prisoner is involved, and the man is apparently as old as dirt. We have no reason to believe Crockett was so old and decrepit that he walked stooped over. In fact, after a brisk engagement on February 25, 1836, William Barret Travis wrote: "The Hon. David Crockett was seen at all points, animating the men to do their duty."[13] No doubt the days in the Alamo were cruel to the men involved; but in eleven days did Crockett become a venerable old man who stooped when he walked and had to be led by the hand? It doesn't seem possible. It appears more probable that Urriza was trying to tell the Texans what he thought they wanted to hear, or possibly Labadie fabricated the entire incident to support the cause for executing Santa Anna, something many Texans were most interested in seeing happen.

Kilgore makes no mention of the part about the Mexicans calling the man Coket. It would be interesting to hear his explanation of exactly how the Mexicans knew it was Coket or Crockett or anyone else. There is absolutely no information available to suggest the Mexicans would have known who Davy Crockett was or how to identify him. It seems precarious at best to consider Urriza's statement as any sort of verification that the old man was David Crockett.

Kilgore also cites the account of Ramon Martinez Caro, the personal secretary to Santa Anna, whom Kilgore called the most prestigious Mexican source. Caro relates how five men hid themselves and were discovered and brought before Santa Anna and subsequently killed. Kilgore uses this account as corroboration that some did survive, but he fails to address the matter that Caro mentioned no names. Does it not seem totally logical that if Crockett had been identified to Santa Anna and Caro witnessed it, that he would have made some mention of the incident? It would seem in this case that the absence of any name would be in favor of the theory that Crockett was *not* among the men brought before Santa Anna.[14]

Of course, there is still the problem of the Pena account which may be the basis for the entire story. But like all the others, Pena's version is not without some highly suspicious elements, not the least of which is how he knew it was Crockett. It is very doubtful, perhaps even impossible, that Pena would have known who Crockett was, and he offers no clue as to how he might have known the Tennessean. Kilgore, unfortunately, failed to include even a guess to explain Pena's knowing it was Davy. Also, Pena did not arrive in San Antonio until March 3.[15] March 4 and 5 were very busy days, and it seems very likely Pena would not have even known Crockett was in the Alamo. It's difficult, considering the trying times, to picture Pena sitting around a campfire and saying "So, my brothers, tell me about these gringos in the Alamo." More than likely, Pena later heard of Crockett's presence and simply used his name.

In his highly excerpted quotation from the Pena story, Kilgore fails to include the narrative about Crockett "finding himself in Bejar at the moment of surprise" and taking refuge in the Alamo because he feared his foreigner status might not be respected. By omitting that portion of the quotation, which is pure fiction, the problem of trying to prove the passage was true and then explaining how Pena would have known it is avoided. By all accounts, whatever happened to the survivors happened very quickly. There was apparently no sitting around chewing the fat and discussing reasons for people's presence in the Alamo. It seems almost certain that Pena added the "innocent bystander" part of the story, which leads to the inevitable question, how much more fiction did he include in his "true narrative?" It would seem historically prudent not to place too much faith in the Pena account, but then historians, as a group, are not always prudent.

An interesting point about the passages Kilgore omitted is that they may offer a clue to explain Pena's account. We know that Pena's complete narrative was not written until after the hostilities, probably after San Jacinto and, as even Kilgore admits, throughout his narrative Pena was strongly critical of Santa Anna's actions during the war. We also know that Pena flowered his account of the captives with hearsay, so it is reasonable to suspect that he fictionalized the account of the survivors in an attempt to disgrace El Presidente, who in all probability, was a prisoner of war when the account was written. What better way to disgrace someone than by claiming he executed a famous "innocent bystander?" Carmen Perry, who translated the Pena narrative, admitted in her preface that Pena was "eager to hold important positions."[16] Making Santa Anna look bad, Pena might have reasoned, could have catapulted himself into a more important position.

Pena is also the only reference we have that claims the men were tortured before they were killed. All the other accounts seem to indicate that whatever happened was over in a furious, matter-of-fact moment. Also, some of the other accounts expressed horror that the men were murdered, so why did they not express even more horror if the men were tortured? If Pena's motive was to make Santa Anna look bad, then a little torture would have been a nice touch, like icing on the cake.

Another problem with Kilgore's treatment of the Pena narrative is that he fails to review the entire document for overall validity. Some glaring problems should be noted. Pena clearly says that Travis died in the Alamo courtyard after the Mexicans had breached the walls and after he had traded his life dearly.[17] Joe, Travis' slave, said his master died quickly after firing only one shot and then fell to the base of the wall. It seems if anyone were going to lie about the death of Travis, it would have been Joe, who was loyal enough to his master to pilot Susanna Dickinson to Gonzales after the battle.[18] Francisco Ruiz, who identified Travis' body for Santa Anna, said his remains were found on a gun carriage, which would not be anywhere near the courtyard.[19]

Pena also included a story that on March 5, Travis promised the men that if help did not arrive on that day, they would surrender or try to escape under cover of darkness. Supposedly these "facts" came from a lady from Bejar (a suspected turncoat spy who left the Alamo a few days before the end) and a Negro (probably Joe) and some women who were rescued in the fortress. Neither Joe nor the spared women mentioned such a story, and the details could not have come from the spy since she escaped before March 5. It is also very doubtful Travis would have thought of surrender or escape since either would have been fruitless.[20] It should also be noted that apparently Travis sent out a final messenger on the night of the fifth seeking help from Fannin, an action which seems unlikely for a man on the verge of surrender.[21]

Pena, on the other hand, claimed it was said Santa Anna heard of the story and decided to attack on the sixth "because he wanted to cause a sensation and would have regretted taking the Alamo without clamor and without bloodshed, for some believed that without these there is no glory." It doesn't seem unreasonable to suspect Pena simply included a provocative rumor, or possibly an out-and-out fabrication, to strengthen his personal campaign to make Santa Anna look bad.

Doubtless other examples from the Pena book could be noted but the point has been made. The Pena story is an embellished narrative based on brief and sketchy notes, hearsay, innuendos, undoubtedly some pure fiction, and perhaps some plain old self-serving lies. The book may be entertaining and enlightening to those sympathetic to the Mexican side of the revolution, but, like much of the material written by Texans, the Pena story appears to fall far short of being totally reliable, and, consequently, should be subject to close scrutiny. Dan Kilgore offered no such close examination but rather simply accepted the Crockett tale as fact. Somehow, that does not seem at all fair to poor ol' Davy.

In an ironic twist of historical fate, Kilgore may have stumbled onto some evidence which might—just barely might—explain the entire Crockett affair. At the center of this possible evidence is a character well known to students of Texas history, one William P. Zuber, the very man who gave us the story of Louis Rose's escape from the Alamo and of Travis's drawing the line in the dirt.

Kilgore correctly identifies Zuber as the sole source of another tale of Alamo survivors that included Crockett as one of the victims. Supposedly, a Dr. George M. Patrick interviewed General Cos while he was a prisoner after San Jacinto. When asked about Crockett, Cos related his version of how the Tennessean died. Patrick later related the story to Zuber, who refused to accept it, preferring to believe that none of the Alamo defenders survived the final assault. In fact William P. Zuber actually used the story to illustrate how legends of the Alamo might have gotten started.

In a soft-shoe sort of way, Kilgore attacked Zuber's credibility and even suggested that William "sometimes relied too much upon his memory in stating historical facts."[22] And yet, after attacking Zuber (who did not believe the story), Kilgore concluded, "Still, Zuber's letter documented a significant fact: General Cos told Dr. Patrick that Crockett was captured and then executed." That seems like Kilgore went to some length to prove the fox wasn't in the chicken coop and then admitted it ate a chicken. If Zuber's letter "documented a significant fact," as Kilgore claimed, perhaps it also is the key to unlock the Crockett mystery. The following is the tale told by Zuber:

> When the Mexican prisoners were quartered at Anahuac, in 1836, Dr. Patrick visited them and obtained an interview, through an interpreter, with General Cos. He asked Cos if he saw Colonel David Crockett in the Alamo, and if he knew how he died.

Cos replied: "Yes, sir. When we thought that all the defenders were slain, I was searching the barracks, and found, alive and unhurt, a fine-looking and well dressed man, locked up, alone, in one of the rooms, and asked him who he was. He replied: I am David Crockett, a citizen of the State of Tennessee and representative of a district of that state in the United States Congress. I have come to Texas on a visit of exploration; purposing, if permitted, to become a loyal citizen of the Republic of Mexico. I extended my visit to San Antonio, and called in the Alamo to become acquainted with the officers, and learn of them what I could of the condition of affairs. Soon after my arrival, the fort was invested by government troops, whereby I have been prevented from leaving it. And here I am yet, a noncombatant and foreigner, having taken no part in the fighting.

I proposed [Cos is narrating] to introduce him to the President, state his situation to him, and request him to depart in peace, to which he thankfully assented. I then conducted him to the President.[23]

Zuber continued that Cos presented Crockett to Santa Anna and told the whole story. The President refused to allow Crockett's release and turned to leave whereupon Davy drew a knife and tried to kill the dictator but was, instead, bayonetted himself. Zuber concluded that the story was a falsehood but added it "shows what Santa Anna would have done if it were true."

Even though Zuber denounced the entire story, Kilgore selected the part about Crockett as documentation "when considered with statements of other eyewitnesses" of his being found and executed.[24] The interesting part of the story, however, is that Cos, like Pena, claims Davy was what amounted to an innocent bystander. The stories of Cos and Pena are as different as a hog and a horse but only those two men used the innocent bystander portion, which is most curious.

One of the real problems with the Pena story is how he would have known of Crockett being an innocent by-stander. Since Cos gave the interview shortly after San Jacinto and Pena didn't write his narrative until sometime later, perhaps Pena heard the tale of Crockett, as related by Cos, and simply included his own embellished version in his personal narrative. It seems very likely that Pena either made up the story or heard it from someone else, so perhaps Cos is the real culprit. If that were the case, does it mean the story is true? No way, Jose de la Pena.

An interesting part of the Cos story is that he says he is responding to a direct inquiry about Crockett and how he died. It seems logical that Cos would have assumed the Texans might have been more sympathetic with someone who had tried to save Davy and thus he came up with the wild story to make himself look like the angel of the Alamo. Patrick, and perhaps Cos himself, then repeated the story to one or two people, who also told one or two people, and so on, until it got back to Pena, who had no way to know it was a fake and thus he included it in his narrative.

In all probability, some of the Texans did survive the final assault, were then discovered by Castrillon and subsequently executed.25 Whether or not Pena actually witnessed the events is a matter of some dispute. Based on what he wrote, it seems more probable that Pena simply took parts of two stories he heard and combined them into his "true" account. That is the most reasonable explanation for why Pena had Castrillon discovering the men and then added substantially the same story told by Cos as to the fate of Crockett. If that possibility is true, and from this distance it appears to be, then the entire Pena account must be viewed with a jaundiced eye and should not be relied on as unquestionable fact. Discounting the Pena version as probable fiction would seem as reasonable a deduction as Kilgore's accepting the version as fact, perhaps more so.

Based on all of the above, it appears that Kilgore's "valid documentation" might be considered as suspect by some people. It seems very possible that the entire Crockett story is the product of one very fertile Mexican mind, perhaps Cos' or Pena's, and that all the other stories are simply different versions of the same fabrication. Is it not possible that Pena made up the whole thing, added the Crockett part from Cos, then told some other people, and the story, in one form or another, spread as fact?

Consider the case of one Sergeant Francisco Becerra, whose story of Crockett's end was labeled "bizarre" by Kilgore. According to Becerra, he killed James Bowie and then discovered Travis and Crockett in another room. Supposedly Travis was trying to buy his freedom with money and Crockett was lying on the floor asleep and exhausted by the battle. Then General Cos, not Castrillon, discovered the men and took them before Santa Anna, who ordered them killed.[26]

This story is, of course, pure horse feathers even though Becerra later admitted he could have been wrong about the names. Kilgore admitted Becerra was probably being self-serving and may have even come to believe that he was associated with three of the most famous Alamo defenders thanks to years of story telling, and yet Kilgore fails to acknowledge the possibility that Pena might have done something similar. The point in even presenting Becerra's version here is to show how crazy the story of Crockett's death actually became. But it is worthy of some note that Becerra said it was Cos who took the captives to Santa Anna. Since the other Mexican accounts claimed it was Castrillon, it sounds suspiciously as if Becerra might have heard the Cos story and simply embellished it for his own purposes, just as Pena probably did.

Kilgore does take the time to relate the story of the travelers arriving in New Orleans on March 27, 1836, with the news Crockett had surrendered and was killed. But Kilgore, like so many other writers who quote this story, failed to hazard a guess as to how those travelers might have known the individual to be Crockett. News traveled very slowly on the 1836 Texas frontier. It was five days after the fall before Sam Houston first heard the story. It was another two days, or an entire week in total, before he got confirmation of the fall and even then, he did not hear of the Crockett story. In fact he never mentioned having heard the Crockett story.

Since the mysterious travelers, who must have been Americans, arrived in New Orleans about three weeks, or sooner, after the fall, how could they possibly have heard about the fate of the Alamo unless someone who was at

Gonzales with Houston passed on the story? The problem is that the people of Gonzales did not hear the wild Crockett rumor, so how did the travelers have that news? Of course, it is possible other Mexican citizens slipped out of San Antonio after the fall and spread the word elsewhere. But how would they have known Crockett was one of the men who surrendered? If the Pena story is to be believed, it would seem the entire Army would have been buzzing over the cruelty and it would have become common knowledge. Yet, the Mexicans who reported to Houston said nothing. It seems very probable that one of those travelers knew the Tennessean had gone to the Alamo, and the narrator conveniently added Crockett's name to the story either for some perverted headline or, more probably, to help build sympathy for the Texas cause.

Not only does Kilgore use his supposed "valid documentation" as evidence, he also uses what was not said as possible confirmation. Consider the case of Santa Anna himself. At about eight o'clock on the fateful morning, El Presidente dictated his official report of the battle.[27] Although he mentions seeing the bodies of Travis, Bowie, and Crockett, he says nothing about captives or ordering their execution. Kilgore concludes, "But Santa Anna would have sought, of course, to avoid mentioning that it ever occurred."[28] That sounds a bit presumptuous, especially when the entire events of that day are considered.

It sounds as if Kilgore is assuming that Santa Anna felt some remorse for the execution but the author offers no explanation. It is a lead-pipe cinch Santa Anna had no qualms about ordering the men killed. He was, after all, on a mission to exterminate all the Anglos in Texas. He raised the blood red flag and sounded the tune *Deguello* signifying no quarter would be given. Killing a few survivors would not have given the general a moment's pause. Remember, Santa Anna is also the man who ordered Fannin and 420 men executed just twenty-one days after the fall of the Alamo. Yet Kilgore would have us believe that General Santa Anna felt remorse over executing five pitiful Texans who had just participated in the slaying of several hundred Mexican soldiers.

The fact is, it's hard to imagine any of the Mexicans feeling remorse as indicated in some of the reports. It must be recalled that whatever happened occurred just as the bloody fighting subsided, and probably while most Mexicans were still searching through the Alamo grounds for more Texans. It is a certainty that many wounded Mexican soldiers were screaming in pain and begging for help when the captives were discovered, and to think the Mexicans had second thoughts about killing the captives is a bit far fetched.

As for Santa Anna, the fact that he omits any mention of the executions is almost curious if Crockett was actually involved. We know Santa Anna was obsessed with proving that *norteamericanos* were active in helping the Texans. In his official report of the battle, he makes sure he mentions that the flag captured in the Alamo was from the New Orleans Grays. If the great American naturalist David Crockett had surrendered himself, it seems consistent with Santa Anna's character that he would have bragged about it. He didn't. That may not be proof of anything, but it is curious.

It is also strange that Kilgore bothers to point out that in his autobiography Santa Anna says, "not one soldier [Texan] showed signs of desiring to surrender, and with fierceness and valor, they died fighting." Kilgore maintained that "All indications are that he [Santa Anna] tried to absolve himself of any blame for the heartless executions."[29] Although the general is certainly less than a reliable witness thanks to the misinformation he often gave out, there is no real indication he was the least bit concerned about any "blame" for carrying out his avowed purpose of extermination. It is just possible that the general was telling the truth and all the Texans, including Crockett, died fighting.

As for Richard G. Santos, he is more flagrant in his acceptance of the Mexican versions. He simply states: "According to Colonels de la Pena, Sanchez Navarro, Almonte, and Urriza, 'David Crockett, a well known naturalist from North America' was among the captured." Mr. Santos apparently accepted the reports as gospel because he offers no proof or any explanations for the many problems with those accounts.

One odd part of the Santos story is his mention that Almonte identified Crockett. Santos offered no note as to where he got the information, so it is possible he made a classic mistake and assumed George Dolson's informant was Almonte. It is easy to see how the mistake could have occurred when you consider the quotation from Dolson as it appeared in the *Journal of Southern History* as follows:

> Colonel Crockett was in the rear, had his arms folded, and appeared bold as the lion as he passed my informant [Almonte] Santa Anna's interpreter, knew Colonel Crockett, and said to my informant, "The one behind is the famous Crockett.

At first glance, it might appear Almonte was the informant, but the passage actually does not make sense as written. Since Almonte was, in fact, Santa Anna's interpreter, it appears the passage should have been ". . . appeared bold as the lion as he passed my informant. Almonte, Santa Anna's interpreter, knew Colonel Crockett, and said to my informant. . . ." Since Almonte made no other mention of Crockett, he should not be listed as directly saying Crockett survived the battle. Since Santos offered no evidence to support his case, the counter arguments against the Mexican accounts, as already presented, would apply to Santos as well as to Kilgore.

Just as Kilgore and Santos seem quick to accept the nebulous Mexican versions without serious challenge, so do they seem inclined to discount or even ignore the scant evidence we have that Crockett might have died as legend would have us believe.

The primary sources of that evidence are Mrs. Susanna Dickinson, the wife of Captain Almaron Dickinson, and Travis' slave Joe, both of whom survived the final battle. Of their accounts, Kilgore says, "Even their earliest recorded statements reflected heavy editorial assistance aimed at building the Crockett legend."[30] That may be true as to their glorifying Crockett, but it does not change the possibility that the substance of what they said contradicts Kilgore and the Mexicans.

Susanna said, in one report, "I recognized Col. Crockett lying dead and mutilated between the church and the two story barrack building and even remember seeing his peculiar cap laying by his side."[31] Now Kilgore might claim that statement is rife with editorial prompting, but it seems doubtful. From later statements by Susanna, we know she was well acquainted with Crockett and he was a frequent visitor in her home.[32] The fact that she mentions his cap may be significant since her description squares with the accounts left behind by two enemy soldiers.

One Mexican, Captain Rafael Soldana, mentions in his account of the siege, "A tall man with flowing hair, was seen firing from the same place on the parapet during the entire siege. He wore a buckskin suit and a cap of a pattern entirely different from those worn by his comrades." The captain goes on to describe the man's prowess with a rifle and concludes with "This man I later learned was known as Kwockey."[33] He does not say how he learned the man's name, only that he learned it later. Perhaps he was with Santa Anna when Crockett's body was pointed out.

Sergeant Felix Nunez related details of the death of a Texan on the palisade as follows:

> He was a tall American of rather dark complexion and had a long buckskin coat and a round cap without any bill, made of fox skin with the long tail hanging down his back. This man apparently had a charmed life. Of the many soldiers who took deliberate aim at him and fired, not one ever hit him. On the contrary, he never missed a shot. He killed at least eight of our men, besides wounding several others. This being observed by a lieutenant who had come in over the wall, he sprang at him and dealt him a deadly blow with his sword, just above the right eye, which felled him to the ground, and in an instant he was pierced by not less than 20 bayonets.[34]

Of course Nunez does not identify the man, but how could he? The Mexicans did not know the Texans by name. However, his description and location seem to correspond with accepted facts.

Susanna's description of the location of the body as being opposite the low palisade is the spot Crockett and the Tennessee boys were assigned to defend. Kilgore does not argue with Susanna's description of the location and here Kilgore appears to be off the mark completely when he implies that her description of the position of Crockett's body was consistent with where it would have been found had Davy been brought before Santa Anna and executed. Kilgore himself surmised that the survivors were marched into the open Alamo yard, but that is nowhere near the spot between the chapel and the two story barracks identified by Susanna.[35]

Furthermore, if the position described by Susanna is the location where Crockett was executed, that would seem to indicate the back room where he was discovered was the

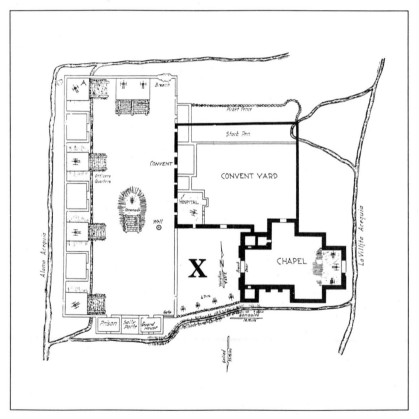

The X marks the spot where Davy Crockett is thought to have died while bravely fighting with his fellow Tennesseans. (*Map courtesy of the Archives Division of the Texas State Library in Austin.*)

chapel. The only problem is, Susanna was in the chapel, and she made no mention of any capture in that building. The accompanying graphic chart of the Alamo grounds shows the discrepancy regarding the position of the body.

As for Joe, Travis' slave, any flowers attached to his testimony were almost certainly added by some creative editor. William Fairfax Gray, a traveler in Texas, heard Joe interviewed on March 20 and recorded what was said in his diary. According to Joe, Crockett and a few of his friends were found together, with twenty-four of the enemy dead around them.[36] By the time that testimony was printed in the *Telegraph and Texas Register* four days later, phrases like "the great hunter of the west; immolated on the alter of Texas liberties; and freshness of hue, which his exercises of pursuing the beasts of the forest and prairie had imparted to him" had been added to the account.[37] Anyone who would believe Joe the slave used such language would probably believe Davy Crockett surrendered.

Kilgore omitted the testimony of Joe the slave, as recorded by William F. Gray, concerning possible Alamo survivors. According to Joe, "The handful of Americans retreated [as the Mexicans poured over the walls] to such covers as they had, and continued the battle until one man was left, a little, weakly man named Warner, who asked for quarter. He was spared by the soldiery, but on being conducted to Santa Anna, he ordered him to be shot, and it was done."[38] It should be noted that Joe's account closely matches that of Colonel Fernando Urriza in that both men say only one defender was found, and he apparently an old, weak man.

Joe did say the man's name was Warner, and there is no record of anyone by that name having died in the Alamo. Perhaps he confused the name, but would he have said Warner if it were Crockett, someone he knew and whom he had already identified as having died among his friends? For all anyone knows, Kilgore and Santos included, there could have been an unknown oldster named Warner who was found and perhaps confused for Crockett. Despite the name problem, Joe gave his testimony within two weeks of the fall, and the Mexicans who seemed to name Crockett did not record their thoughts or opinions until several weeks, months, or years later after they had plenty of time to pick up a wild rumor about the famous Davy Crockett. And yet Dan Kilgore never mentioned Joe's account.

As for Joe's placing Crockett among his friends, it is widely believed that the Tennessee boys would have stood together to fight and thus would have died together. It is considered very doubtful that Crockett would have deserted his friends, and it is equally doubtful that, had he later surrendered, he would have been found dead among his friends. For the record, Susanna also said he was found dead "amongst his companions."[39] Of course, Kilgore seems to dismiss such similarities in the statements as editorial prompting.

Kilgore also says the fact that Susanna claimed Crockett had been mutilated "adds further substance" to his theory that Crockett was taken alive and executed.[40] He completely ignores the very real possibility that had Davy died fighting in violent hand-to-hand combat, his body also surely would have been mutilated by numerous stab wounds. Nunez said that Davy was slashed above the eye and his body was pierced by twenty stab wounds, which would be about as close to mutilation as you could get.

The evidence may be fragile, but when the stories of Susanna, Joe, Captain Soldana, and Sergeant Nunez are considered together, it seems to be every bit as convincing as all the Mexican evidence, probably more so. The accounts of Susanna and Joe may have been flowered by overly zealous editors, but the bare essentials seem acceptable. As to the two Mexicans, their accounts seem authentic and no possible motive for their lying can be contemplated. Perhaps it is significant that Kilgore mentions neither Soldana nor Nunez. It's hard not to wonder why.

A final bit of evidence comes from Francisco Ruiz, the alcalde of San Antonio, who was called upon by Santa Anna to handle the burial of Mexican troops, the burning of the Texas troops, and for identification of the bodies of Travis, Crockett, and Bowie. After carring out his duties, Ruiz recorded his thoughts. In part he wrote:

> He [Santa Anna] directed me to call on some
> of the neighbors to come with carts to carry
> the [Mexican] dead to the cemetery and to

A traditional view of Davy Crockett fighting until the bitter end. From *The Fall of the Alamo,* a 1903 painting by Robert Jenkins Onderdonk. *(Courtesy of the Archives Division of the Texas State Library in Austin.)*

accompany him, as he desired to have Colonels Travis, Bowie, and Crockett shown to him.

On the north battery of the fortress convent, lay the lifeless body of Col. Travis on the gun carriage, shot only through the forehead. Toward the west and in a small fort opposite the city, we found the body of colonel Crockett.[41]

This statement can be confusing and might be interpreted to prove Crockett was found toward the west, which would have been the Alamo yard where Kilgore claimed the body was found. The curious thing is Kilgore only mentions the report as it was quoted, incorrectly, by Reuben Porter. Naturally Kilgore's quoted passage ends simply with "the body of Crockett was found in the West battery. . . ."

The alcalde's statement is curious because he mentions a small fort opposite the city. The only logical explanation is that the palisade where Crockett and the Tennesseans were stationed was separated from the Alamo yard and could have been considered a small fort all its own. If that were the case, Ruiz may have meant the western part of the palisade. Since his original statement is missing, we cannot verify the possibility that the translator erred saying west instead of east. Either way, the only area which could be construed as a small fort was the exact area where Susanna said Crockett was found.

Ruiz's statement also offers other valuable clues. He says Santa Anna ordered him to accompany the general and point out the bodies. If that is what happened, which is the indication, then the fact that he does not mention the executions seems to indicate they had already occurred before he joined the general. If so, this would seem to mean Crockett was not among the survivors. The alcalde clearly says "we found Crockett" which seems strong evidence that Santa Anna and Ruiz were together when Crockett was found, thus dealing a damaging blow to the theory that Crockett survived, was pointed out to Santa Anna, and then executed.

Dan Kilgore might dismiss the alcalde's statement with something like "even though Santa Anna already knew where Crockett was, he let Ruiz carry out the identification because he was ashamed of the executions." Such logic would be consistent with many of his other arguments.

Santos, on the other hand, has his own interpretation of the Ruiz account. He claims Ruiz was not called until half an hour after the fighting ended and concluded that Ruiz's explanation meant Crockett's body was "probably in the vicinity of the southwest corner of the mission compound." He offers no explanation as to how the huge Alamo compound could be construed as a "small fort opposite the city."[42]

The real truth is, we may never know how Davy died. Anyone can hazard his own guess as to how it happened and probably support his case with his own logic. But caution must be exercised. Perhaps Carmen Perry said it best in her translator's preface of, you guessed it, Jose Enrique de la Pena's *With Santa Anna in Texas*. Ms. Perry said, "The sacred function of the researcher is to keep constant vigil for the verification of facts."[43] It would seem that unless the facts can be absolutely verified, any guesses should be labeled as just that, guesses.

Unless conclusive proof is located, it would appear consistent with the memory of Crockett to believe a quotation attributed to Reuben Porter, "David Crockett never surrendered to bear or tiger, Indian or Mexican."[44] Without better proof than Dan Kilgore, Richard Santos, et al., could muster, let the record show Davy Crockett won his last fight and died fighting like a tiger. Nothing else seems fitting or proper.

Other Obituaries

The questions about how certain Alamo defenders died do not end with the controversy over whether Davy Crockett did or did not surrender. There are also serious questions about how William B. Travis, James Bowie, and others met their end. No one doubts that the end was a violent death but the way the men died is open for some speculation.

The case of William B. Travis is perhaps the most controversial. Some people believe that on the morning of March 6, 1836, when Travis was certain the Mexicans would overrun the mission, he took his own life rather than face fate at the hands of the enemy. Although the possibility that Travis committed suicide has never gotten the press coverage of the Crockett surrender issue, staunch, freedom-loving Texans should nevertheless be just as appalled at the proposition.

The origin of the Travis suicide theory apparently can be traced to Sam Houston. When the two Mexicans, whom Houston considered spies, arrived in Gonzales on March 11, 1836 with the news that the Alamo had fallen, they also apparently said Travis had taken his own life. In a letter of March 13 to Henry Raquet Houston said, "Travis, tis said, rather than fall into the hands of the enemy, stabbed himself. . . ."[1] As the information in Houston's letter was disseminated, the story of Travis' possible suicide was picked up and repeated in various sources around the nation.

In the ensuing years, however, many historians chose to discount the suicide theory and preferred instead to report the popular notion that Travis died early in the fighting while commanding on the north wall. Although the exact circumstances of his death often vary from source to source, the net result was always that Travis died at the hands of the enemy, and not by his own hand.

More recently, the controversy over a possible Travis suicide has been revived by a precious few historians in an effort to capture some coveted headlines to promote their literary efforts. Fortunately, all the headlines in the world will not change what appear to be the true facts in this case.

The problem of how Travis died has three parts which must be explored before any reasonable prediction about the Colonel's death can be made. First, there is the question of the validity of the information provided by the Mexican spies. Second, there is a considerable amount of information which contradicts the Mexicans' version. Finally, there is the character and spirit of Travis himself.

As to the validity of the information provided by the Mexican spies, the phrase "extremely suspicious" is perhaps most applicable. If, as the Mexicans supposedly maintained, they were friendly to the Texas cause, then how would they have known the details of Travis' death? Unless the Mexicans were actual combatants themselves, which is so far beyond belief that it is not worthy of any mention, then they must have been told of the Travis suicide. So who told them?

There is some speculation that the two Mexicans were indeed spies dispatched secretly by Santa Anna (or one of his representatives) to spread the word of the fall of the Alamo and to attempt to incite fear and panic in the ranks of the remaining Texas army. While such a theory is not supported by irrefutable facts, it does not seem beyond the realm of possibility. And if that theory is true, then what better way to incite fear and panic than with wildly provocative stories such as all the men of the Alamo were killed and their bodies burned; that some of the men tried to surrender and were executed; and that some men, including Travis, committed suicide rather than face the

In this 1953 painting by Ruth Conerly Zachrisson, William B. Travis is depicted, probably correctly, as having died with sword in hand while manning a cannon on the north wall. *(Courtesy The Alamo — Daughters of the Republic of Texas.)*

wrath of the mighty Mexican army. In our modern vernacular, we might call such information propaganda. In 1836, it may have been nothing more than a scare tactic.

In defense of the propaganda theory, much of the provocative information supplied by the Mexican spies was not true. The spies claimed all the men were killed and it is now widely believed that some of the men did survive. It is now generally accepted as fact that some of the men in the Alamo did survive the final assault and were quickly executed. However, the number of men involved and the exact circumstances vary among several sources.

As to the matter of suicide, the spies not only claimed that Travis took his own life, but that Bowie, Despallier, Parker, and others followed suit. While we have very few particulars of how the individual men died, no other sources even allude to the possibility that Bowie took his own life. The spies also apparently claimed that Captain Almaron Dickinson, when he decided all was lost, strapped his son to his back and leaped from a high point to his death. That is an interesting claim since Dickinson did not have a son and his infant daughter, Angelina, was one of the Alamo survivors.2

It seems probable that the two Mexicans were either reporting what they had been told to report or simply what they had heard from the "rumor mill." Either way, to accept their testimony as fact would appear to be a dangerous proposition from the standpoint of historical accuracy.

The credibility of the information provided by the Mexican spies would appear to be further damaged if other evidence concerning the fate of Travis is considered. Joe, Travis' slave, was one man who should have known what happened to the acting commander of the Alamo. On March 20, 1836, Joe was interrogated in Washington, Texas and he gave his account of the fate of Travis. William Fairfax Gray, a traveler in Texas at the time, witnessed the interrogation and recorded the gist of what was said. According to Gray, Joe claimed that Travis mounted a wall when the attack began and then encouraged the men to give the Mexicans hell. Unfortunately he was shot down an instant later.

Joe also maintained that the gallant Travis fell within the walls of the fortress and then sat up. When the Mexicans finally penetrated the walls, General Mora attempted to stab Travis but the commander managed to thrust up with his own sword and mortally wound the Mexican general. According to Joe, both men then expired. The slave supposedly witnessed the event while hiding in a nearby building and firing on the Mexicans.[3]

While Joe's account may be correct in every respect, it does seem a little melodramatic, perhaps the result of some skillful editorial prompting. The most serious challenge to Joe's story comes from the San Antonio Alcalde Francisco Ruiz. It was Ruiz who was detailed by Santa Anna to find and identify the bodies of Travis, Crockett, and Bowie. He reported that Travis was found on the north battery and that his body was ". . . on the gun carriage, shot only through the forehead." If Travis had fallen to the ground, as Joe reported, his body would not have been found on the gun carriage.

The Ruiz report may have also inadvertently contributed to the suicide theory. Amelia Williams, in her 1930 Ph.D. thesis at the University of Texas, cited the Ruiz account but concluded Travis' wound was a "pistol shot through the forehead."[5] Many people may have concluded that a pistol shot through the forehead would be the type of wound consistent with a suicide. There are two problems with that conclusion. First, Ruiz never mentioned a pistol shot but rather simply said "shot through the forehead." Second, Ruiz is specific with his use of forehead. Knowledgeable experts advise that it would be rare (and difficult) for anyone to attempt suicide with a shot through the forehead because making such a shot would require holding a gun at a difficult angle.[6]

Even though the accounts of Joe and Ruiz vary dramatically, they both appear to indicate Travis suffered his fatal wound at the hands of the enemy while defending the north wall. That might be enough said if it were not for some contradictory evidence from Mexican participants.

Jose Enrique de la Pena, in *With Santa Anna in Texas*, claimed that Travis lived until the enemy was storming the fortress and, unlike many of the Texans, Travis refused to seek shelter in the rooms surrounding the fortress. As to the fate of the commander, Pena wrote:

> He would take a few steps and stop, turning his proud face toward us to discharge his shots; he

fought like a true soldier. Finally he died, but he died after having traded his life very dearly. None of his men died with greater heroism, and they all died. Travis behaved as a hero; one must do him justice, for with a handful of men without discipline, he resolved to face men used to war and much superior in numbers, without supplies, with scarce munitions, and against the will of his subordinates.

Pena seems to be saying that Travis continued the fighting until almost the very end and then died in the open part of the Alamo compound. Unfortunately, such a possibility is totally contradictory to the accounts of Joe and Ruiz. Since much of the information in the Pena book is suspicious from an accuracy standpoint, it would appear Pena either lied about how Travis died or, since he probably did not know what Travis looked like, he simply had Travis confused with another soldier who did die fighting in the open courtyard.

The Pena version is also contradicted by another Mexican whose identity is not known. The April 5, 1836 edition of *El Mosquito Mexicano*, a Mexican newspaper, contained an account of the fall of the Alamo by a young Mexican soldier that was supposedly written while the soldier watched the funeral pyres burn at the Alamo. According to the unnamed soldier, "Travis died like a brave man with his rifle in his hand at the back of a cannon. . . ."[7] Another Mexican, Sanchez Navarro, wrote that Travis "died like a hero."[8]

Based on the accounts of Joe, Ruiz, Pena, Navarro, and the unknown soldier, it would appear foolish to conclude that the original spies were correct in their assessment that Travis died from a self-inflicted stab wound. We may never know whether the suicide story was planted or just a rumor but either way, it does not appear to be accurate.

Even if we did not have any evidence to the contrary, the prospect that Travis would have taken his life rather that fight for all he was worth would be difficult to accept. It was, after all, Travis who proclaimed to the world that his stand in the Alamo would result in either victory or death. He also proclaimed "I am determined to sustain myself as long as possible & die like a soldier who never forgets what is due to his honor & that of his country."[9] The young acting-commander wrote those words eleven days before he died.

On March 3, just three days before he died, the Travis spirit was still not broken. In a letter to the government on that day he wrote:

> I will, however, do the best I can under the circumstances, and I feel confident that the determined valour and desperate courage, heretofore evinced by my men, will not fail them in the last struggle, and although they may be sacrificed to the vengeance of a Gothic enemy, the victory will cost the enemy so dear, that it will be worse for him than a defeat.

In another letter of the same day, Travis said, "I have held this place for ten days against a force variously estimated from 1,500 to 6,000 and shall continue to hold it till I get relief from my country or I will perish in its defense." It is difficult—no impossible—to believe that the man who wrote those words would, just over two days later, take his own life rather than fall into the hands of the enemy. In fact, the possibility that Travis would have had doubts about his fate once the attack began is ridiculous. Travis knew, as all the men did, that their reward would be death. There is absolutely nothing about the man's character to suggest he would not have preferred to die only after giving a good account of himself before the enemy. The truth is, if Travis was shot down early in the fighting, as it certainly appears, he probably died angry at not having been able to kill more Mexicans. You can believe Crockett surrendered if you want to, but do not ever think for a moment that William Barret Travis took his own life.

In the case of the death of James Bowie, there is a similarity to that of the death of Travis in that the Mexican spies apparently said the great knife fighter also took his own life. In the letter to Henry Raquet where Houston reported Travis had stabbed himself, the general also wrote, ". . . our dear friend Bowie, as is now understood, unable to get out of bed, shot himself as the soldiers approached."[10] As with Travis, the Mexican spies are probably responsible for any other reports of Bowie taking his own life.

One aspect of the case of James Bowie that is generally not debated is the fact that the colonel[11] died in his bed. There is, however, some controversy over why Bowie was confined to his bed and unable to fight with the rest of the men. The question is whether Bowie was desperately ill or was injured as the result of a fall from a cannon platform.

The fall theory originated with Reuben Potter, the early Alamo historian who provided valuable research to later generations. In his first essay on the Alamo, in 1860,[12] Potter advanced the theory that Bowie was injured seriously in a fall. Potter repeated the theory in his 1868[13] essay and the legend was born. Other historians picked up the story and repeated it and there are probably historians out there today who believe the story. If so, those historians should change their mind just as Potter did.

Sometime between the publishing of his 1868 essay and 1874, Potter apparently learned the truth about James Bowie's illness. Since Potter continued to research the Alamo for the rest of his life, it is possible he learned the truth in an interview with Juan Seguin who had been in the Alamo during part of the siege. When Potter's friend H. A. McArdle was researching the Alamo in preparation for completion of his famous painting "Dawn at the Alamo," Potter reported his error and advised that Bowie had been ill and not injured. In Potter's best essay on the fall of the Alamo, in 1878, he listed Bowie's affliction as an illness.[14]

Once historians began to agree that Bowie had been ill, the debate switched to the nature of the illness. Potter suggested in his 1878 essay that the illness was pneumonia. Other guesses include typhoid fever, tuberculosis, and even the deadly typhoid-pneumonia. Whatever the affliction was, it apparently baffled the physicians on hand in the Alamo. Dr. John Sutherland, in his essay *The Fall of he Alamo*, reported that Bowie's illness, being, "of a peculiar nature, was not to be cured by an ordinary course of treatment."[15]

It would appear that James Bowie was a very sick man on the morning of March 6, 1836.[16] But was he so

A traditional view of James Bowie's death as illustrated by Louis Betts for the January 1902 issue of *Clure's Magazine*. Many historians speculate that after Bowie emptied his pistols he managed to kill one additional Mexican soldier with his famous knife. *(Author's collection.)*

desperately ill that he took his own life rather than face the Mexicans with whatever energy remained? Popular Texas legend, of course, implies that Bowie waited for the Mexicans to advance on his position and killed several of the enemy before he himself was brutally murdered.

Part of the controversy over Bowie's death may have been derived from the inadequate information available to the Mexican participants. The unknown Mexican soldier who wrote that Travis died like a hero also wrote in the same letter, ". . . that perverse and haughty James Bowie died like a woman, in bed, almost hidden by the covers." Sanchez Navarro wrote, "Buy [Bowie], the braggart son-in-law of Beramendi [died] like a coward." Without doubt, the brave Mexican soldiers who stormed the Alamo would have perceived any man that died in bed as a coward because they would have had no way to know Bowie was ill and unable to stand and fight like the true man he was. The animosity felt by the Mexican soldiers toward Bowie shows through in their writing but neither man implies that the famous knife-fighter took his own life.

Although the accounts of Bowie's actual death vary widely, only the two Mexican spies implied that the colonel died by his own hand. The most bizarre report on Bowie's death came from William P. Zuber who supposedly heard the story from a Mexican fifer named Apolinario Saldigna. According to the story, long after the fighting subsided and the funeral pyres had been built, an unscathed Bowie was carried out of his quarters. Supposedly the defiant colonel berated his captors and the Mexican soldiers promptly cut out his tongue then "lifted the writhing body of the mutilated, bleeding, tortured invalid from his cot, and pitched him alive upon the funeral pyre."[17] Such a story is virtually beyond comprehension. We know the funeral pyre was not lighted until late in the afternoon of March 6. Since the fighting was over about dawn on the same day, it is unthinkable that Bowie would have remained alive for several hours.

The most popular, and probably the most accurate, theory is that Bowie somehow managed to kill two or perhaps three enemy soldiers before he was slaughtered. As E. Alexander Powell wrote in 1915, "Bowie, propped up on his pillows, shot two soldiers who attempted to bayonet him as he lay all but helpless and plunged his terrible knife into the throat of another before they could finish him."[18] Madame Candelaria, who long claimed to have attended to Bowie while he was sick, said, "A dozen Mexicans sprang to the room occupied by Colonel Bowie. He emptied his pistols in their faces and killed two of them . . . I implored them not to murder a sick man, but they thrust me out of the way and butchered my friend before my eyes."[19] Although Candalaria's actual presence in the fortress is often questioned, the spirit of her account tracks with what is widely believed to have been the death of Bowie.

As to what happened to the body, William Brooker wrote in 1897 that Bowie was killed in his bed and the body was "hoisted on the bayonets and his remains savagely mutilated."[20] Apparently Brooker's account was derived from information provided by Juana de Navarro Alsbury, Bowie's sister-in-law, whom it is believed was in the Alamo for some time during the siege.

There is some question as to whether or not Bowie's body was unceremoniously cremated with the rest of the Alamo defenders. Martha McCullough-Williams wrote, in an 1898 story for *Harper's Magazine*, that the Mexican soldiers honored the great Bowie by burying his body apart from all the rest.[21] Although McCullough-Williams offers no clue as to the source of the material, she probably found the basis for her story in the October 1852 issue of *DeBow's Review*. A story in that issue entitled "Early Life in the Southwest—The Bowies," by John L. Bowie, a relative of James, included the information that the colonel was honorably buried by the Mexicans because "he was too great a man to be buried with common soldiers."[22]

The possibility that Bowie's body was afforded Christian burial is about as ridiculous as the possibility that he committed suicide. Every known Alamo historian accepts as fact that the bodies of the Alamo victims were cremated. Since the Mexicans had a passionate dislike for the "braggart" Bowie, the idea that his body was treated with honor of any kind is too far outside the scope of believability to be given any credence. Since the author of the story was apparently a Bowie relative, apparently the information was a self-serving attempt to expand the legend of James Bowie.

Colonel James Bowie fought to the end and was butchered; his body was mutilated and subsequently burned with all the other defenders. Nothing else makes sense. As J. Frank Dobie said, "Imagination and patriotic sympathy rebel at the idea of Bowie's dying except in the climax of hand-to-hand combat."[23] James Bowie's mother may have summed up the general feelings of most Texans about the famous knife-fighter. According to Walter Worthington Bowie, when the iron-nerved old woman was told that her son James had met death at the hands of the Mexicans, she took the news calmly and remarked that she "would wager no wounds were found in his back."[24] Mrs. Bowie, along with most Texans, would probably bet the entire farm that Colonel James Bowie did not take his own life.

It would appear that the Mexican spies who reported to Sam Houston on March 11, 1836, were totally wrong in their opinion that Travis and Bowie committed suicide. It probably follows that the spies' claim about Charles Despallier, Christopher Parker, and "others" also taking their own lives is false. There is no evidence whatsoever that any of the Alamo defenders chose self-destruction as a means of avoiding the final engagement with Santa Anna's army. Perhaps that issue can finally be put to rest for all time.

One related issue that probably will never be put to rest is the matter of what happened to the remains of the Alamo defenders. We know that all Santa Anna did was order the defenders' bodies stacked among layers of branches and logs and then burned. The dictator did not bury the ashes and other remains after the fires burned themselves out. And yet stories remain that the ashes of the gallant Alamo defenders were later buried.

There are several versions as to what happened to the ashes of the victims. In one account, Francisco Ruiz buried the remains shortly after the fires stopped smoldering; but that seems a little too convenient since Santa Anna would have still been in town at that time, and he probably would not have allowed the Texans to be buried in any manner. In another story, Dr. John Sutherland claimed that two or three months after the battle (in April or May of 1836, when the Mexican army was gone from San Antonio) a company of rangers under the command of a Captain Lockhardt found the remains and promptly buried them.

The most accepted story of the burial of the defenders is that on February 25, 1837, Juan Seguin, one of the Alamo messengers, paid tribute to the fallen heros and buried the remains. Supposedly the remains were gathered and taken to a church and then were carried to the place of interment. The following is a translation of the eulogy offered by Seguin in his native Castillian:

> These remains, which we have had the honor to carry on shoulders, are the remains of those valiant heroes who died at the Alamo. Yes, my friends, they preferred to die a thousand times than to live under the yoke of a tyrant.
>
> What a brilliant example! One worthy of inclusion in the pages of history. From her throne above, the spirit of liberty appears to look upon us, and with tearful countenance points, saying, "Behold your brothers, Travis, Bowie, Crockett as well as all the others. Their valour has earned them a place with all my heroes."
>
> Yes, fellow soldiers and fellow citizens, we are witness to the meritorious acts of those who, when faced with a reversal in fortune, during the late contest, chose to offer their lives to the ferocity of the enemy. A barbarous enemy who on foot herded them like animals to this spot, and then proceeded to reduce them to ashes.
>
> I invite all of you to join me in holding the venerable remains of our worthy companions before the eyes of the entire world to show it that Texas shall be free, and independent. Or to a man, we will die gloriously in combat, toward that effort.[25]

The ceremony was followed by the actual burial of the remains and it would be fitting and proper if that were where the story ended. Unfortunately, that is not the end of the story.

The largest question any historian has about the Seguin account is how the colonel was able to locate the ashes after they had lain, supposedly neglected, on the south

Texas prairie for just a few days short of an entire year. Supposedly, the ashes were found in three places and the two smallest piles were placed in a coffin with the names Travis, Bowie and Crockett carved inside the lid. If the story is true, then someone—some unknown Samaritan— must have taken care to preserve the ashes. But who? And why, if care was taken to preserve the ashes, were they not properly buried long before Seguin arrived? Perhaps one of the stories about earlier attempts to preserve the remains is true and Juan Seguin merely formalized the ceremony. We will probably never know exactly what happened.

The next largest question about the Seguin story is the matter of where the remains were buried. Incredibly, even though Juan took care to preserve the remains, he did not adequately mark the ultimate grave site. The March 28, 1837 edition of the *Telegraph and Texas Register* contained a story indicating the remains were buried "in a peach orchard near the fortress." Dr. John Sutherland and Reuben Potter confirmed the burial site was a peach orchard near the fortress although Sutherland said it was "not far" from the fortress and Potter said it was "a few hundred yards" from the Alamo. Several other sources place the burial site near the fortress but do not mention the peach orchard.[26]

Juan Seguin actually complicated the issue. In 1899, while responding to an inquiry about the burial site, Seguin wrote, "I collected the fragments, placed them in an urn and buried it in the Cathedral of San Fernando, immediately in front of the alter—that is in front of the railing near the steps."[27]

For the most part, Seguin's version of where the remains were interred was dismissed as the ramblings of an old man with a frail memory. Then, in July 1936, a coffin was unearthed in the Cathedral at the exact spot Seguin suggested. Inside the rotting old casket were charred remains, some bones, and even uniform fragments. There was some excitement that the actual burial site for the Alamo defenders had been located until astute historians pointed out that the men of the Alamo did not wear uniforms. Certainly some burial took place in the cathedral, and Seguin was aware of it, but the identity of the person or persons whose remains were buried there will probably never be known.

We also will never know the exact location of the burial of the Alamo victims. However, it seems prudent to accept the probability that wherever the remains lay, there are no ashes of any suicide victims included.

The Travis Account Book Mystery

Much to the delight of historical researchers, William Barret Travis was very fond of taking up his quill and putting words on paper. One of his letters, the famous plea for help from the Alamo on February 24, 1836, is considered by many to be the most patriotic document in the annals of American history. In reality, however, that one letter was but a small part of the writings of Travis. The young lieutenant colonel from North Carolina left behind a wonderful collection of written documents that has helped us gain considerable insight into the man.

Two years after he escaped a marriage gone sour in Alabama, Travis sailed to Texas and settled in Anahuac. In 1833[1] the young attorney relocated his law practice to San Felipe, the seat of government and the perfect place for an ambitious young man to further his fortunes. Travis' writing ability, coupled with his persuasive nature, almost certainly contributed to his being named secretary to the local community council (the *ayuntamiento*).

On August 30, 1833, just a few months after arriving in San Felipe, Travis began recording the highlights of his life in a personal diary.[2] He continued making almost daily entries in the journal until June 26, 1834, when, for unknown reasons, he abruptly stopped. Even though the diary covers less than a year of his life, the information provides many clues into Travis' personality.

Based on the entries in his journal, we know Travis had a passion for reading, sometimes completing an entire volume in a single day. His readings included H. St. John Bolingbroke's *Letters on the Study and Use of History*; P. C. Headley's *Life of Empress Josephine*; an anonymous 1831 work entitled *The Court and Camp of Buonaparte*; Jane Porter's *Scotish Chiefs*; Benjamin Disraeli's *Vivian Grey*; and *Rob Roy, Guy Mannering*, and *The Black Dwarf* by Sir Walter Scott.

What we do not know is whether Travis' reading material was a matter of personal preference or simply availablity. On the early Texas frontier, books were certainly in short supply, and it seems probable that Travis, like anyone else who enjoyed reading, was destined to read whatever was available. Regardless of the reasons for his choices in titles, it seems a fair assessment to assume that the romantic novels he read had a profound effect on his personal philosophy and writing.

His diary also provided glimpses into the day-to-day activities of Travis. We know he occasionally took a drink, risked some of his money gambling (and usually lost), and enjoyed the pleasures of a frontier party. He was also a reasonably successful lawyer. In one of his cases, he successfully sued Green B. Jameson on behalf of a client and won a $50 judgement. Jameson was the same man who later served as engineer for the garrison at San Antonio and was in charge of fortifying the Alamo. History does not tell whether there was any deep-seated animosity between the two men.

Without doubt, the most intriguing entry in Travis' diary was the simple notation "duel &c."[3] This entry seems to imply that the young lawyer was involved in an affair of honor, but we have no information as to who else might have been involved or what could have precipitated the action. About all we know is that if Travis did fight a duel, he survived to fight another day.

Even though, sadly, Travis abandoned his diary project, he continued to write letters. When he led an attack against the custom house in Anahuac and public opinion condemned the action as inciting war, Travis wrote of his personal disappointment. When the Mexican army advanced on Texas and public opinion swung the other

This Wiley Martin sketch is thought to be the only known likeness of William B. Travis to have been drawn from life. Even though the drawing is clearly dated December 1835, Frank Templeton, who used the drawing in his 1907 novel *Margaret Ballentine,* claimed to have found it in an 1834 Tennessee newspaper. *(Courtesy The DRT Library at the Alamo.)*

way, Travis was elated. "Huzza for Texas! Huzza for Liberty," he wrote, "Texas is herself again."[4]

On August 17, 1835, Travis wrote one of the most interesting letters of the entire Texas revolutionary period. The letter was addressed to the *New York Christian Advocate and Journal*. The text was as follows:

> My Dear Sir; —
> I take liberty of addressing you from this distant quarter of the world for the purpose of requesting you to receive my name as a subscriber of your widely circulated Advocate. We are very destitute of religious instructions in this extensive fine country, and the circulation of your paper here will be greatly beneficial, in the absence of the stated preaching of the gospel. Although the exercise of religion in any form is not prohibited here, but is encouraged by the people, yet but few preachers have come among us to dispense the tidings of salvation to upwards of sixty thousand destitute souls. I regret that the Methodist church, with its excellent itinerant system, has hitherto sent the pioneers of the Gospel into almost every destitute portion of the globe, should have neglected so long this interesting country. I wish you would do me and the good cause the favor to publish such remarks as will call the attention of the reverend Bishops, the different Conferences, and the Board of Missions, to the subject of spreading the gospel in Texas. About five educated and talented young preachers would find employment in Texas, and no doubt would produce much good in this benighted land. Texas is composed of the shrewdest and most intelligent population of any new country on earth; therefore, a preacher to do good must be respectable and talented. In sending your heralds in the four corners of the Earth, remember Texas.[5]

Apparently, Travis was concerned about the spiritual well-being of the people in Texas. We have no record that the Methodist church responded to this request and sent missionaries to the "benighted" land.

In late January of 1836, Travis was assigned to take a group of volunteers to San Antonio. Thanks to letters he wrote enroute, we know he was unhappy with the assignment. On January 29, in a letter written to the Texas governor from Burnam's Landing on the Colorado, River, Travis wrote:

> I am willing, nay anxious, to go to the defense of Bexar, and I have done everything in my power to equip the enlisted men and get them off. But sir, I am unwilling to risk my reputation (which is ever dear to a soldier) by going off into the enemies country with such little means and so few men, & them so badly equipped — the fact is there is no necessity for my services to command so few men. The company officers will be amply sufficient. They should at all events be sent to Bexar or to the frontier of Nueces. They may now go on to San Antonio under command of Capt. Forsythe, where they can be employed if necessary, and if they are not needed there may be sent to San Patricio or some other point. I am now thoroughly convinced that none but defensive measures can be pursued at this inclement season. If the Executive or the Major-General desire or order it, I will visit the post of San Antonio or any other for the purpose of consulting or communicating with officers in command there — or to execute any commission I may be entrusted with, but I do not feel disposed to go to command a squad of men, and without the means of carrying on a campaign. Therefore I hope your Excellency will take my situation into consideration and relieve me from the orders which I have hitherto received, so far as they compel me to command in person the men who are now on the way to Bexar. Otherwise I shall feel it due to myself to resign my commission. I would remark that I can be more useful at present, in superintending the recruiting service.[6]

Travis was not relieved, he did not resign, and three days later he was in the Alamo. While in San Antonio, Travis wrote no fewer than fourteen documents, beginning on February 12, when he assumed command after James C. Neill departed and culminating on March 3, when he made a lengthy, last-ditch effort to get help from the colonies. His Alamo writings have helped historians piece together much of what transpired during the final days of the Alamo.

In his letter of February 12, Travis provided intelligence on rumored enemy movements and predicted the garrison was ill-prepared to meet the Mexicans. His patriotic feelings also emerged. He wrote, in part:

> . . . we consider death preferable to disgrace, which would be the result of giving up a Post which has been so dearly won, and thus opening the door for the invaders to enter the sacred Territory of the colonies . . . we hope our countrymen will open their eyes to the present danger. . . I fear that it is to waste arguments upon them — The Thunder of the Enemys Cannon and the pollution of their wives and daughters — The cries of their Famished Children, and the smoke of their burning dwellings, will only arouse them.
>
> For God's sake and the sake of our country, send us reinforcements. . . .

He concluded the letter with his first statement of purpose about defending the Alamo, "I am determined to defend this place to the last, and, should Bexar fall, your friend will be buried beneath the ruins."[7]

The next day, February 13, Travis reported some hint of intrigue in the garrison. James C. Neill had left and installed Travis as acting commander, an action that did not set well with the volunteers. So Travis, in a show of fairness to the men, called for an election. Reporting results of the voting, Travis wrote:

> Bowie was elected by two small company's & since his election he has been roaring drunk all

the time; has assumed all command & is proceeding in a most disorderly & irregular manner — interfering with private property, releasing prisoners sentenced by court-martial & by the civil court & turning everything topsy turvey — If I did not feel my honor & that of my country compromised I would leave here instantly for some other point with the troops under my command — as I am unwilling to be responsible for the drunken irregularities of any man. . . .

Travis also added an ominous note when he said, ". . . by the 15th of March I think Texas will be invaded & every preparation should be made to receive them. . . . "[8] Obviously, Travis was off considerably in his prediction of when the enemy would invade. By March 15 Travis and the other men of the Alamo were nine days dead.

Apparently Travis' troubles with a "drunken" James Bowie were resolved quickly. On February 14, in a letter signed by both men, they said, "By an understanding of today Col. J. Bowie has the command of the volunteers of the garrison, and Col. W. B. Travis of the regulars and volunteer cavalry. All general orders and correspondence will henceforth be signed by both until Col. Neill's return."[9]

We next hear from Travis on February 15, when he sent a note introducing Erastus Smith to the government. Smith had been wounded in the Texans' storming of San Antonio and was appealing to the government for financial aid with Travis' help. Known popularly as "Deaf," Smith survived his injuries to play a key role in the battle of San Jacinto.[10]

The following day Travis attached a cover letter to a report of the post engineer, Green B. Jameson—the same Jameson whom Travis once sued—and asked that the proposed improvements suggested by Jameson be approved. He also again urgently requested men, money, and provisions and predicted that with the needed supplies, Texas might "be saved from the fatal effects of an invasion."[11]

The only other letter we have from Travis before the invasion was dated February 19, when he wrote to Captain J. L. Vaughn concerning recruiting matters. Apparently

Travis enjoyed his short tour of duty in the recruiting service and, as he even speculated, may have felt that duty was where he actually belonged.[12]

Once the Mexicans arrived on February 23, Travis again provided us with interesting, insightful documents. On that date he sent a short notice to Andrew Ponton informing him of the arrival of the enemy and requesting aid at once. Nine days later, in response to that plea, thirty-two men from Gonzales joined the Alamo garrison. It was the only help they received.[13]

Also on February 23, Travis and Bowie together sent an urgent call for assistance to James Walker Fannin in Goliad. In response to that message, Fannin did attempt a march with more than three hundred men, but it faltered within two hundred yards of Goliad, and Fannin never again attempted to go the aid of the Alamo.[14]

On February 24, Travis issued his now famous appeal "To the People of Texas and all Americans in the World."[15] The following day, Travis reported a victory in a major skirmish with the Mexicans. We did not hear from him again until March 3, three days before his death.[16]

On the third, Travis apparently sensed, correctly, that the end was near. He actually issued at least three documents, perhaps more, that day. One letter was long and detailed and was addressed to the president of the constitutional convention, whoever that might have been. He detailed his position and recapped the events of the siege. He was particularly harsh on Fannin, who had not marched in reply to Travis' urgent calls for help. Travis also predicted that the local Mexicans were "all our enemies" and included information about large numbers of enemy reinforcements being received. He concluded the letter, his last-ditch effort for help, with "God and Texas! — Victory or Death!!"[17]

His other two letters of March 3 were more personal. One was to David Ayers, requesting he take care of Travis' young son Edward. "If the country should be saved," Travis wrote, "I may make for him a splendid fortune." He also predicted that if the country was not saved and he perished, then young Edward, "will have nothing but the proud recollection that he is the son of a man who died for his country."[18]

Travis' final letter of the third was to Jesses Grimes, and it began with a tantalizing sentence that has intrigued historians for generations. "Do me the favor," he asked, "to send the enclosed to its proper destination instantly." Travis then went quickly into a discussion of how long he had held the fort and an urgent plea for the convention to go on and declare independence. He had no way of knowing independence had already been declared.[19]

The big question about the letter regards the enclosure that was to be forwarded to its proper destination. The most popular theory is that Travis wrote a farewell letter to his sweetheart, Rebecca Cummings. If that's true, young Rebecca apparently did not preserve what might have been the most famous letter of all from the Alamo. You can be sure any Texan with even an ounce of romance in his heart would give the deed to the ranch to know what private thoughts Travis might have sent to Rebecca. Above all others, that one letter (if to Rebecca) might give us clear insight into exactly what Travis was thinking just three days before he died.

Although Travis' letters provide historians with considerable information, they are not the entire story. One part of the writings of Travis that has often escaped the historical microscope are entries he made in a small notebook used to record expenditures made on behalf of the army. One reason the notebook is often overlooked is that it was stolen from the Archives of the Texas State Library many years ago.[20] Thanks, however, to the efforts of Ruby Mixon, we know at least some of what was contained in the notebook.

Mixon completed her Masters thesis at the University of Texas in 1930, and her subject was William B. Travis. In her appendix to the thesis, she included typed transcripts of all the Travis documents she could find. In some cases, since the original documents are now missing, Mixon's transcripts are the only records that remain. Fortunately for historians, she was very thorough in her research.

Despite the efforts of Ms. Mixon, the circumstances of the Travis account book are still shrouded in mystery. We know (from her thesis) that John R. Jones, the executor of Travis' will, used information from the book to substantiate claims on behalf of the estate against the

Republic of Texas. In December 1837, Jones submitted the following claim:

The Republic of Texas
To the Estate Wm. Barret Travis
1836

Jany 21st	Paid for		flour	$5.00
	do	do	Tin ware	2.50
	do	do	Twine	1.00
			3.00 2.00	
	do	do	Leggins & spurs	5.00
			5.00 1.00	
	do	do	Flag & powder flask	6.00
			4.00 15	
	do	do	Bridle 3 blankets	19.00
			12.00 1.25	
	do	do	Tent frying pan	13.25
			6 ft	
	do	do	rope	.75
Jany 22nd	do	do	Corn to Made	1.00
	do	do	to Burnam for corn	1.00
23	do	do	do do	1.00
24	do	do	Mouly for corn	2.00
25	do	do	Burnams for blankets for 2 soldiers	10.00
			4.00 3.00	
do	do	do	coffee sugar	7.00
26	do	do	Jackson for blanket for soldier	5.00
do	do	do	Winburn for do 2 blankets	8.00
do	do	do	McDaniel	2.50
do	do	do	to soldiers for bounty (see orders)	17.00
	Amount Carried over			$107.00
1836				
Jany 28th			To Chadorn for corn	3.00
30	do	do	Dement for shoeing horses	6.00
	do	do	Kimballs bill for corn	2.00

Feby 3rd			For Corn&wood	
			(at St.Antonio)	4.50
7th	do	do	for Forsyths company	6.00
	do	do	cash to soldiers bounty	4.00
8	do		corn for horses	2.00
			2.00 3.00	
12	do		paper bread	5.00
			1.50 2.00	
16	do		Firewood	
17th			corn	3.50
				$143.00

Note Horses, saddles & arms — in q Masters
books

The foregoing is taken from the original entries in
Col. Travis' hand writing made in a small blank
morocco bound book with his name in it. The
deceased Wm Barret Travis has other claims for
money expended horses &c. while in the army as
will appear by the books of the Quarter Master
Jackson.

Jno R. Jones, Exr[21]

Unfortunately for current historians, the claims against
Travis' estate are also missing. In all probability the entire
file, including the claims and the Travis account book,
were stolen at one time and as yet have not been
recovered. Since Ms. Mixon obviously relied on the claim
file for her information, we do not know if she had access
to the actual account book in 1930, or if it was already
missing at that time. If in fact the book disappeared long
before any historian had a chance to review it, there is also
the possibility that it contained much more information
than simple notations on expenses. Given Travis' writing
habits, it does seem out of character that he would keep a
record without at least some editorial comments. Unless
the book is recovered, some perhaps vital Alamo information is lost to all historians.

The disappearance of the account book is actually only
part of the mystery. The scant amount of information
provided by the claim has tantalized historians for generations. Without doubt, the single most interesting item is
the $5.00 flag purchased in San Felipe on January 21.

There are Alamo historians who would give their eye teeth to have a description of the banner Travis bought and undoubtedly carried with him to the Alamo. Unfortunately, we'll probably never know.

Since flags of many styles and types were for sale on the Texas frontier, we have no way of knowing what the Travis flag looked like since no description has survived. In his famous letter of February 24, Travis said, ". . . our flag still waves proudly from the walls—I shall never surrender or retreat."[22] Was the flag that still waved the Travis flag? No one knows. After the final battle, in his official report, Santa Anna implied there was more than one flag when he said, "The bearer takes with him one of the flags of the enemy's Battalions. . . ."[23] As far as is known, only the flag of the New Orleans Greys was actually captured after the battle. What happened to Travis' $5.00 flag has been lost to history. If it were not for the account book, we would never have even known Travis had a flag.

The biggest single mystery concerning the account book is how it survived to be used in claims on behalf of Travis. The last date noted in the diary is February 17, six days before the Mexicans arrived. There is no record that Travis himself left the Alamo on or after the 17th and then returned by the 23rd. In fact there is no mention anywhere that Travis ever left San Antonio after arriving on February 3. So how did the diary survive?

Apparently, someone left the Alamo with the account book before the fortress was overrun by Mexicans on March 6, 1836. If the book had still been present when the Mexicans stormed the fort, it would have been captured by the enemy and it is doubtful the book would have been back in the hands of Texans barely a year later. We have no record that any Mexican soldier recovered the account book, so it must have been gone before March 6.

Some historians believe James C. Neill carried the account book with him when he left the Alamo in search of funds for the men. The theory, apparently, is that Neill would have used the account book as verification of expenses. The problem with that theory is that Neill almost certainly left on February 11, six days before the final account book entry, to attend to his sick family. There is the possibility that Neill left to take care of his family, returned, and then left again, with the book, to try and secure the funds. Unfortunately, no record whatsoever exists to support that theory.

It would appear someone else carried the account book, and there are several possibilities. Travis sent out many couriers, including James Butler Bonham, John Smith, John Sutherland, and Albert Martin, and any one of them could have carried the book to safety. But why? The couriers were sent in search of help, so what would been the point of sending along an accounting of $143 in expenses? It is difficult to imagine that while the drumbeat of history was quickening, Travis would have been concerned with the loss of $143. The man was worried about saving his life, not getting reimbursed.

Travis, himself, never specifically mentioned the account book in any of his writings, so speculation about the disposition of the book is purely conjectural. Still it is difficult not to think of the perplexing "enclosed" statement in his letter to Grimes of March 3. Certainly it may have been a letter to Rebecca. But what if, on that dark day, Travis did, indeed, surmise that the end was near and thus developed a strong desire to have his personal documents and records preserved? Since, as far as we know, the mysterious "enclosed" is the only unknown item Travis sent out of the Alamo, perhaps it was the account book. For all we know, the enclosed could have been a package of items including, possibly, a final love note, the account book, and even other documents.

Even though it is not nearly so romantic a notion, the possibly that the mysterious "enclosed" was a last love letter seems a bit remote. If Travis did write to Rebecca, it seems unthinkable that the letter would not have been preserved. Remember, Travis and the boys quickly became martyrs in the cause of Texas freedom, so how could Rebecca have been careless in handling the last letter of a genuine hero? The truth is, she probably would have published the letter in a newspaper as was the custom of the day.

In fairness to Miss Cummings, Travis was technically a married man when he began calling on her. Perhaps, given the moralistic tendencies of the period, Rebecca was more interested in preserving her own reputation than the letter of a hero. Maybe the intriguing "enclosed" was indeed a last love letter. We'll probably never know.

One fact seems fairly certain about the mysterious account book. Travis probably had no motivation to send it out prior to March 3. If that's true, then it seems almost certain that John Smith carried the account book with him when he left the Alamo on that date. What Smith actually did with the book is anyone's guess. Perhaps it was the unknown "enclosed" delivered to Grimes; perhaps it was delivered to David Ayers to be passed down to Travis' son; or perhaps Smith carried the book with him to the convention. Take your pick.

The mysteries surrounding Travis' book will probably never be solved. Was it simply a ledger of expenses or did it contain other valuable information? Did Travis send it out of the Alamo on March 3, or was the "enclosed" really a last love note? Perhaps someday the stolen account book will resurface and the questions can be resolved. Maybe what we need is to assign a few good Texas Rangers to the case. If they could track down Bonnie and Clyde, surely they could find one little notebook.

What Happened to Lt. Col. James C. Neill?

In early December of 1835, it was Texans who were laying siege to San Antonio de Bexar. A small army under the leadership of General Edward Burleson was intent on taking the town and the Alamo away from General Martin Perfecto de Cos, the brother-in-law of General Santa Anna.

Burleson favored starving out the Mexicans, but the men in his command wanted to fight. Consequently, the Texans followed "Old Ben Milam into San Antone" on December 5. After five days of fighting, in which Milam was killed, General Cos surrendered, and the first battle for the Alamo was over.

Shortly thereafter Burleson left, and Francis W. Johnson assumed command of the volunteers. By the end of the month, sentiment in Texas was running high for an invasion of Matamoros, Mexico to take that strategic point and loot the town of supplies. After Sam Houston refused to command the expedition, Francis Johnson was selected. He and two hundred men then departed from the Alamo on December 30. Lt. Col. James C. Neill, whom Sam Houston had appointed commandant of the Alamo garrison on December 21, was left to pick up the pieces.[1]

Neill proceeded to do his duty as best he could, but he needed much help from the shaky government and such help was not forthcoming. Still, the colonel struggled on. He welcomed the arrivals of James Bowie, James Butler Bonham, William Barret Travis, and Davy Crockett. But on February 11, 1836, James Neill abruptly departed from the garrison and did not return. He left William B. Travis in command during his absence and the rest is, as they say, history. But what became of Neill?

Most contemporary accounts of the fall of the Alamo simply ignore Neill after he left, although some historians argue over the date of his departure and the reason for his speedy exit. Most say February 11, but some use the fourteenth, and doubtless other dates are out there somewhere. So what day did he leave?

The best evidence is found in a letter written February 11, by Green B. Jameson, the engineer of the garrison. Green says: "Col. Neill left today for home on account of an express from his family informing him of their ill health."[2] On the 12th, in another letter, William B. Travis wrote, "In consequence of the sickness of his family, Lt. Col. Neill has left this post, to visit home for a short time, and has requested me to take the Command of the Post."[3] On the 13th, in still another letter, Travis said, "I wrote you an official letter last night as Comdt of this post in the absence of Col. Neill. . . ."[4]

Such evidence seems conclusive that Neill left on February 11, so why would anyone use the 14th? The reason may be that a document exists, under that date, supposedly issued by Neill from the Alamo. On February 1, the men in Bexar held an election and selected Samuel Maverick and Jesse Badgett to represent them at the constitutional convention to be held in Washington-on-the-Brazos on March 1. Because Badgett had enlisted in the Army, Neill discharged him so he could attend the convention. His discharge papers were issued on February 14, three days after Neill supposedly left.[5] Thus the discrepancy over dates.

Do the discharge papers mean Neill left, came back, then left again? Probably not. After he left the first time, a dispute erupted between Bowie and Travis over who should command. It was resolved that they should both command, and on February 14, they notified the governor:

"All general orders and correspondence will henceforth be signed by both until Col. Neill's return."[6] No mention is made of Neill's returning and subsequently leaving again. While it is possible he returned after that dispatch was issued and then left again, that seems rather doubtful. More than likely the date on the discharge is simply an error, perhaps owing to his haste in leaving to be with his family. We know Badgett was still in the post on February 17, since he purchased wine for the hospital and some powder on that date,[7] so he was in no hurry to leave; but Neill might have been in such a hurry that he erred on the date. Based on the squabble over the command, it seems certain that neither Bowie nor Travis would have issued the discharge with Neill's signature.

It is probably safe to conclude that Neill left on February 11. So why did he leave? Many, if not most, writers cite the Jameson and Travis references to an illness in the colonel's family and pronounce the matter closed. Others, however, believe that the illness story was a simple ruse. They maintain that Neill had become so frustrated over not receiving desperately needed help for the garrison that he finally determined to go directly to the government leaders and either get some assistance or resign. The story about an illness was, they said, an effort not to alarm the men.

For years very little evidence existed to support that theory. The only reference to Neill's possible resignation appears in a letter from William B. Travis to the governor, dated February 13, 1836. He said, ". . . Col. Neill has applied to the Commander in chief to be relieved and is anxious for me to take the command. . . ."[8] Apparently that shred of evidence was enough to cause some to deduce that Neill's motive for leaving was not to attend to a family illness.

Recently more conclusive evidence has come to light. In the Daughters of the Republic of Texas library on the Alamo grounds, an old receipt seems to solve the mystery. The receipt reads, "Received San Felipe 28th Feby 1836 of Henry Smith Gov of Texas Six hundred dollars of public money for the use of the troops at Bejar." The receipt is signed J. C. Neill, Lt. Col. of Artillery.

In consideration of such evidence, it seems possible Neill did leave the Alamo in search of support for the garrison. The irony is that other proof as to Neill's purpose always existed but it was just a little hard to find. Another story is required to explain the obscure evidence.

In February of 1836, the Texas government was in shambles. A governor, Henry Smith, had been appointed to run things under the watchful eye of a general council of elected citizens. The governor generally favored fighting for independence, and those who sided with him were in the "war" party. The council generally favored having Texas become a separate state under either the reinstated Mexican Constitution of 1824, or a new Mexican constitution. Those siding with the council were in the "peace" party, although either way, there was sure to be fighting.

An almost inevitable rift developed between the governor and the council, and the differences exploded into internal warfare over the Matamoros expedition, which the Governor saw as the main cause of the weakened condition of the Alamo garrison. The disagreement led Governor Smith to demand that the council disband; and the council, in turn, promptly impeached the governor. The council also demanded that Governor Smith relinquish all official documents and the $5,000 in the treasury. Smith refused and, for all practical purposes, while the men of the Alamo were preparing to fight for their lives, there was no government in Texas to support them.

Almost two years later, on December 5, 1837, former governor Smith submitted a report on the account of the $5,000. An item for February 28, 1836, shows he gave James Neill $600 for the use of the troops at Bexar.[9] The entry coincides with the Neill receipt in every respect. The difference is that while the Neill receipt was only recently uncovered, the governor's report has been in the state archives for generations.

The fact that Neill was in San Felipe seventeen days after leaving the Alamo is not necessarily conclusive proof that he did not originally leave on account of illness in the family. It would not have taken seventeen days to travel from Bejar to San Felipe. There would have been time to visit his family and then venture off in search of help for the garrison. The fact that he signed the receipt Lt. Col. of Artillery is curious. Most of his documents were signed Lt. Col. commanding, so if he really did leave in an official capacity to seek money for the troops, why didn't his signature on the receipt for that money indicate he was in command?

It seems highly probable that Neill left because of family illness and was returning to the Alamo when he stopped in San Felipe to try to secure funds for the men in the garrison. The theory that Neill used the illness story as a ruse seems very hollow since, if his intention had actually been to secure funds, he surely would have told that to the men so they might be somewhat encouraged. In addition, Green Jameson clearly said Neill reacted to an express received. If the express concerned an official call, no record survived. It therefore appears Neill left to be with his family.

What became of Neill after he left is the more important question. In most accounts, the story of his involvement in the struggle for Texas independence resumes on April 11, when the Texas army received the now famous "Twin Sisters," a pair of cannons that arrived as a gift from the people of the city of Cincinnati, Ohio. James Neill was placed in command of the artillery when the "sisters" arrived. Frank X. Tolbert, in *The Day of San Jacinto*, describes what happened to Neill on April 20, 1836, in the first exchange of artillery fire between the Texans and the Mexicans: "Their [the Mexicans'] first shot fell directly into the Texas position and hit the artillery commander, Lieutenant Colonel Neill, on the rump."[10] Neill was then taken by boat to Lorenzo De Zavala's house across Buffalo Bayou, and he missed entirely the events of April 21, when Texas' independence was won.

So most historians ignore Neill from February 11 until April 11. Does that mean Neill ignored the Alamo? Apparently not. We know the colonel was in San Felipe on February 28, getting money for relief of the Alamo. He next surfaces on March 5, in Gonzales. On that date, the colonel signed one of the strangest documents of the revolutionary period in Texas. The document, which follows, was designed to solve the mystery of five pair of shoes missing from the Alamo.

> John W. Smith Public Store Keeper for the Garrison of Bejar you will issue to the bearer five pairs shoes and place them at the disposition of Mr Fitch to be sold for the use of this garrison

said shoes was delivered between the 16th & 24th of January 1836.[11]

This receipt was issued to clear up a discrepancy in the inventory of the Public Stores in the Alamo. On December 31, 1835, John Smith took inventory in the Alamo and found 102 pairs of shoes. Then on February 3, Smith took another inventory and could account for only 97 pairs of shoes. Smith noted that the discrepancy would be resolved when Mr. Fitch returned from San Felipe. Apparently, Fitch had disposed of the shoes and was most anxious to have Neill resolve the issue. The incredible thing about this affair is that amid all the turmoil of the times, there was still concern over the missing five pair of captured Mexican shoes.[12]

The day after Neill resolved the mystery of the missing shoes was one of the most fateful days in Texas history— Sunday, March 6, 1836, the day the Alamo fell. While his comrades in arms were lying dead in the dirt of the Alamo, the ever faithful Neill was in Gonzales spending $90 of the $600 he had received for medical supplies. The receipt he issued is as follows:

Gonzales
March 6th, 1836

Received of Horrace Eggleston a Set of medicines of the amount of Ninety Dollars which sd medicines I have this day purchased from him for the use of the Post of Bexar.

J.C. Neill
Col. Comdt. of
the Post of Bexar[13]

Although the men of the Alamo no longer needed medical help, Neill had no way to know that. It would be five days before word spread that the Alamo had fallen. What Neill did know was the garrison had a severe shortage of medical supplies. He had said as much in a January letter, and he would have known no help had arrived after he left, thanks to his visit with the governor. He also would have surmised there had been casualties as

a result of the siege. So, Neill was trying to help as best
he could.

No written proof exists to show what Neill did with the
supplies he purchased, but there is strong evidence that
the day after the fall of the Alamo, fifty men left Gonzales
and headed back to the Alamo. Most certainly they would
have carried the supplies with them since that would
account for Neill's making the purchase. It also appears
likely Neill was among the group.

On March 6, 1836, Captain Moseley Baker and 110 men
arrived in Gonzales. On the 8th, in a personal letter, Baker
stated, "I found about one hundred and sixty men here,
which, with our force, made about two hundred and
seventy, fifty of which started on yesterday for the
Alamo."[14] It is very hard to imagine that fifty men started
for the Alamo without Neill, the man who had purchased
the medical supplies and who still claimed command of the
post. One small shred of evidence exists that actually
suggests Neill was in the group. On March 6, Acting
Governor James W. Robinson wrote to James Fannin. In
part he said, "This moment information has been given
that about 30 men has thrown themselves into Bears for it's
relief from Gonzales, that many more is on the way under
Coll. Neill Genrl. Barlison & to raise the siege if possible."[15] This line, reproduced exactly as it was written and
showing poor spelling—especially Bears for Bexar—
presents some perplexing problems in trying to determine
Neill's movements.

Robinson seems to be saying that Neill and Burleson,
with thirty more men, were on their way to break the
siege. Break a siege by several thousand with thirty men?
The governor must have been as much an optimist as he
was poor speller. Be that as it may, it appears he had just
received news that thirty-two men from Gonzales had
gone to the aid of the Alamo garrison and in the same
dispatch was information that Neill and Burleson were on
their way to the Alamo. Based on the dates involved, it
appears Neill left Washington shortly after obtaining his
$600 and went immediately to Gonzales, arriving perhaps
on the 1st or 2nd. He and Burleson must have made
immediate plans to march and sent word to that effect at
once back to the governor. Otherwise, the information
could not have reached Washington by March 6. Whatever

communication the governor was referring to apparently did not survive.

The next question becomes: If Neill and Burleson decided no later than the 2nd or 3rd to return to Bexar, why did they wait until the 7th to leave when the governor was under the impression they were on the way by the 6th? Had they left immediately, they probably would have been in the Alamo when it fell, and it surely would have still fallen. Fifty or so more men would not have helped the Texas cause that Sunday morning other than perhaps to slay a few more of the enemy before falling.

We can only guess at the reason for the delay. It seems doubtful they were waiting for men, since more than fifty were on hand at the time. They certainly were not waiting for Houston since he did not receive his orders to march until March 6, the same day Robinson got word that Neill was on the way to Bexar. We'll never know for sure, but it's just possible that Neill waited until Horrace Eggleston arrived with the medical supplies which Neill surmised were desperately needed.

Regardless of the reason, it appears the fifty left on the 7th. What happened after that becomes difficult to determine. The next thing we know for sure is that Neill was back in Gonzales on March 10. The three missing days are most difficult to fill with facts.

Sam Houston apparently did not know of Neill's plan to break the siege. On March 9, while en route to Gonzales to take command of the army, Houston issued orders to Neill, as commander of Gonzales, and, in turn, to Fannin for the two armies to link up and prepare to go to the relief of Bexar.[16] On the 10th, Neill replied, "I have received with great satisfaction your communication of the 9th inst. . . . I shall forward your communication to Colonel Fannin by express agreeably to your instructions, giving him due time to concentrate his forces with mine at the time and place I shall designate."[17]

Neill's presence in Gonzales on March 10 is a complication. The infamous fifty men could not have marched all the way to Bexar and back in three days. Furthermore, had that occurred, they certainly would have had word of the fall of the Alamo. Such was not the case. The first news of the fall did not reach Gonzales until the 11th, when two Mexicans arrived shortly after Sam Houston with the horrible news. Official confirmation did not arrive until the 13th, when "Deaf" Smith arrived piloting Susanna Dickinson and her child, along with Travis' slave Joe, all of whom had been spared by Santa Anna. It is, therefore, positively shown that Neill and the fifty men did not march all the way to Bexar and return. They must have turned back before reaching the Alamo. But why?

No less a character than Sam Houston gives us the answer. On March 13, before receiving official confirmation of the fall of the Alamo, Houston was trying to outfit a company to go to Bexar and ascertain the truth. He wrote, "The scarcity of horses, and the repulse of a party of twenty-eight men, the other day, within eighteen miles of Bexar, will, I apprehend, prevent the expedition."[18] That information seems to confirm that Neill and his men got close to Bexar before being driven back by a superior force. But why only twenty-eight when Moseley said fifty went out? Again Sam Houston comes to the rescue.

On the 11th, Houston reported that he felt the worst for the Alamo because Travis had said he would fire signals each day that he was safe, and the signals had stopped. Houston wrote, "No signal guns have been heard since Sunday, though a scouting party have just returned who approached within twelve miles of it, and remained there forty-eight hours."[19]

Based on the Houston clues, it appears the following is what happened to the Neill force of fifty: The group moved out on March 7, and closed to within eighteen miles of Bexar before being repulsed by a Mexican patrol. At that point a small scouting party broke off from the main group. Perhaps it contained twenty-two men; perhaps fewer since the number fifty was probably an estimate rather than an actual head count. The scouting party then closed to within twelve miles and waited two days hoping to hear the signal guns. When no such signal was heard, they returned. Houston mentions the two groups and two distances because, at the time, he was probably unaware they were all part of one group originally. Apparently, Neill returned with the twenty-eight since he was in camp on the 10th and the scouting party did not return until the 11th.

There is another wild story about the whereabouts of Neill worthy only of passing mention. The story comes from none other than William P. Zuber, the very man who gave us the tale of Louis Rose escaping from the Alamo and of Travis' speech and line in the dirt.

In 1877, Zuber was asked by the adjutant general of Texas, William Steele, to help determine who had died in the Alamo. In a letter to Steele, Zuber included a fanciful tale about Neill. Zuber claimed that on March 13, he was camped with a detachment of troops on the Colorado River near present-day La Grange. Supposedly about nine o'clock that night Neill came riding into camp with the news the Alamo had fallen. As Zuber told it, Neill had carried an express from Travis to either San Felipe or Washington and was returning to the Alamo when, on March 7, he met Susanna Dickinson on her way to Gonzales and she told him of the fall. Zuber concluded, "Of course, Colonel Neill returned with Mrs. Dickinson, to the Colorado. He first went to Bastrop, to inform the citizens of the great calamity, & was proceeding down the river, for the same purpose." Zuber claimed he kept a diary and witnessed and noted what he saw.[20]

This story is so full of erroneous information that it almost defies description. And it gets worse. In another letter, dated 1904, Zuber told a different version of the story. In the second letter he dropped the part about Neill's spreading the word of the disaster and said, instead, "He [Neill] seems to have passed Gonzales without halting to inform General Houston, our little force at that place, nor the people of the town of the great calamity. I know not why, for while he was stating the facts to us—at that precise moment—Mrs. Dickinson was stating the same to General Houston at Gonzales. . . ."[21]

This Zuber tale appears to be total fantasy. Colonel Neill was the commander of the Alamo and would not have carried dispatches for Travis. Susanna Dickinson knew Neill very well and never mentioned meeting him on the trail. The possibility that Neill would have passed by Gonzales without informing anyone of the calamity does not even warrant comment. We know that Neill was in Gonzales on March 10, waiting for Houston, and that he had been assigned to command the men in that location in a link-up with Fannin's men and subsequent march to Bexar. The possibility that Neill was forty-five miles east of Gonzales and riding alone on the 13th seems too far fetched to receive serious consideration.

William P. Zuber either erred in placing Neill in this story or he out-and-out lied. Either way, because he said he witnessed and recorded the event, his misinformation must cast suspicion on the man's credibility. The natural question that follows is, did he make up the Rose story? The irony of the Zuber tale about Neill is that in the 1904 letter, Zuber was attempting to explain how misinformation about the Alamo became accepted fact. In one part of the letter he said, "I happen to know how some of the absurd stories of alleged Alamo incidents originated." It's difficult not to wonder just how much he really did know.

As for James C. Neill, the reliable evidence seems to fit like a glove on a hand and should perhaps be considered conclusive. The history books tell us that, as a result of his being wounded at San Jacinto, Neill was awarded a headright certificate for a league of land in Harrisburg County in 1838. He led an expedition against the Indians of the upper Trinity River in 1842 and was assigned to treat with the Indians in 1844. He was awarded a pension of $200 per year for life in 1845, but died shortly thereafter at his home on Spring Creek in Navarro County. He apparently never left a written account of his involvement in the Alamo and his attempts to return.

One additional point worthy of note. On March 6, 1836, Lt. Col. James C. Neill was still the commander of record for the Alamo garrison, and he was actively participating in the affairs of the day. The history books should all be re-written to show Travis as *acting commander* out of respect for Lt. Col. Neill, who apparently did his best to throw himself back "into Bears."

The Missing Alamo Letter That Toppled a Government

Historians have known for generations that a single letter from the Alamo garrison was largely responsible for bringing down the shaky government of Texas in early 1836. Many, if not most, of those historians have believed the letter that did the deed was written by Lt. Col. James C. Neill on January 6, 1836. A review of the facts indicates that those historians are dead wrong.

As 1835 drew to a close, the meager army of Texas was on somewhat of an undefeated roll. Victories had been won at Gonzales, at Goliad, at Mission Concepcion, and at San Antonio de Bexar, where the ultimate prize was the Alamo garrison. There was strong sentiment to take the war to Mexican soil, and an expedition against Matamoros was undertaken.

F. W. Johnson, the commander of the volunteers in San Antonio de Bexar, was a champion of the Matamoros expedition. He looted the Alamo garrison of vital supplies and selected about two hundred volunteers (more than two-thirds of the total available men) for the adventure. At the end of 1835, the expedition, under command of Johnson and John Grant, marched into the Texas sunset leaving behind a naked and undermanned Alamo garrison.

Lt. Colonel James C. Neill, commander of the regulars in the Alamo garrison, was left the unenviable task of trying to pick up the pieces of his command after Johnson and Grant had left. Even though the few remaining men under Neill's command swore an allegiance to stand and defend the important post of Bexar, they lacked the bare essentials of life and war with which to effect that defense. Frustrated and angry, Neill took the only course open to him. He wrote an urgent plea for help to General Sam Houston, the commander in chief of the army of Texas. Neill's letter set off a chain reaction that ultimately toppled the Texas government.

On January 6, Houston, who was not in favor of the Matamoros expedition, received Neill's dispatch at army headquarters in Washington-on-the-Brazos, Texas. He forwarded it, along with an urgent plea of his own, to Henry Smith, governor of Texas. Houston requested the governor's "serious attention" and asked that the Neill letter be presented to the general council in secret session so that they might adopt some course "that will redeem our country from a state of deplorable anarchy." The general predicted that, "Manly and bold decision alone can save us from ruin" and he included a plea for help with, "Oh save our poor country! — send supplies to the wounded, the sick, the naked, and the hungry."[1]

Governor Henry Smith received Houston's package of dispatches at San Felipe de Austin on January 9, and it is easy to surmise his blood pressure jumped fifty points. Smith also did not favor the Matamoros adventure, believing it could cost Texas the support of liberal Mexican citizens living in the province of Texas, and news that Texas troops had been left starving on the prairie would certainly have provoked the governor. Accordingly, Smith took up his own pen and addressed a letter to the general council.

The letter Smith wrote has to rank as one of the boldest of the Texas revolution period. He called the Matamoros expedition "predatory" and flatly predicted the general council had "Judas in the camp" and "base corruption." He said there were scoundrels and parricides on the council that had left their country "bleeding at every pore."

The governor also had a "balm" for the country's wounds. He announced that the members of the council had done all that was required of them and that their services were no longer needed. Smith boldly announced that, until the constitutional convention convened on March 2, he alone would continue to run the country as governor and commander in chief.[2] Unfortunately for the governor, there was no real basis in law for his actions.

The council met in secret session, as Houston had requested, on January 10, and received with much despair, the governor's attack and charges. On the 11th, the council members went public with the "secret" proceedings and demanded that Governor Smith cease the function of his office. Lt. Gov. James W. Robinson was sworn in as acting governor.[3]

On January 12, Governor Smith announced that perhaps his language had been too harsh and that he was willing to compromise if the council would admit their errors and correct them, which would mean cancelling the Matamoros expedition.[4] The council countered with an announcement that it was too late, the damage had been done; and they demanded Smith relinquish all the state papers and the $5,000 in the state treasury.[5] Smith refused to comply, and an impasse developed. The council appointed a five-man advisory committee to run the government, and by January 17, a quorum could not be reached in the general council so, in effect, the government of Texas ceased to operate. While the men of the Alamo desperately needed help, there was no one left to help them.

Students of Texas history often refer to the following Neill letter of January 6, 1836, as the ax which felled the shaky tree of Texas government:

> Sirs: Having informed officially the Commander in chief of the Federal Army of Texas at Washington, the condition and situation of my command, I deem it my infinite duty to make a corresponding representation to you, altho' so far as regards the social intercourse desired between the Civil Authorities, the citizens, and our Army, every thing has been harmonized Since the Command has devolved upon me, to my Complete satisfaction, and far beyond my most sanguine expectations.
>
> You have doubtless heard from various

Sources of the arbitrary rule of the aides de Camp of Genl. E. Burleson, F. W. Johnson, and James Grant the Town was surrendered on the 9th Decr. and so long as they remained in command there was not a move made by them to restore or organize harmony, or to reestablish the civil functions of Govt. which continued up to the 30th ulto, and on that day and the next through the aid of major G. B. Jameson, I had on the first day of this month all of the civil functions of this department put in power — under the Constitution of 1824, and all things are now Conducted on a permanent basis, the Army aids and sustains the civil authority, while the Civil Authority aids us in getting horses, and such supplies as the greatly impoverished vicinity affords.

It will be appalling to you to learn, and see herewith inclosed our alarming weakness, but I have one pleasurable gratification which will not be erased from the tablet of my memory during natural life, that those whose names are herewith inclosed are to a man those who acted so gallant in the 10 weeks open field campaign, and then won an unparalleled victory in the five days siege of this place — Such men in Such a condition and under all the gloomy embarrassments surrounding, calls aloud upon you and their country, for aid, praise, and sympathy.

We have 104 men and two distinct fortresses to garrison, and about twenty four pieces of artillery. You doubtless have learned that we have no provisions or clothing since Johnson and Grant left. If there has ever been a dollar here I have no knowledge of it. The clothing sent here by the aid and patriotic exertions of the honorable Council, was taken from us by arbitrary measures of Johnson and Grant, taken from men who endured all the hardships of winter and who were not even sufficiently clad for summer, many of them having but one blanket and one shirt, and what was intended for them given away to men, some of whom had not been in the army more than 4 days, and many not exceeding two weeks. If a divide had been made of them, the most needy of my men could have been made comfortable by the stock of clothing and provisions taken from here.

About 200 of the men who had volunteered to garrison this place for 4 months left my command contrary to my orders and thereby vitiated the policy of their enlistment and should not be entitled to neither compensation, nor an honorable discharge, leaving this garrison destitute of men, and at all times within 8 or 10 days reach of an overwhelming Enemy, and at all times great danger was apprehended from want of Civil order and Govt among the lower class of the Mexican soldiers left behind, they have not even left here for our Government an english Copy of the Treaty, so derogatorily made.

I want here for this garrison at all times 200 men and I think 300 until the repairs and improvements of the fortifications is completed, a chart and index of which has been sent to Headquarters at Washington, with the present Condition of the Fort, and such improvements suggested by Mr Jameson as has met my approbation, and I hope will be accorded by my Commander.

As I have stated to you before our exact situation here, I know you will make no delay to ameliorate our condition. The men have not even money to pay their washing, the hospital is also want of stores and even the necessary provisions for well men was not left the wounded by Grant, and Johnson, send us money in haste, the men have been here many of them more than three months and some of them have not had a dollar during the time.

I shall say to you as I have to my Commander in Chief, the services of Major Jameson to this army, and to his Country, cannot be too highly appreciated, the present army owes in a great part its existence to his exertions, and management, and so far as I am concerned in my Command, I assure you I cannot get along without him. I hope he will be continued in the army.

There are many subjects, that owing to the bearer of this letter being on the Eve of leaving, that has passed my attention of which you should be advised, and I will from time to time give you such information as may transpire here, and hope you will use all the exertions necessary in your power, to stimulate the men now under my Command to remain, and to award to each, and Every one of them, such praise as your patriotism may dictate, and I particularly recommend to your notice the officers now under my Command.

I further add that owing to our having no correspondence with the interior, that we Know not what day, or hour, an enemy of 1000 in number may be down upon us, and as we have no supplies of provisions within the fortress we could be starved out in 4 days by anything like a close siege.

I will say to you I know about the feelings of the Citizens of this place on the subject of Independence — they Know not whose hands they may fall into, but if we had a force here that they Knew could sustain them I believe they would be 3/4ths American and go for Independence and claim all to the Rio Del Norte as they Know we want it and will have it —

The extent to which the impressment of Cattle and Horses, has been carried to by Johnson and Grant, has been the Cause of great Complaint and very much distress among the poorer class of the inhabitants, as several of them have been deprived of the means of cultivating their Crop for the ensuing Season, and which is their only means of support, owing to their Cattle being taken from them.

I beg leave to tender to his excellency the Governor and the Honorable Council the high regard I have for their patriotic exertions, in sustaining the present Federal Army of Texas, in my own name, and also in the name of all those I have the Honor to command at this post. . . .

P.S. The troops who Engaged to Garrison this place for the term of 4 months, did so with an understanding that they were to be paid monthly and unless money comes in time there are several of them will return home —

I am just informed through a private source, that there are one Thousand Troops now on their march from Laredo towards this place, Should I receive any further information as to their proceedings or destination I will advise you without loss of time by express. . . .[6]

This letter, addressed to the governor and the general council, pointed out the appalling and alarming weaknesses of the Alamo garrison and almost begged for help. The facts, however, indicate it is not the "express" letter that did the damage to the government of Texas.

In 1836, communications were difficult at best on the rugged frontier of Texas. Letters were handwritten and carried from point to point via horseback. The courier trip from San Antonio to San Felipe could easily take four days or more. Some historians have pointed out that Neill's letter of the 6th could easily have been in San Felipe on the 10th when the governor presented his case to the council. Those same historians seem to overlook the fact that the governor wrote his scathing attack on the 9th and Neill's letter of the 6th could not easily have been there on that date. It would have taken a spirited ride for a courier to cover the distance in three days; and in the absence of enemy activity, it is doubtful such a swift ride would have been contemplated.

Sam Houston, on the other hand, wrote his letter to the governor on January 6, from Washington-on-the-Brazos. He clearly states he is enclosing a report from Neill; and since it is not physically possible for that report to have been the one Neill wrote on the same day more than 180 miles away, there must have been an earlier Neill letter. Houston's package of dispatches written in Washington on the 6th could easily have been in San Felipe on the 9th. Since the governor honored Houston's request and asked for a secret session of the council, it seems certain he was reacting to the Houston dispatch and not the Neill letter of the 6th.

It is likely that most historians simply assumed that the Neill letter of January 6 was the culprit since that is the earliest surviving message from Neill after he assumed command of the Alamo. The colonel himself gives us a clue, however, that his initial report was issued earlier. In another letter to Sam Houston dated January 14, Neill states, "Fourteen days has expired since I commenced informing my superior officers of my situation. . . ."7 Simple math tells us that if he were writing on the 14th and fourteen days had expired, then his first message must have been dated on the 1st, shortly after Johnson and the Matamoros expedition departed San Antonio. A letter of that date could easily have been in Houston's hands on the 6th and subsequently in Governor Smith's possession on the 9th.

The only complication to that theory—and one that may have thrown many historians off the trail—is that in his letter of January 14, Neill begins with, "This is my third official since my command at this place and they are all of the same nature, complaining of Provisions, men and money. . . ." We know Neill wrote on the 6th, then again on the 8th (to inform the government that Indians around San Antonio wanted to talk treaty) and then again twice on the 14th. That would seem, at first glance, to indicate the three letters he mentions were accounted for, making the letter of the 6th the culprit. Probably not.

Apparently, Colonel Neill used the word "official" as a designation only for his correspondence to his commander in chief Sam Houston. Neill opened his letter of January 6 by saying he had already "officially" notified his commander. On the 14th, he actually wrote two letters, one to Houston and one to the government, but only the Houston correspondence was marked official. Since his letter of the 14th was his third official, it appears the one he wrote fourteen days earlier—the one that brought down the government—and another one written between the 1st and the 14th, are both missing. Another Neill letter, apparently written on the 13th to the government and referenced in his letter of the 14th, is also missing.

The questions now become, what did that January 1 letter say and what happened to it? Unfortunately, we are left with nothing but speculation for the answers, but the surviving evidence suggests what might have transpired.

We know that on the date the letter was written, Neill was not in a good frame of mind. His post had just been looted, and he was left wanting for men and supplies. If the letter was to be private and not official, Neill may not have intended his words to actually reach the council so he could have named names and pointed the ugly finger of guilt at specific members of the council or at Johnson and Grant. Such a possibility might account for the governor's subsequently calling some council members Judas and scoundrels. We do know the words Neill chose were strong enough to prompt Houston to use the phrase, "What will the world think of the authorities of Texas?"

As to what happened to the letter, that is another mystery which may never be solved. It is strange, however, that much of the written material from that period survived and yet one of the most important documents did not. The fact that the letter disappeared may be testimony to the fact that Neill did name names—that he did offer proof of the contemptuous acts of the council. The letter was ultimately turned over to the council members themselves; and if it were so inflammatory as to bring down a government, it does not take much imagination to guess that perhaps the evidence was either destroyed or simply conveniently misplaced. Any copy Neill might have kept for himself would have fallen into Mexican hands when the Alamo fell.

No matter what the letter said and no matter what happened to it, let history show that an imposter has been blamed for toppling the fledgling Texas government of early 1836. The real culprit has escaped and whatever information it might have contained has been lost with it. The students of the history of the Republic of Texas have been denied a key that might have unlocked some valuable secrets.

The Alamo Mystery Letter

The period of the Texas revolution produced many heroes and noteworthy people. One of the participants in the activities of those days, Phillip Dimitt,[1] achieved sufficient notoriety to have a Texas county named for him. But was Dimitt of the mettle to qualify for such an honor? Perhaps not. One letter Dimitt left behind suggests he deserted the Alamo in the very hour of need.

Dimitt, a native of Kentucky, was twenty-one years old when he ventured into Texas in 1822. In 1828, he took a Mexican wife and became a naturalized Mexican citizen. A year later he applied, as head of a family, for a league of land, and six years later, in 1835, he received title to the land. He then established Dimitt's Landing, a trading post on Lavaca Bay, and received the contract to supply the Mexican garrison at San Antonio de Bexar.[2] Life couldn't be better!

When hostilities erupted between the colonists in Texas and the Mexican government, Dimitt was a willing participant. In October of 1835, he and George Collinsworth took command of a small group of volunteers and seized the garrison at Goliad. Dimitt remained in command with the rank of captain and called upon the inhabitants east of the Guadalupe River to rally in support of the Texas cause. The young captain must have performed well, initially, since his commander in chief, Stephen F. Austin, took time to commend him. On October 22, Austin wrote to young Dimitt, ". . . I am much pleased with your exertions to send us supplies of which we are greatly in want."[3]

The good times did not last long for Captain Dimitt. Apparently his fitness for command and leadership was somewhat lacking, and those deficiencies did not escape the notice of his superiors. General Austin began receiving disturbing reports on Dimitt's activity and was finally forced to take action. On November 18, Austin wrote the following letter to Dimitt in Goliad:

> On receipt of this you will deliver to Capt. Geo. M. Collinsworth the command of that fort and town. I regret to say that I am compelled to adopt this measure, owing to complaints made by Govr. Viesca and also by the Acting Alcalde of that place and other sources. These complaints show that great harshness has been used towards the inhabitants of Goliad. This conduct is the reverse of what I had expected and had ordered and is well calculated to injure the cause we are engaged in.[4]

On the same day Austin wrote to Collinsworth informing him that he was to take command. The general also included a note, in Spanish, to be presented to the local citizens and the alcalde, which explained his actions and to make it clear Collinsworth would work in accordance with the civil authority. There was no doubt Austin was concerned that Dimitt's actions might cost Texas the cooperation of loyalist Mexicans sympathetic to the Texas cause.[5]

Whether or not Dimitt actually complied and relinquished command is not clear. It appears the captain did depart Goliad for some time and participated in the siege of Bexar by the Texas army under Austin. He did not stay to see that conflict through to conclusion on December 10, however, since by December 2, Dimitt was back in Goliad and apparently back in command. On that date he authored a long narrative concerning a proposed expedition to Matamoros, Mexico. In part, he predicted:

> If this [the Matamoros Expedition] or some other
> movement like this, is not adopted, which will
> enable us to hurl the thunder back in the very
> atmosphere of the enemy, drag him, and with
> him the war out of Texas, her resources and her
> blood must continue to flow from the centre to
> the frontier. If this is done, the paralyzing effects,
> and the immediate calamities of war will be
> greatly mitigated.[6]

Young Dimitt was, in all likelihood, a headstrong young
man and not prepared to relinquish his position easily. On
December 9, he was recognized as being in command
when the General Council authorized payment for horses
Dimitt had pressed into service for Texas.[7] But it was not
long before his old problems of handling that command
reappeared. Evidence of that fact can be found in a letter
dated December 16, 1835, from H. M. Fraser to James
Power. Although Fraser's English was rather poor, his
intent was clear. He said:

> This is will inform you that I am still under
> Confinement in prison and no hopes of my
> release until Dimmet pleases — he wount give
> me a Trial nor give me the satisfaction of know-
> ing my crimes — or give me no Correct answer
> whatever — only sais he is waiting from head
> Quarters for a Answer . . .[8]

Dimitt's problems were not isolated to imprisoning one
man. He seems to have gained the ire of many people in
Goliad and elsewhere, including some rather influential
folks. On December 17, without knowledge of the Fraser
letter, F. W. Johnson, who was selected to lead the
Matamoros expedition, wrote to the governor with some
serious charges. He said:

> I have the honor to acquaint you that strong
> representations have been made to Generals
> [Stephen F.] Austin & [Edward] Burleson, & lat-
> terly to me against Captn. Dimitt of Goliad for
> Arbitrary Conduct in the execution of his duty,

for repeated attacks on individual property And for a total disregard of the civil authorities & civil rights of the citizens of Goliad & Guadalupe. In consequence of these representations my predessors in Command ordered his removal from the Charge of Goliad, but these orders have been treated with Contempt & I feel myself in Consequence called upon to draw the attention of the Executive to this matter, as a continuance of such violent measures will seriously injure the cause of Texas particularly & of liberty generally. To Col. James Bowie, who lately visited Goliad I beg to refer Your Excellency, for further particulars of Captn. Dimmitt's Conduct.[9]

Incredibly, Phillip Dimitt again avoided a bullet and maintained command. There is no record the governor ever embarked on a course designed to strip Dimitt of his position; and as for the prisoner Frazer, the council simply ordered him released or forwarded to San Felipe with appropriate charges.[10]

Emerging basically unscathed, the captain continued his patriotic ways when he and Ira Ingram drafted a declaration of independence in Goliad on December 20, 1835. In consequence of that declaration, Dimitt even designed what may have been the first flag of Texas independence, a white banner with an arm raising a sword dripping with blood. The banner was hoisted over Goliad on a flagstaff made of a sycamore tree cut from the banks of the Guadalupe.[11] Although the action of Dimitt and the others in Goliad was actually the first effort of any group of Texans to declare themselves free of Mexican rule, the governing council of Texas was still fighting for restoration of the Mexican constitution at the time, and the declaration was suppressed.

By January 1836, Dimitt not only still held command of Goliad but was being requested to continue to do so by the government. In the proceedings of the General Council of Texas, part of the entry for January 6, 1836, from the committee on military affairs reads: "Your committee would further recommend that Captain Dimit [sic] be earnestly requested to remain commandant at Goliad, and to keep as many of the troops at present under his command, as will remain at that post."[12]

In the span of less than a month, young Dimitt went from having half of Texas looking for his scalp to the government's "earnestly requesting" he remain in command. That would have to rank as an incredible turnaround. Also, by January 10, Dimitt had done an about face on the Matamoros expedition. On that date Dr. John Grant, a leader of the expedition, had arrived in Goliad and confiscated all available horses. An apparently angry Dimitt fired off a note to the governor complaining, "The Volunteers who were the first to open the war, who have taken this post and maintained it, and who were on the eve of being relieved from garrison duty, are by this act left without the means of transportation to their homes."[13]

The firebrand captain was still in Goliad in mid-January when Sam Houston, who succeeded Austin as commander of the military, arrived to try to make some sense out of the Texas army, which had been sharply split over the Matamoros fiasco. Houston's top priority was to strengthen the Alamo garrison. His first order was to James Bowie, who was instructed to march to Bexar with twenty to fifty men. As for Captain Dimitt, he was ordered to raise one hundred volunteers and "march to Bexar forthwith, if it should be invaded, and if not to repair to headquarters with his company."[14]

In very early 1836, volunteers were scarce as hen's teeth in Texas, and the probability that Dimitt was able to carry out his orders is slim. No record exists to suggest Dimitt arrived at the Alamo with anywhere near one hundred men, but we know he at least went himself. It is remotely possible Dimitt went with a small party to deliver supplies in fulfillment of a trade for cannons.

In January the Alamo garrison was in desperate need of supplies and provisions and, despite many pleas to the government, no help was forthcoming. Lt. Col. James C. Neill, commander of the post at Bexar, decided to try a trade for supplies since he had something a lot of other people wanted—cannons, lots of cannons. In a letter of January 14 to Sam Houston, Neill said, "I have sent to the command of Major Dimitt, three pieces of artillery and must have in return three loads of supplies, as per contract with the owners of said wagons."[15] We have no record that the deal was ever consummated, but the time frame would have been about right if Dimitt was in Bexar in the latter part of February.

There is also the very slight possibility that Phillip Dimitt was among the group who went to the Alamo with William B. Travis. On January 30, while enroute to San Antonio, Travis recorded in a small notebook that he paid "Dement" six dollars for shoeing horses. If Dement was Dimitt, there is the possibility either that the captain was a part of Travis' group or that Dimitt simply tagged along and arrived at the Alamo on February 3.[16]

We do know that before the end of February, the young captain was in neither Bexar nor Goliad but rather was back at Dimitt's Landing on Lavaca Bay along the Gulf coast. He arrived at that location on February 28, five days after the Mexicans laid siege at the Alamo, and quickly wrote to fellow Kentucky transplant James Kerr. Captain Dimitt said:

> I have this moment, 8 p.m., arrived from Bexar. On the 23d, I was requested by Colonel Travis to take Lieutenant Nobles and reconnoiter the enemy. Some distance out I met a Mexican who informed me that the town had been invested. After a short time a messenger overtook me, saying he had been sent by a friend of my wife to let me know that it would be impossible for me to return, as two large bodies of Mexican troops were already around the town. I then proceeded to the Rovia and remained till 10 p.m. on the 25th. On the 24th there was heavy cannonading, particularly at the close of evening. I left the Rovia at 10 p.m. on the 25th, and heard no more firing, from which I concluded the Alamo had been taken by storm. On the night of the 24th, I was informed that there were from four to six thousand Mexicans in and around Bexar. Urrea was at Carisota, on the Matamoros road, marching for Goliad. If immediate steps are not taken to defend Guadalupe Victoria, the Mexican will soon be upon our families.[17]

If taken at face value by the casual observer, the letter appears to be another in the long list of documents expressing concern over the advancing Mexican army. But when examined under a historical microscope, the letter takes on somewhat more of a sinister overtone.

Dimitt's remark that on February 23 he was requested by Travis to "reconnoiter" the enemy seems very strange indeed. It is well documented that the Mexican arrival of the 23rd was a surprise to Travis and the men of the Alamo. Travis himself expected the Mexicans about March 15 so why would he send two men to reconnoiter an enemy he did not know was near? Travis did send out a few scouts, but if that had been Dimitt's charge, why did he not say "scout for" in place of reconnoiter?

There are also some serious questions about Dimitt's remark that "some distance out I met a Mexican who informed me that the town had been invested." If Travis had sent him out on the morning of the 23rd, whether to reconnoiter or scout, he surely would have sent him south, the direction from which the Mexicans were expected. On the morning of the 23rd as many as two thousand Mexicans, with a long line of baggage cars, were moving toward San Antonio from eight miles out. Are we to believe Dimitt could have gone south and missed an entire army practically in the town's backyard? That doesn't seem possible.

Dimitt's account of what supposedly followed is certainly suspect. He said he stayed in the area for two days after being told he could not return to Bexar for his wife. On the 24th, Dimitt claimed, he heard heavy cannonading, especially heavy at the close of day and then left on the evening of the 25th and, hearing no more cannon shots, assumed the Alamo had fallen. From other reliable sources we know the Mexicans began cannon fire on the 24th, but the first major engagement did not occur until the afternoon of the 25th.[18] We also know that the cannon fire continued unabated until March 5.

The known facts just do not square with Dimitt's account. Some might say he was simply confused about dates and the heavy firing he heard was really the battle of the 25th. If that were true, surely he was not confused about staying in the area for twenty-four hours after the battle which would mean, if the dates were confused, he did not really leave until the night of the 26th. That being the case, he could not have been at Dimitt's Point on the 28th. It seems highly unlikely that problems with the facts in the letter can be explained away with a "mistaken date" theory.

Dimitt's remark that all firing ceased after the battle is also most suspect. Some of the men in Fannin's command at Goliad, ninety miles away from San Antonio, claimed they could hear Mexicans firing at the Alamo. Other troops, in Gonzales, seventy miles away, said the same thing. Since the cannon fire continued almost unabated, it doesn't seem possible Dimitt could have traveled fast enough and far enough on the evening of the 25th to get completely out of hearing range of the cannon shots.

Perhaps the most damaging part of the letter is the matter of dates and times. If, as Dimitt says, he did not depart the area until 10 p.m. on the 25th, how is it possible he arrived home on the gulf coast, more than two hundred miles away, exactly seventy-six hours later. He would have had to average almost three miles per hour round the clock for virtually three days. Knowledgeable horsemen advise that while such a ride is barely possible, it would require a horse well trained for long distance endurance riding. We have no reason to suspect Dimitt would have had such a mount. The possibility that he might have changed mounts several times along the route seems remote since horses were in short supply and not easily obtained on the trail. On the other hand, had Dimitt left San Antonio on the afternoon of the 23rd and ridden all the way to the coast, he could easily have arrived by the afternoon of the 28th.

Another small matter with the letter is that he apparently is saying he abandoned his wife and the cause of Texas and simply went home. If Dimitt was such a patriot, as he had previously indicated, why didn't he ride for Goliad where Colonel Fannin had over four hundred men and warn them of impending danger? Better still, if he really felt the Alamo had fallen, why didn't he ride directly to San Felipe de Austin, the seat of government, and warn the provincial leaders of the advance of the Mexicans? Why didn't Dimitt do something, anything, to go to the aid of his wife?

Dr. John Sutherland, one of the Alamo messengers who lived to tell his story. (*Courtesy The Archives Division of the Texas State Library Austin.*)

Based on the evidence, it is almost tempting to surmise that Captain Dimitt was never at the Alamo and made up the entire letter. But, thanks to one of Travis' couriers, John Sutherland, we do have confirmation of Dimitt's presence in the area near the Alamo on February 23.

Sutherland played a couple of key roles in the events surrounding the Alamo. He, along with Dr. John Smith, rode out of Bexar on the morning of February 23 to check on reports that the Mexicans were near; and by racing back to town after spotting the enemy, they provided the slim margin of notice that allowed the men to withdraw to the Alamo fortress before the enemy arrived. Travis then selected the Sutherland-Smith duo to carry a dispatch to Gonzales with an urgent plea for help. Fortunately for historians, Sutherland survived the ordeal and lived to tell his story. Unfortunately, Sutherland's account of the events of the 23rd casts serious doubt over the material in Dimitt's letter.

According to Sutherland, after discovering the Mexicans, he raced his horse back to Bexar to spread the alarm and encountered Captain Dimitt and Lt. Nobles at a ford of the San Antonio River near the Alamo. Dimitt inquired as to where Sutherland was going, and the doctor informed him of the approach of the Mexican army. Supposedly, the captain remarked that "there were not men enough at Bexar to defend the place, that it was bound to fall" and he encouraged Sutherland to leave with him, promising to "see him to safety" so they could "go and bring reinforcements to the garrison."[19]

Sutherland refused the offer saying he had to report to Travis. Dimitt replied that he would wait for the doctor at Southerland's house which was supposedly "just down the road." Sutherland completed his mission and made his report to Colonel Travis. Later in the afternoon, the doctor was dispatched with a message and, in his words, "I first rode down the river a short distance, thinking to meet Dimitt, but he had gone, taking the main Goliad road."

It is obvious someone is lying. But who? The account by Sutherland was not actually written until many years after the fact, and Dimitt's letter was supposedly written at the time of occurrence. Still, it seems doubtful that Sutherland's memory would have dulled to the point of missing the facts completely. That, plus what possible motive could Sutherland have had for falsifying the information? Time may have fogged Sutherland's memory as to minor points, but it is doubtful he could have erred in placing Dimitt near the Alamo at the critical moment.

If John Sutherland was even close in his account of Dimitt's claiming the Alamo could not stand up against the Mexicans without reinforcements, then why didn't Dimitt do as he proposed and return with help? If Dimitt left as presented, he would have passed through Goliad where Fannin and his men were waiting. There is no record of Dimitt trying to convince Fannin to march to Bexar, much less warning him of danger. All we know for sure is that Dimitt turned tail and ran — all the way back home. The only record we have of his spreading the alarm was the one letter to his old friend Kerr. Very strange, indeed.

Two days after Dimitt wrote his letter, the constitutional convention opened in Washington-on-the-Brazos, Texas. On March 2, independence from Mexico was declared and by March 6, Sam Houston was confirmed commander in chief of the army and was on his way to Gonzales to coordinate the war effort. On March 11, Houston was informed of the fall of the Alamo by two alleged Mexican spies. The next day, General Sam wrote to none other than Phillip Dimitt and ordered the captain to bring all available men to Gonzales. In an official post script to that letter, Houston said: "I am induced to believe from all the facts communicated to us that the Alamo has fallen, and all our men are murdered. We must not depend on forts; the roads and ravines suit us best."[20]

So one of the first things Houston did, on learning that perhaps the Alamo had fallen, was to notify Dimitt and even offer advice that forts should not be used. And yet Dimitt, by his own admission, had already deduced the Alamo was lost fourteen days earlier and apparently made no effort to warn Houston or the convention. Most of the records of the convention were carefully preserved, and there is no mention anywhere of any notification from Dimitt that the Alamo might have fallen.[21]

According to what we know, it is hard not to imagine that Dimitt's letter was some sort of preconceived alibi. It appears he was in San Antonio when the Mexicans arrived. It seems he hightailed it out of town and went all the way home without going for help and without trying to warn his fellow countrymen. But once he was safe and sound, what if he wondered if someone, anyone — perhaps an old friend like James Kerr — had known he was in San Antonio at the critical moment? That could be a complication.

If Dimitt assumed, as he supposedly told Sutherland, that the Alamo could not withstand an attack, he would probably have also assumed that the final assault would have come quickly, perhaps on February 24 or 25, and that none of the Texans would have survived. The complication is that if someone, say Kerr, knew he had been in San Antonio, then Dimitt could reasonably expect he would have to explain why he did not participate in the defense of the Alamo. His letter (which, considering the inconsistencies, must have been concocted) may have been his attempt to explain how he survived. What better excuse for still being alive than, "I concluded the Alamo had been taken by storm." He had no way to know the Alamo could survive for thirteen days and that John Sutherland would live to tell his story.

Of course, the problem with that theory is that Dimitt would also have to explain why he did not go for help or spread the alarm. Since Dimitt wrote his letter so quickly, however, the question is whether he had time to fully ponder all the ramifications. We don't know. There is also the possibility that he could simply say he had to get home to protect the vital provisions and supplies in his care.

Whatever the true story is, the Dimitt letter surely signifies that something strange happened to cause a man perceived to be a patriot to change colors. Many Texans would have a word for a man who ran out on his wife, his friends, and his country. Whether or not that word should aptly be applied to Phillip Dimitt is open for some conjecture. Perhaps, there is another explanation, just as plausible, to clear up the discrepancies in Dimitt's letter. Maybe Dimitt did issue other warnings and the records were simply lost. Or maybe not.

According to *The Handbook of Texas*, edited by Walter Prescot Webb,[22] Dimitt and three companions were captured by Mexicans in 1841, while working near Corpus Christi Bay. Supposedly the men were taken to Mexico where they were told they would be executed. Some in the group of captives escaped, but as for Dimitt, the handbook says, "It is supposed that Dimitt committed suicide after he was told that he would be shot if the escaped men did not return." Phillip Dimitt is gone, but the letter he left behind will forever be another Alamo mystery.

Fannin's Follies

On March 27, 1836—Palm Sunday—a detachment of Mexican soldiers entered the room in Goliad Mission where Colonel James Walker Fannin, Jr., was being held captive. It was time for Fannin to die. Most of the more than 400 men in his command had already been marched out and murdered. Now it was the leader's turn.

Already wounded and thus unable to stand to face the firing squad, Fannin was seated in a chair and blindfolded. He handed his watch and money to a guard with, some say, the forlorn hope the items would be forwarded to his family. He had but two additional requests. He asked that he be shot directly in the breast and not the head and that when the deed was done his body be afforded a Christian burial. In a moment, it was over. The Mexicans, firing from close range, shot Fannin in the head and then dumped his body into a pile with some of his men to be burned. There is no record of what happened to his watch.[1]

Thus ended the life of one of the most perplexing characters of the entire Texas revolution. Among other things, James Walker Fannin was, perhaps, the one man in all of Texas who might, just might, have saved the Alamo.

On the afternoon of February 23, 1836, General Santa Anna entered San Antonio de Bexar with an attack force of perhaps 1,500 men to lay siege to the Alamo which was being held, at the time, by fewer than 150 Texans. At the moment of Santa Anna's arrival, Colonel Fannin, with a command of more than 400 men, was barely over ninety miles away in LaBahia, better known as Goliad. At that particular moment, Fannin's force was by far the largest contingent of soldiers on the entire province of Texas.

There is little wonder that William B. Travis turned first, and often, to Fannin for help. Even before Santa Anna arrived, Travis had dispatched the trusted James Butler Bonham to meet personally with Fannin and seek his help. Bonham returned from that mission empty-handed and was subsequently sent out a second time with a personal note to Fannin signed by both Travis and James Bowie. It read:

> We have removed all the men to the Alamo where we make such resistance as is due our honor, and that of the country, until we can get assistance from you, which we expect you to forward immediately. In this extremity, we hope you will send us all the men you can spare promptly. We have one hundred and forty six men, who are determined never to retreat. We have but little provisions, but enough to serve us till you and your men arrive. We deem it unnecessary to repeat to a brave officer, who knows his duty, that we call on him for assistance.[2]

James Fannin, who had ignored the first plea, responded, somewhat half-heartily, to the written request for a "brave" officer to do his duty. On February 26, he marched with about three hundred men toward Bexar. His march lasted for about two hundred yards. The colonel's official report to the acting governor of Texas on one of the world's shortest relief marches was as follows:

> I have to report, that yesterday, after making all the preparations *possible*, we took up our line of march, (about three hundred strong, and four pieces of Artillery,) towards Bexar, to the relief of those brave men now shut up in the Alamo, and to raise the siege, leaving Captain Westover in command of this post. Within two hundred yards of town, one of the wagons broke down, and it

was necessary to *double teams* in order to draw the Artillery across the river, each piece having but one yoke of oxen—not a particle of breadstuff, with the exception of half a tierce of rice, with us—no *beef*, with the exception of a small portion which had been dried—and not a head of cattle, except those used to draw the Artillery, the ammunition, &c.: and it was impossible to obtain any until we should arrive at Seguin's Rancho, seventy miles from this place. After crossing the river, the troops camped.[3]

In all candor, Fannin's excuse of a broken down wagon as the primary reason he failed to complete the march is a little hard to swallow. It has to be asked why he was even taking wagons and cannons in the first place. If there was one thing the Alamo had plenty of, it was cannons—so many in fact that not all could be mounted on the walls. What Travis needed, and quickly, was men, so it would appear Fannin should have at least sent some troops on their way with or without artillery.

Sam Houston apparently felt the same way. In one of his early communications after learning of the fall of the Alamo, the general said, "Colonel Fannin should have relieved our brave men in the Alamo. He had 430 men with artillery under his command, and had taken the line of march with a full knowledge of the situation of those in the Alamo, and owing to the breaking down of a wagon abandoned the march, returned to Goliad and left our Spartans to their fate."[4] It's not hard to envision sarcasm literally dripping off the paper as the General authored those words.

The fact that Fannin did not go to the aid of Travis and the boys, leaves historians with two tantalizing questions to ponder. First, why *didn't* Fannin march to the Alamo? Second, had he marched, would he have made any difference in the final outcome? They are not easy questions to answer.

In exploring the first question, we need to examine the man himself. Not much is known of Fannin's life before he migrated to Texas in late 1834 from Georgia. We do know that Fannin attended the West Point Military Academy

James Walker Fannin, Jr., from a painting probably done while he was a cadet at West Point Military Academy. Even though Fannin was the only officer in the Texas revolution with West Point training, he failed in his attempts to lead the Matamoros expedition and refused to march to the aid of the Alamo. *(Courtesy The Dallas Historical Society.)*

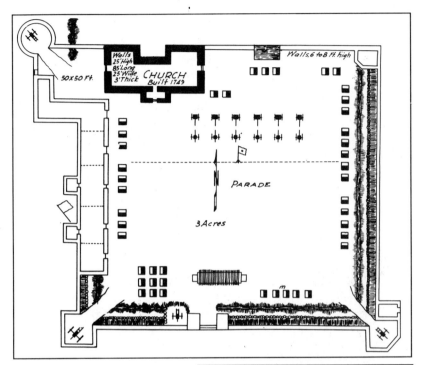

Map of LaBahia Mission, more commonly referred to as Goliad. When Fannin's men finished fortifying the mission in preparation for an anticipated attack, they held a lottery to select a proper name for the fortress. The entries were Fort Milam, Fort Independence, and Fort Defiance. The winner was Fort Defiance. *(Courtesy The DRT Library at the Alamo.)*

under his adopted name of James Walker from July 1819, until November 1821. He never rose above the class of Plebe, or freshman, and ultimately left under clouded circumstances. Still, his brief stay earned him the distinction of being the only officer, and perhaps the only soldier, in the Texas revolution to have West Point experience.[5] That experience did not do him much good.

One reason Fannin may have come to Texas was perhaps to perpetuate his trafficking in African slaves. By the time James arrived in Texas, direct importation of slaves was illegal in the United States. Many enterprising slavers solved that problem by simply bringing their slaves into Texas, where it was still legal, and then smuggling them into the United States through Louisiana. Evidence indicates Fannin was a part of that illicit business. As late as mid-January 1836, just a month before the Mexicans arrived in force, Colonel James W. Fannin and Joseph Mimms entered into a partnership in which Fannin's contribution was slaves valued at more than $17,000.[6]

When the differences between Texas and Mexico boiled over into open conflict, Fannin was an active participant. As a captain he was with James Bowie at the Battle of Concepcion in October of 1835, and later was in charge of handling volunteers at Velasco. When the Texans decided to launch an expedition against Matamoros, Mexico in late December, F. W. Johnson was named leader. Johnson subsequently withdrew because the governing council refused to commission some of his officers. Although Johnson quickly changed his mind about resigning, James Fannin had already been promoted to colonel[7] and named to head the expedition. Ultimately, he and Johnson both embarked on setting up the expedition and both issued calls for volunteers. Fannin's version, issued January 8, was as follows:

ATTENTION, VOLUNTEERS !

To the West, Face: March !

An expedition to the west has been ordered by the General Council, and the Volunteers from Bexar, Goliad, Velasco, and elsewhere, are ordered to rendezvous at San Patricio, between

the 24th and 27th instant, and report to the
officer in command. The fleet convoy will sail
from Velasco, under my charge, on or about the
18th, and all who feel disposed to join it, and aid
in keeping the war out of Texas, and at the same
time cripple the enemy in their resources at
home, are invited to enter the ranks forthwith.

J. W. Fannin, Jr.[8]

Of course, four days after the public call for volunteers
Fannin entered into his partnership with Joseph Mimms,
so it is difficult to believe the colonel was totally focused
on the cause of Texas. Still, he pressed on. By January 28,
Fannin had sailed to Aransas Bay with two hundred men.
On that date he wrote to the acting governor, James
Robinson. He passed along the intelligence that he had
heard Santa Anna was at Matamoros and predicted, if
true, a vigorous onset of hostilities could be expected. He
encouraged the governor to order all members of the Texas
militia into the field and incredibly prompted Robinson to
"Do your duty as you have done, and you need not fear
the consequences." Interesting that a colonel encouraged
the acting governor to do his duty. Also, in that letter
Fannin passed along what he believed was a rumor that
2,500 men were on their way to Bexar. It was not a rumor.[9]

By February 4, Fannin was in Mission Refugio near
Copano and he again wrote the governor. The colonel
passed along intelligence received from F. W. Johnson that
Santa Anna's troops were somewhat in disarray and
Johnson flatly predicted Matamoros could be taken without
a shot. Fannin predicted that, if the Johnson intelligence
was true, there was no need to withdraw the cannons and
abandon Bexar as had been contemplated.[10]

Fannin again turned to his pen on February 7 and 8 to
apprise the governor of developments. He advised that
there could no longer be any doubt that Santa Anna intended to overrun the country and exterminate all the
Anglo population. He encouraged the governor to call out
all available men and even encouraged the construction of
floating bridges over the rivers. An interesting aspect of
the letter is that Fannin again referenced the suggestion
that all unneeded cannons be removed from the Alamo.

He concluded, "I now feel authorized to give orders to that effect, and shall forward an express to him [Colonel Neill, commandant at Bexar] today." Fannin offered no clue as to what gave him such authority. There is also no record that he forwarded the orders.[11]

In response to Fannin's letter, the governor replied with somewhat less than specific orders. "You will occupy such points as you may in your opinion deem most advantageous . . . ." and "Fortify & defend Goliad and Bexar if any opportunity fairly offers, give the enemy battle as he advances. . . ." In addition, since General Sam Houston had departed for treaty talks with the Indians, Robinson advised Fannin that "all former orders given by my predecessor, Gen. Houston or myself, are so far countermanded as to render it compatible to now obey any orders you may deem expedient."[12] It seemed obvious the mantel of command for the entire army of Texas was being passed to Fannin. The question is, did he want such a responsibility?

The Matamoras expedition was basically in shambles by late February and although Johnson attempted to carry on, Fannin took his command and marched to Goliad. From that location he responded to Robinson with a strange letter. "I do not desire any command, and particularly that of chief. I feel, I *know*, if you and the council do not, that I am incompetent. Fortune, and brave soldiers, may favour me and save the State, and establish for me a reputation. I do earnestly ask of you . . . to relieve me and make a selection of one possessing all the requisites of a commander . . . If General Houston will give up all other considerations, and devote himself to the military, I honestly believe he will answer the present emergency. I ask of you all, not to obtrude my name or rank upon the approaching convention: for I would feel truly happy to be in the bosom of my family, and rid of the burden imposed on me." Despite rejecting command, Fannin implores the governor to "*kick for the moon, whether we hit the mark or not;* send us men, provisions, and ammunition; haste is requisite."[13] There seems little doubt that Colonel Fannin was nowhere near ready to assume command of all the forces in Texas.

In another letter of that same day, Fannin apparently changed his mind about the prospects of command. "I am well aware," he said, "that during the General's furlough, the command naturally, and of right, devolves upon me;

but the fact has not been communicated to me officially, either by the General or the Governor." He went on to ask for specific orders and promised to obey them even if sacrificed in the process.[14] Fannin seems to have been somewhat confused about his intentions and desires.

Throughout his correspondence, Fannin is consistent on one point. He seemed to have believed San Antonio de Bexar was a critical point that had to be maintained no matter what. On at least two occasions he urged the governor to send men and supplies to the Alamo. On February 16, Fannin informed the governor, "I have taken measures to forward provisions to Bexar, and forwarded orders there to-day to place that post in a state of defense, which if attended to will make it safe."[15] We have no sur-viving record that Fannin ever sent any provisions to the Alamo. If he did send the orders to Bexar that would make the place safe, they either never arrived or didn't work.

In that same letter, Fannin also states that if General Houston did not return from furlough, he would make headquarters at Bexar and take as many men with him as practical. He even predicts that Bexar would be one of the posts of "danger and honour." It seems very clear that Fannin was wrestling with the prospects of total command.

By February 21, Fannin's predicament was becoming critical. He was now convinced that Goliad was also a position of great danger, and he assured the governor that he was fortifying the place to make it tenable for a reasonable force. In a letter to Robinson that day,[16] Fannin apprised him of the taking of some prisoners, including a priest who was the "blackest of old villains." He implored the government not to trust Mexicans since to do so would be a "fatal decision." Although he said he would attend to the enemy, he wrote, "I hope you will soon release me from the army, at least as an officer."

Incredibly, in the same letter Fannin informed Robinson he was sending the old priest—the blackest of villains—to "officiate as your chaplain, during the Convention." Perhaps he was kidding, but he did send the prisoners to the convention. William Fairfax Gray, a traveler in Texas during the time of the revolution, was in Washington observing the convention and recorded in his diary on March 5: "This evening two Mexican prisoners were brought here from Goliad charged with improper communications with the enemy and pointing out to them a place to build a bridge over the San Antonio. One of them is an old priest. . . ."[17]

Was Fannin joking? Or, did he really intend for the old Mexican priest who was believed to be a spy to officiate at the convention? Or was his comment pure sarcasm, intended to prod the convention just a bit for what he perceived as a total lack of cooperation? We'll never know his real motive.

The next day, the eve of the Mexicans' arrival in San Antonio, Fannin advised Robinson that the fortifications in Goliad would be complete by March 3, and in honor of that occasion he had christened the place Fort Defiance.[18] It seems clear that Fannin was becoming dedicated to defending Goliad and had abandoned the prospect of relocating to Bexar. It should also be noted that by this date, Bonham had arrived in Goliad with a request for help from Travis. Fannin makes no mention of that request in any of his surviving correspondence.[19]

By February 22, some of Fannin's old fears had reared their ugly head. In a letter on that day, he said:

> I am critically situated. General Houston is absent on furlough, and neither myself nor [the] army have received any orders as to who should assume command. It is my right; and, in many respects, I have done so, where I was convinced the public weal required it. I well know that many men of influence view me with an envious eye, and either desire my station, or my disgrace. The first, they are welcome to—and many thanks for taking it off my hands. The second will be harder to effect. Will you allow me to say to you, and my friends of the old or new convention, that I am not desirous of retaining the present or receiving any other appointment in the army. I did not seek, in any manner, the one I hold, and, you well know, had resolved not to accept—and but for Colonel Burnet and Clements, and Kerr, would have declined. I am a better judge of my military abilities than others, and if I am qualified to command an Army, I have not found it out. I well know I am a better company officer than most men now in Texas, and might do with

Regulars, &c. for a Regiment. But this does not
constitute me a commander.[20]

By his own admission, on the day before Santa Anna
arrived and after he had received a call for aid from the
Alamo, Colonel James Walker Fannin was still doubting his
ability to command. At the very hour that Travis and the
boys needed him most, Fannin was wallowing in the
depths of self-pity and indecision. There was no longer
any doubt that he was committed to holding Goliad.

A couple of days later Fannin wrote to the governor, "I
learn from several sources, that as soon as Bexar is retaken,
they [the Mexicans] next march here, and thus complete
their chain of communication to the Interior and Gulf. . . .
I again repeat to you, that I consider myself bound to await
your orders." It would seem the good colonel was writing
off the Alamo and asking for help with what to do about
his own situation. He went on to state, ". . . I am desirous
to be erased from the list of officers, or expectants of office,
and have leave to bring off my brave, foreign volunteers in
the best manner I may be able."[21]

Fannin definitely wanted no part of command and the
associated responsibility of making decisions. But then
James Bonham appeared again, this time with the drastic
news that the Mexicans had arrived in San Antonio.
Apparently the urgent plea, signed by Travis and Bowie,
spurred Fannin into at least temporary action. He wrote to
the governor, as he prepared to march, "It may be well to
inform you, that I am aware that my present movements
towards Bexar is anything but military. The appeal of
Colonels Travis and Bowie, however, cannot be resisted,
particularly with the description of the troops now in the
field—sanguine, chivalrous volunteers. Much must be risked
to relieve the besieged. If, however, I hear of the fall of
Bexar before I reach them, I shall retire on this place, complete the fortifications already commenced and in a state of
forwardness, and prepare for a vigorous defence, waiting
anxiously, in any event, for the arrival of reinforcements."[22]

So the brave Fannin marched to the relief of the
"sanguine, chivalrous volunteers" and he made a total of
two hundred yards. Then owing to the breaking down of a
wagon, he returned to Goliad. Following that aborted

attempt, Fannin's men demanded a council of war to determine their course of action. Fannin granted the council and, for all practical purposes, the decisions doomed the Alamo. Fannin reported that the council of war "unanimously determined that, inasmuch as a proper supply of provisions and means of transportation could not be had; and as it was impossible, with our present means, to carry the Artillery with us; and as by leaving Fort Defiance without a proper garrison, it might fall into the hands of the enemy, with the provisions, &c. now at Matagorda, Demit's Landing, and Coxe's Point, and on the way to meet us; and, as by report of our spies we may expect an attack on this place, it was expedient to return to this post and complete the fortification &. &c."[23]

This one paragraph actually gives us many clues as to why Fannin did not march to the Alamo. He clearly is not in total command or he would not have depended on a council of war requested by his officers to make the ultimate decision. He obviously feels Fort Defiance is in a clear and present danger and that it must be maintained to protect the vital supplies in warehouses along the Gulf coast. Therefore, he reversed himself and retreated the entire two hundred yards back to Goliad. We do not know just how much Fannin's mental vacillations affected his judgment but the damage was apparently significant since he did not even attempt to send a small detachment to the Alamo. Travis, Bowie, Crockett, and the rest of the Alamo defenders were left watching the horizon toward Goliad, looking for a friend and an ally that was never coming.

Fannin also, apparently, left some of his men wondering about their leader and his motives. Joseph G. Ferguson, a private in Fannin's command, perhaps summed up the feelings of the men, when he wrote in a letter to his brother: "I am sorry to say that the majority of soldiers don't like him [Fannin,] for what reason I don't know, unless it is because they think that he has not the interest of the country at heart, or that he wishes to become great without taking the proper steps to achieve greatness."[24]

Fannin's rantings also perplexed his commander in chief, Sam Houston. In a letter of March 13, Houston said: "I am informed that Colonel Fannin had about seven hundred men under his command; and, at one time, had taken up the line of march for the Alamo, but the breaking down of a wagon induced him to fall back . . . since then, he has written letters here, indicating a design to march upon San Patricio, and also the occupation of Copano. So that I am at a loss to know where my expresses will find him. . . . On seeing the various communications of Colonel Fannin at this point, I could not rely on any co-operation from him."[25]

It is also possible that General Sam Houston himself inadvertently caused Fannin not to march promptly. It is obvious that Fannin had trouble making up his mind and possibly he wanted to take his time and be sure he was right. If so, perhaps he was adhering to advice given him by Houston. On November 13, 1835, Houston advised Fannin he had been appointed Inspector General of the Army. In that letter, the general said, "Remember one Maxim, it is better to do well, *late;* than *never!*" [26]

So Fannin didn't march because he felt Goliad had to be protected and the Alamo defenders ended up on Santa Anna's funeral pyre. The question now becomes, If Fannin had marched, would it have made any difference in the outcome? The answer, sadly, is probably no.

The Alamo was a dilapidated, falling down old relic of a Spanish mission that was anything but a fortress. It was a huge affair with an outer courtyard almost as big as an entire city block.[27] To be properly defended, Colonel James C. Neill, former commander of the garrison, once predicted a force of 600 to 1,000 would be required.[28] Even if Fannin's entire force had marched to Bexar, the addition of his men would have created a total garrison of about 600 men, which probably would not have been enough.

We know that Travis and the boys held their own for ten days and sustained a continued bombardment without losing a single man and, according to Susanna Dickinson, only one horse.[29] The old walls remained generally cannon-ball proof, primarily because the Mexican cannons were almost out of range. But on March 3, Santa Anna received considerable reinforcements including more artillery. On the 4th, the Mexicans established a new battery barely over four hundred yards away and suddenly, as the last messenger out of the Alamo reported, "every shot goes through, as the walls are weak."[30] It seems likely that had Santa Anna simply kept up the fire a few days longer, he might have taken the fort with much less dramatic action than an all-out assault. In fact, within a couple of days

Santa Anna received even more men and artillery. In all likelihood the Mexicans could have eventually taken the fortress no matter how many men were on the inside.

The irony of Fannin's follies is that even if he had completed the march they started on February 26, he and his men probably would not have made any difference. Santa Anna, thanks to an excellent spy network, knew Fannin had marched but he did not know the Texans managed to travel only two hundred yards. In anticipation of Fannin's probable arrival, the Mexican general dispatched a crack cavalry brigade to intercept the Texans in the open prairie.[31] Quite probably the Mexicans would have shredded Fannin's forces long before they reached the Alamo.

There is, however, one bare possibility that Fannin might have made a difference. If he had marched immediately upon receiving Travis' first request, then his force would have been in San Antonio shortly after Santa Anna's arrival. We know the Mexican troops had just completed a grueling forced march and were undoubtedly worn out. Plus, the General probably had only 1,500 to 1,800[32] men when he first arrived. Perhaps the first day or two after arriving at San Antonio were the only times the Mexicans were vulnerable. Perhaps.

If Fannin marched immediately and attacked promptly on arrival, supported by Travis and the boys from the Alamo, then it is possible they could have routed the enemy. However, since many more Mexicans were closing rapidly on San Antonio, the Texans' window of opportunity was small indeed, perhaps only hours. Had they failed to rout the enemy and perhaps capture Santa Anna, the entire force of Texans probably would have ended up in the Alamo; and when additional Mexicans arrived, the outcome would have been about the same.

Fannin's indecision ultimately cost him his life. When Sam Houston received confirmation of the fall of the Alamo, he ordered Fannin to destroy Fort Defiance and fall back.[33] True to form, Fannin faltered and did not march immediately. When he finally did begin a retrograde movement, he failed to destroy the fort. Once on the move, Fannin again had trouble with baggage wagons; and, over the objections of his men, he actually halted the march in an open prairie instead of seeking the cover of nearby woods. His position was detected by the enemy and a skirmish ensued. On March 19, in consideration of his untenable position, Fannin surrendered. He and all his men, except a bare few who were able to escape, died in a massacre on Palm Sunday, March 27.

It would appear Fannin was correct when he said he was no commander. It also appears his actions cost the lives of most of his men and may, just may, have cost the lives of Travis and the boys. Just as we'll never know what happened to Fannin's watch, we also will never know if he, and he alone, could have saved the Alamo.

Military Malpractice

One Alamo legend that appears to be absolutely factual is that neither side displayed any abundance of military intelligence in carrying out the campaign. The tactical decisions made in both camps were so poor, in fact, that it is difficult to determine who made the most critical errors. If military chieftains were subject to the same scrutiny as physicians, some of the antics of the Mexican and Texan leaders in the revolution would surely be labeled as malpractice.

In the case of Santa Anna retaking San Antonio and the Alamo, about the only thing the general did right was win. Unfortunately for the general, the victory was, as William B. Travis had predicted, about as costly as a defeat.[1] And it all could have been so easily avoided.

Probably the largest single mistake Santa Anna made was in even marching to San Antonio in the first place. In the early months of 1836, the Texas army was little more than a myth. There was a small garrison in San Antonio under the command of Travis, a much larger garrison at LaBahia mission in Goliad under the command of Colonel James Walker Fannin, and small groups of assorted volunteers scattered about the province. Thanks to intelligence provided by sympathetic Mexican citizens acting as spies, Santa Anna was well informed on the poor organization and lack of strength of the enemy in Texas. And he was very much aware that the traitorous rebels were planning a constitutional convention for March 1, 1836, at Washington-on-the-Brazos, Texas.

Armed with such information, a proper battle plan for the Mexican general would have been to split his force in three parts: one large force to seek out and destroy Fannin, one small force to cut off any retreat from the Alamo, and the bulk of his force to slice through the heart of Texas and march all the way to Washington-on-the-Brazos. There is some evidence that such an invasion plan was once considered by Santa Anna. In a February 16, 1836 letter to acting Governor James Robinson, Colonel Fannin stated:

> It [the Mexican invasion] is designed to enter our country in Three Divisions—One to take Bejar, commanded by General Sesma, Filisola, Cos— one against Goliad under Urrea (recently Gov. of Durango) and Col Garay. The Third under Santa Anna himself, to pass either above Bejar, or between that post, & Goliad, and proceed directly into the heart of the Colony. . . . [2]

Fannin listed his source for such intelligence as two well-known gentlemen who had just arrived at Goliad in five days from Matamoros, Mexico. Concerning the validity of the information, Fannin claimed that most people in middle Texas knew the two men and that even the smallest detail in their intelligence could "be confidently relied on."[3]

If such a plan was Santa Anna's intention in early February, it probably would have been immensely successful. Had the Mexicans marched directly through Texas they could have easily smashed any meager resistance found at Gonzales and continued on to Washington, arriving well before the March 1 convention convened. Such a course of events would have prevented the convention, disrupted the Texans' plan for a declaration of independence and a constitution, and destroyed what little unity existed among the Anglo population. Since Fannin and his men would surely have still fallen and the men in the Alamo would have been totally cut off, Santa Anna seemingly could have crushed the rebellion in short order

An artist's interpretation of what a young Antonio Lopez de Santa Anna might have looked like. The plumed, Napoleon-style hat favored by Santa Anna is not shown. *(Courtesy The DRT Library at the Alamo.)*

and restored Texas to its proper place as a Mexican state. But the general chose to march boldly into the insignificant little village of San Antonio.

Why the general made such a critical decision is open for some debate. Perhaps Santa Anna felt, as most Texans did, that San Antonio was a vital outpost which was necessary for the success of the campaign. As events actually unfolded, San Antonio did become a critical position. The Mexican army was stalled for thirteen days awaiting a victory they did not even need. During that time the people of Texas did meet in convention and declare their independence, an act which solidified the cause for all Texans.

A better explanation for Santa Anna's action is that his thinking was clouded by an overwhelming desire for swift and brutal revenge. It had been the dictator's brother-in-law, Martin Perfecto de Cos, that was forced to surrender the Alamo to the Texans three months earlier. Undoubtedly the general had a burning desire to make the upstart Texans pay dearly for causing embarrassment to his family. The revenge motive may have even been bolstered by reports that the Alamo garrison was small in number and poorly supplied. Santa Anna probably reasoned that a quick and decisive victory could be had in San Antonio and that the remainder of the campaign would be something close to what modern military strategist might call a "mopping up" action. Of course, thanks to the antics of Santa Anna, such was not the case.

Once Santa Anna made the decision to attack San Antonio, he continued to make critical tactical errors. In his haste to surprise the enemy and gain a quick victory, Santa Anna ordered twelve to fifteen hundred troops to separate from the main army and move toward San Antonio in a forced march. Unfortunately, the main army that was left behind to move forward at a normal pace included most of the artillery and almost all the physicians and medical supplies. Apparently the general felt that the battle for the Alamo would be such a small affair that no artillery would be needed and that no Mexican soldiers would be wounded. The advisability of such a move was questioned by some of the Mexican soldiers. Sanchez Navarro wrote of Santa Anna, "He is going to Bexar with inconceivable, rather, astonishing haste. Why is His Excellency going in such haste? Why is he leaving the entire army behind?

behind? Does he think that his name alone is sufficient to overthrow the colonists?"[4]

Regardless of what his motive was, Santa Anna did arrive unexpectedly in San Antonio on February 23, 1836, and it should have become clear almost immediately that any thought of the campaign being a small affair with an associated quick victory was a foolish notion. William B. Travis punctuated some aborted surrender talks with a cannon shot and the first real skirmish between the two armies, on February 25, resulted in a Texas victory. As a result of the loss, Santa Anna made his first solid decision of the Alamo campaign when he decided to await the arrival of more troops before storming the fortress. Unfortunately for the soldiers of the Mexican army, the general did not wait quite long enough.

On March 3, 1836, approximately one thousand Mexican reinforcements arrived in San Antonio with a few more pieces of artillery. The bulk of the army with all the medical supplies and most of the big siege guns was still out on the Texas prairie trudging their way slowly toward the Alamo city. Even though many more men and several more cannons were expected within a few days, Santa Anna decided not to wait. The general called a council-of-war on March 4 to complete plans for the final assault that would bring glorious victory to the Mexican army.

Apparently there were two contributing motives for the general believing that an all out assault had to be made on the Alamo. In his diary *With Santa in Texas*, Jose Enrique de la Pena explained:

> He [Santa Anna] believed as others did that the fame and honor of the army were compromised the longer the enemy lived . . . It was therefore necessary to attack him [the enemy] in order to make him feel the vigor of our souls and the strength of our arms.[5]

So Santa Anna felt that an assault was necessary to avoid the embarrassment of further delay and to teach the Texans a lesson that might serve as an example for other rebels. Whether or not his personal vendetta against the

Texans played a part in the ultimate decision will never be known.

According to Pena, most of the officers present at the council-of-war favored assaulting the fortress. However, there was some dissention among the troops as to exactly how the assault should be carried out. General Castrillon and Colonels Almonte and Romero favored waiting for the big guns to arrive and then using the increased fire power to open a significant breach in the walls. It was predicted that with more guns a large breach could be opened in eight or ten hours of spirited fire and thus the army could avoid the prospect of having to scale the walls amid murderous enemy fire. Pena even predicted ". . . it was necessary only to await the artillery's arrival at Bejar for these [the Texans] to surrender; undoubtedly they could not have resisted for many hours the destruction and imposing fire from twenty cannon."[6]

There is some historical evidence that the opinion of Pena, Castrillon, and the others was exactly correct. On March 3, in his letter to the government, Travis wrote, "I have so fortified this place, that the walls are generally proof against cannon balls. . . ." With the few new cannons that arrived on March 3, the Mexicans were able to establish a new artillery battery closer to the Alamo than ever before with damaging results. On March 9, John S. Brooks, who was with Fannin at Goliad, wrote in a letter to James Haggerty, "We have again heard from Bexar, Santa Ana has arrived there himself, with 3000 men, making his whole force 4800. He has erected a battery within 400 yards of the Alamo, and every shot goes through it, as the walls are weak."[7] The only possible explanation for the walls of the Alamo going from cannon-ball proof to weak in two days is that the new Mexican artillery was doing significant damage.

There appears little doubt that had Santa Anna been content to await the arrival of more guns, the Alamo fortress could have been reduced to rubble in short order and more than likely the Texans would have had no choice but to surrender. But the general's overpowering belief that victory without significant bloodshed is victory without honor prevailed. It was a critical mistake as summed up by Pena. He wrote:

> We [the Mexican army] were in a position to
> advance, leaving a small force on watch at the
> Alamo, the holding of which was unimportant
> either politically or militarily, whereas its acquisi-
> tion was both costly and very bitter in the end.[8]

So Santa Anna vetoed the opinions of his men and
ordered the attack to commence before dawn on Sunday,
March 6, 1836. Before the last shot was fired that chilly
morning, the consequences of Santa Anna's foolhardy
action became evident. By refusing to open a breach in the
walls, his gallant men were forced to use scaling ladders in
an attempt to enter the fortress. The withering and deadly
fire from the Texans took a significant and probably unexpected toll on the Mexican force. In less than an hour,
Santa Anna lost almost a third of his attacking force
to either the grim reaper or the hospital bed. The lack
of adequate medical attention became an acute and
demoralizing reality.

A significant and often overlooked consequence of the
Alamo assault is that even in death the Texans were able
to continue to impede the advance of the Mexican army.
Because the Texans inflicted such a large number of
casualties, Santa Anna was forced to remain in San
Antonio for an extended period of time while waiting on
reinforcements to replenish his decimated ranks. Had the
general delayed the final attack just a few hours, his men
probably could have taken the Alamo with much more
efficiency and much less loss of life. Such a victory would
have bolstered the morale of the men and the general
could have advanced on Gonzales and Washington almost
immediately. But the general could not wait.

Incredibly, after winning the "great" victory at the
Alamo, Santa Anna continued to make tactical errors, not
the least of which was to give the enemy advance notice of
what was to come. In his quest to reach San Antonio, the
general had moved his army swiftly and quietly across the
Texas prairie. Once victory was his at the Alamo, the
general could have quietly replenished his army and then
advanced as rapidly as possible against Sam Houston.
Instead, while in the process of rebuilding his army, Santa
Anna chose to dispatch Susanna Dickinson, her child, and

Travis' slave Joe to spread the word throughout the colony that San Antonio had fallen and other settlements would soon follow suit.

It seems certain that Santa Anna's motive for such a bold course was to possibly incite panic among the Anglo-Texas population and perhaps put an end to the revolution without firing any more shots. And that is almost what happened. The settlers east of San Antonio did abandon their homes and flee toward the Sabine river in what has become known as the "Runaway Scrape." But Santa Anna apparently failed to realize that while he was giving the citizens advance warning he also giving something precious—time—to men who remained in what was left of the Texas army. As Pena predicted, "If Houston had not received news of the fall of the Alamo, it would have been very easy to surprise and defeat him."[9]

Sam Houston did receive the news that the Alamo had fallen and he reacted quickly. He ordered the town of Gonzales evacuated and burned, then assembled his men and began a retreat to the East. The men who left Gonzales with Houston on March 13 formed the nucleus of the army that would defeat Santa Anna at San Jacinto just five weeks later. If His Excellency had just summoned some patience he could have taken the Alamo almost casually, marched immediately to Gonzales where he would have found little resistance, and then been waiting when Commander in Chief Sam Houston arrived. In the final analysis, perhaps something so simple as impatience cost Mexico the entire province of Texas.

As poor as Santa Anna was in his strategic planning, the Texans were not much better. In fact in some cases the Texans made even more glaring errors. Perhaps *the* most glaring errors on the part of the Texans were overconfidence and underestimating the enemy.

In the early days of the revolution, the meager Texas army scored quick and easy victories at Gonzales, Goliad, Mission Concepcion, and even at the Alamo. Bolstered by such success, the Texans perhaps felt themselves somewhat invincible and even embarked on a provocative scheme to take the war to Mexican soil with an invasion of Matamoros. Some Texans even predicted that Santa Anna would never chance an invasion of Texas for fear he might

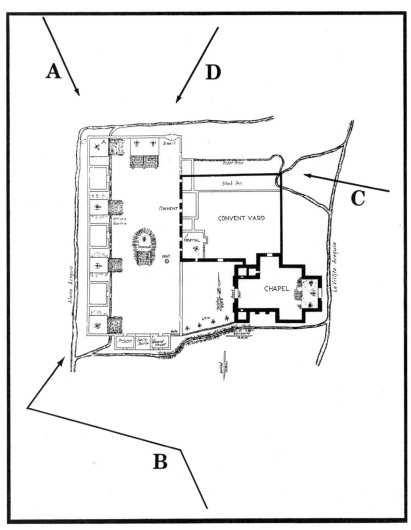

This map shows the approximate charge of the Mexican army. **A.** The movements of General Martin Perfecto de Cos as he attacked from the northwest, which was considered the post of greatest danger and thus the greatest honor. **B.** Morales, who initially charged from the south but was forced to swing west. **C.** Romero's force which came in from the east and swung north. **D.** Duque's troops who came in from the north. Santa Anna's position was above the mission with the reserves. *(Central map courtesy of the Archives Division of the Texas State Library.)*

loose the entire Mexican nation to the Texas rebels. In a letter of January 3, 1836, John Lamar wrote:

> The fall of San Antonio has for the present put a stop to the war—many think it has terminated, that after the single defeat of Genl Cos that the Mexican Dictator will not again dare to invade the country. Others are of the opinion that Santa Anna will make another desperate effort in the spring to subjugate Texas to centralism, at the head of a powerful army; powerful at least in numbers—and I am inclined to the latter opinion but come as he may, he will meet a warm reception and the result will no doubt be favorable to the Texas Arms—5,000 Americans are fully competent to fight and defeat 20,000 Mexicans— numerical force avails nothing against gallant freemen contending for their rights, their homes and their fire sides, aided by the volunteers from the United States. . . .[10]

We now know that such talk was preposterous. Even before the Texans won the Alamo in early December, Santa Anna was already making plans for an invasion. To think that a few relatively minor victories would discourage Santa Anna was indeed foolish. If anything, the early victories only prompted the Mexican leader to move quicker. And to predict that five thousand Americans could easily defeat twenty thousand Mexicans was the ridiculous by-product of over-confidence.

Although the Texans did not have a sophisticated spy network, there was plenty of information available about possible enemy movements. On December 18, 1835, Frank Johnson, the eventual leader of the Matamoros expedition, reported that he had learned of 1,500 Mexicans arriving at Laredo to reinforce General Cos at the Alamo. While the information was accurate, most Texans apparently felt that since Cos had already surrendered, the reinforcements would simply return to Mexico with Cos' army. In fact, some of those reinforcements later participated in retaking the Alamo.

On December 22, 1835, Edward Hall reported to the government that Santa Anna was approaching Texas with an army of 6,000 men. Again, the information was basically correct but largely ignored. One reason the information was ignored was a somewhat general belief that even if the Mexicans were planning an invasion, it would not come until spring. Eli Mercer summed up the feelings of many Texans when he wrote the governor on December 25, 1835. In part Mercer said:

> . . . ample supplies for the support of the army should be laid in, in good time and forward to the proper places, and securely deposited to be in readiness for a spring campaign; as we may expect a strong force of the enemy to march against Texas at that time I deem it necessary for Texas to be ready to meat an army of eight or ten thousand strong in may next. Our army should be well organized and disciplined, to do which they should all be in the field by the middle of March. . . .[11]

Sam Houston echoed the thoughts of Mercer two days later when he issued the following circular to potential volunteers in the United States of the North:

TO UNITED STATES VOLUNTEERS

Washington, Texas, Dec. 27, 1835

To all Volunteers and Troops for the Aid of Texas in her conflict:
I now recommend to come by sea, and to land at Copano, Coxes point, or Matagorda. The time employed will be less than one fourth that which would be needed to pass by land.
To those who would prefer to pass by land, I would recommend to bring Baggage Wagons; and to bring NO HORSES, unless for teams, or for packing.
By the first of March the campaign will open.

Sam Houston[12]

This circular actually provides several clues as to how the military minds were functioning in Texas in late 1835 and early 1836. Houston's prediction that the campaign would open by the first of March was somewhat off the mark. By March 1, Texas had already been invaded and the first disaster of the war was just around the corner. The significance of that date, however, is that Houston himself was gone for the entire month of February holding treaty talks with the Indians. It would appear he either did not believe his own date or that he feared the Indians more than the Mexicans. The fact that Texas was embroiled in political intrigue during February should not have been sufficient cause for Houston to leave if he really believed the campaign would open by March 1.

An apparent contradiction in the circular is that Houston is encouraging volunteers to come to Texas by sea rather than land because the travel time would be cut by seventy-five percent. And yet he seems to be encouraging those who chose to come by land to walk or ride wagons rather than bring horses. Surely the general knew that riding horses would have been faster than walking or riding in a wagon. Perhaps Houston was already aware of acute supply problems and that more horses would be more mouths to feed. He may have felt that there would be ample time to break some of the wild horses that roamed Texas during the days of the revolution. He was wrong because the ultimate war effort was actually hampered by a lack of suitable mounts.

Not only did many Texans continue to ignore the possibility of an advancing enemy, they also chose to ignore the clear and present danger. On January 6, then Alamo Commander James Neill predicted that an enemy of one thousand men could starve out the Alamo garrison in about four days. Despite his plea for help, very little was forthcoming.[13] It was a trend that continued virtually until the Alamo fell—repeated pleas for help fell on deaf ears.

Throughout January and February, reports continued to be circulated and mostly ignored that the enemy was closing fast. Of course, it was one thing for the general populace to ignore the reports but it was another matter when the commander of the Alamo followed suit. Unfortunately, that is apparently what happened.

William B. Travis assumed command of the Alamo when James C. Neill left on February 11, 1836. Two days later, on the thirteenth, Travis wrote that he felt Texas would be invaded by March 15, and that preparations should be made to receive them.[14] Travis certainly underestimated his enemy because by March 15, the men of the Alamo were gone and Houston was in full retreat.

The belief by Travis, Houston, and all the others that the campaign would not begin until March was based on the theory that Santa Anna would not chance crossing the barren South Texas wasteland until the supple grasses of spring were up to allow for feeding stock along the trail. Everyone ignored the fact that mesquite grass, a common plant in South Texas, was a delicacy to mules and horses and that it matures earlier than normal range grass. The Texans also did not allow for Santa Anna's vindictive, tenacious nature. So while the Texans argued among themselves about supplies and volunteers, the Mexican army was closing fast.

It seems a bit harsh to blame Travis for his shortcomings as a commander because, after all, he was a practicing attorney before he enlisted in the army. Unlike his Mexican counterpart at the battle of the Alamo, Travis had little or no formal military training and certainly he had never participated in anything like a close siege. While modern historians may excuse Travis' actions due to his inexperience, it is difficult to imagine why Travis himself did not recognize his own lack of ability and act accordingly.

The single most disastrous event that led to the fall of the Alamo and the loss of the men was the fact that no one knew the Mexicans were even close until they appeared on the horizon. Almost unbelievably, Santa Anna and his army of fifteen hundred men were able to sneak up on the Texans without being detected. In truth, it could have been even worse. On the night of February 22, the day before the Mexicans arrived, the Texans were secure enough with their position to hold a party in honor of George Washington's birthday. Thanks to his spy network, Santa Anna learned of the party and immediately dispatched his cavalry to attempt a quick capture of the entire garrison. Had it not been for a sudden rainstorm that caused a river to rise and prevent the cavalry from crossing, the entire Alamo saga might have ended at a party. But the creek did rise.

Even though Santa Anna's surprise party did not work, he still boldly marched into San Antonio on the afternoon of February 23. By all accounts of the events of that day, the only safeguard Travis had against disaster was a sentry located in the bell tower of San Fernando church. The sentry's warning and subsequent verification by John Smith and John Sutherland was the only notice given. Travis and the Texans were caught totally off guard and left with no other choice but to retreat into the Alamo and start praying for help.

The obvious questions are why didn't Travis have scouts out on patrol watching for the enemy? Was he so secure in his belief that Santa Anna would not even attempt to enter Texas until March that he did not feel the need for scouts? Why didn't he recognize his own lack of military expertise and attempt to allow for every contingency?

It is barely possible that Travis lacked the means with which to send out scouts. Before he left, Colonel Neill reported he was having trouble sending out spies because horses were in short supply. However, there always seemed to be enough horses and the means to send out couriers. It seems if Travis had even remotely considered it possible that the Mexicans were already on the march, he would have found a way to get out the scouts.

The intriguing part of the problem of being taken by surprise is what Travis might have done had he actually been given some advance warning. Suppose a scout had been sent out twenty or thirty miles south with specific instructions to watch for an unexpected enemy movement. It appears highly likely that such a scout would have detected a large army moving across the country side and been able to give the men of the Alamo two, three, or more days notice. We will never know what Travis and the boys might have done had they been given that much of a head start.

If the men of the Alamo were firm in their conviction that San Antonio had to be held at all costs, as they apparently were, then advance notice might have done nothing more than provide some extra time for fortification and for scavenging the town in search of needed supplies. The end result might have been the same except that the

Texans would have been a little better nourished and perhaps a little warmer when they died.

On the other hand, a few precious days notice would have given Travis some time to explore other options. He might have deduced that help was not coming in time and opted to spike the cannons (or at least drop them in the river) to keep them out of Mexican hands and then ordered a retrograde movement. The men of the Alamo could have fallen back to Gonzales or perhaps Goliad to join Fannin. Either way they would have lived to fight another day. It is even possible that given time Travis might have elected to defend one of the nearby smaller and stronger missions as military historians have long argued would have been the best chance for a proper defense of San Antonio. Unfortunately, Travis did not send out scouts, he did not have any advance notice, and the Alamo became his only choice.

Travis' lack of military experience certainly played a major part in the Alamo tragedy, but to the man's credit he apparently recognized his own shortcomings and asked to be relieved. In December of 1835, when the government appointed Travis a major of artillery, he rejected the commission on the grounds that he could not be as useful in the artillery as elsewhere and he asked for a commission in the cavalry.[15] The government obliged him and he subsequently became a lieutenant colonel in the cavalry. So what did the government of Texas do with a colonel of the cavalry? They assigned him to a fort!

When Colonel Neill left the Alamo and passed command to Travis, the cavalry officer notified the governor that he would accept the position "until an artillery officer can be sent here."[16] It never happened and a horse soldier was left to try to effect a proper defense of an old mission that even Neill, who was a proper artillery officer, said was largely indefensible without perhaps a thousand men. Travis never had so many as two hundred men in his command. His lack of experience may have led to the fall but the blame should rest squarely on the lunatic government leaders who left the Alamo in the hands of an inexperienced cavalry officer.

Another major flaw in the military tactics of the Texans was that they even considered using forts as a defense against the Mexicans. As is seen in "Sam Houston and the

Alamo Conspiracy" elsewhere in this volume, Sam Houston decided, after the fall of the Alamo, that it was useless to try to defend forts because there would have been no way to keep the troops properly supplied. It is almost a shame that such a great revelation did not dawn on Houston in time to order the Alamo fortress abandoned. The Texans would probably have fared much better had they chosen a sort of "run and gun" defense against Santa Anna's troops. The theory is that the Texans could have aggravated the Mexicans by staging sporadic and unexpected mini-attacks.

At least one Mexican soldier believed the Texans were wrong to defend the forts. Jose Enrique de la Pena wrote:

> The enemy should have begun to harass the army at the Frio River, for this is an advantageous position, easy to defend with slight loss, since a forest more than five leagues long covers the left bank, adding to the advantage. There is not the least doubt that the foe should have limited himself to a defensive war, which the nature of the terrain indicated, but he was too inexperienced and thus could not utilize its advantages.[17]

The complication to the possibility of the Texans using more of a guerilla type warfare is that such a plan would require a well defined, extensive cavalry force. Although the Texans surely recognized the need for such a mounted force, no real action was taken other then naming some officers to participate. Some of those officers, including Travis, found themselves confronting the Mexicans while mounted on brick walls instead of horses.

There is, of course, one gigantic bit of irony surrounding the military malpractice of the Texans. Had they done everything in strict accordance with sound military logic, they almost certainly would have lost the entire war. If by some miracle, Travis had received advance warning and chosen to abandon the Alamo garrison, there would have been no one to prevent Santa Anna from continuing his march through Texas all the way to Washington-on-the-Brazos. His Excellency certainly would have been able to disrupt (and probably prevent altogether) the constitutional convention. As a consequence, the Texans might never have been able to assemble and declare themselves free and independent. Santa Anna would have driven the rebels out of Texas and then been free to pursue a possible sale of the region to the United States.

On the other hand, had the Texans been sophisticated enough to recognize the inadvisability of forts and opted for open warfare, the far superior numbers of the Mexican army, especially the crack cavalry troops, probably would have led to an eventual victory. It would appear that had both sides in the Texas revolution used sound military logic and neither side experienced any military malpractice, then the Mexicans would have won. About the only way Travis and the boys could have stalled the Mexican advance and *possibly* lived to tell about it is if they had chosen to defend one of the smaller, stronger missions in the San Antonio area. Unfortunately, although we have evidence that Santa Anna expected to find at least some of the Texans at Mission Concepcion,[18] there is no record that the Texans ever considered any position other than the Alamo. It was a tragic decision that saved Texas.[19]

The Alamo Number Game

Those who become infatuated with the saga of the Alamo and who study the events of that epic struggle eventually try to answer an impossible question. How many men died when Santa Anna's troops overran the garrison and put the defenders to the sword? Any Texas historian would give half the mineral rights in the Lone Star state to be the one to establish the definitive list of all who died in the Alamo. It will never happen.

At a quick glance it might appear that 183 men died that fateful morning in March of 1836. Many Alamo stories use that figure as the total, and it is not hard to construct where the number might have come from. When the Mexicans first laid siege to the mission, William B. Travis reported that he had 150 men.[1] After that report, only 32 men from Gonzales and one messenger, James Butler Bonham, joined the garrison. That's a total of 183. An easy confirmation comes form Francisco Ruiz, the San Antonio alcalde in charge of burning the bodies of the Texans. He said he burned 182 and he buried one defender, who was a relative.[2] Again, the total is 183. But is that the correct number?

The question of the total number of men who died is destined to be forever debated. Some, like noted Alamo historian Walter Lord, say 183 (see *A Time to Stand*). In *Roll Call at the Alamo*, Phil Rosenthal and Bill Groneman, long-time Alamo enthusiasts, claim the number is 185; and the official list published by the Daughters of the Republic of Texas includes 189 names. Undoubtedly, many other estimates are out there somewhere.

Many reasons exist for the wide variances, not the least of which is a lack of reliable, undisputable, succinct information. A chronological review of the scant evidence available points to some of the problems in trying to determine the exact number of casualties.

December 30, 1835: On this date F. W. Johnson, Dr. John Grant, and 200 volunteers left the garrison at San Antonio en route for Matamoros, Mexico. Johnson later wrote that he left 100 men in the garrison and predicted another 50 would be required for the defense of the place.[3] So much for his ability to predict.

We do not know whether Johnson's 100 total included any of the men who were wounded in the Texans' assault on the Alamo in early December. We do know that several of the wounded, perhaps more than 15, were still recuperating in the Alamo hospital at the time Johnson left.[4]

January 6, 1836: Lt. Colonel James C. Neill, who succeeded Johnson in command of the garrison, reported in a letter to the governor of Texas, ". . . we have 104 men and two distinct fortresses to garrison."[5] Neill mentions nothing about wounded men and we do not know whether he included officers in his count.

January 14, 1836: In a letter to General Sam Houston, Colonel Neill complained about his men being "almost naked" and very much in need of their promised pay. Of the men, Neill said, ". . . almost every one of them speaks of going home, and not less than twenty will leave tomorrow, and leave here only about 80 efficient men under my command. . . ." It would appear that on this date there were still about 100 men in the garrison. However, Neill says he would have 80 "efficient" men left which seems to indicate he would have others that were not efficient due either to illness or previous wounds, but he gives us no clue as to how many men that might include.[6]

January 15, 1836: The state archives in Austin include a muster roll of men in the Alamo garrison which contains 110 names, including officers and wounded. Many historians have tried to maintain that the list should be dated February 11, the day Neill left the garrison to attend to sick family members. The only problem with that theory is that the names of James Bowie, David Crockett, James Butler Bonham, and William B. Travis do not appear on the roll. Omission of those names means that the roll must have been completed prior to January 19, the date Bowie and Bonham are thought to have arrived. The journals of the General Council of Texas contain the following entry, under date of January 15: "The President presented a communication from J. C. Neill, Lieut. Colonel commandant at Bexar, enclosing a list of the men in that garrison which was read and on motion of Mr. Royall, was referred to the committee on military affairs."[7] There still is, and probably always will be, some doubt as to the date the roll was prepared, but it was probably sent to the government on either the first or sixth of January in conjunction with other Neill correspondence. Aside from the actual total number of troops, the most significant information from the list is that eight men are listed as being either wounded, sick, or simply "in hospital." One man is listed as "taken prisoner," a strange notation since if he was not present, how could he be listed on the roll?

January 17, 1836: Sam Houston advised the governor he was sending James Bowie to the Alamo with a detachment of between 20 and 50 men. He also instructed Captain Phillip Dimitt to advance to Bexar with 100 volunteers.[8] However, no record exists to suggest Dimitt ever completed his mission.

January 18, 1836: Green B. Jameson, the garrison engineer, reported in a letter to Sam Houston, "We now have 114 men counting officers, the sick and the wounded, which leaves us about 80 efficient men."[9] This count is significant because he indicates 34 men are either sick or wounded and not fit for combat, which would seem to mean that sometime between January 1 and January 18, the sick list grew by 26, but we have no explanation for the dramatic increase. One possible reason might be that Neill indicated only the men in the worst possible shape, and Jameson listed anyone with so much as a runny nose.

January 19, 1836: This is the day generally accepted to be the arrival date of Bowie and his men. The problem is we cannot be absolutely certain of the exact number of men in the group although most experts tend to agree on 32. Accepting that number would mean the garrison was then 146 total men or 112 efficient men.[10]

January 28, 1836: William B. Travis advised the governor that he was marching to Bexar with 30 men.[11]

January 28, 1836: James C. Neill was obviously expecting Travis, because in a letter to the government he said that he would use the lieutenant colonel to cut bridges and impede the enemy's advance. Of Travis, Neill said, ". . . with the men, say 25, under that officer's command the force at this garrison will consist of 130 Americans."[12] Simple subtraction of the expected men leaves a total current force of 105 men. Neill says nothing about sick or wounded men and does not use the term "efficient." If we assume the 105 is a total number, then 41 men (or 28 percent) abandoned the garrison between January 19 and January 28. Even given the horrendous conditions and the lack of pay, 28 percent is a considerable amount; so much so, in fact, that it seems likely Neill would have mentioned something about such a mass exodus. On the other hand, if Neill's 105 includes only efficient men, then only seven left, which is a much more believable figure. We cannot, however, be positive as to how many men were in the garrison.

February 2, 1836: James Bowie wrote a letter to the governor wherein he used one of the most quoted phrases from the Alamo period. Concerning the possibility of abandoning Bejar, Bowie said, "Col Neill & Myself have come to the solemn resolution that we will rather die in these ditches than give it up to the enemy."[13]

Bowie also advised that Capt. Patton and "5 or 6 has come in." Concerning the total force, Bowie said, ". . . the returns this day to the Comdt. is only one hundred and twenty officers & men." He also added an ominous line when he wrote, "It would be a waste of men to put our brave little band against thousands."

Even though Bowie did not use the term "efficient" and mentions nothing about sick or wounded men, he does say returns. In all probability, only the men able to fight would have been returned to the commandant. It seems very likely that some men were inefficient on February 2.

February 3, 1836: William B. Travis and 30 men arrived in San Antonio. If Bowie's count of 120 represented the actual total, the garrison was then 151 strong. If Neill and Bowie both omitted the possible 34 sick and wounded, the total might have been as high as 185.

February 9, 1836: The arrival of Davy Crockett and the Tennessee volunteers presents a new complication, because we do not know positively how many men arrived. Estimates vary, but many agree that 17 is an acceptable number. Also, the entire amount is shown here although recent evidence uncovered indicates that as many as eight of the men arrived sometime after Crockett.[14] Adding 17 new arrivals, the garrison is now either 168 or 202, assuming none have deserted which may be an incorrect assumption. It should also be noted that the continued use of 34 for sick and wounded is probably incorrect. Even though recuperation periods on the harsh prairie were often very long, undoubtedly some of the men had regained their strength.

February 11, 1836: Following Neill's departure, engineer Jameson said in a letter to Governor Smith, "We are now 150 strong. . . ."[15] Unlike his earlier report, Jameson makes no mention of sick or wounded so the disposition of the original 34 remains a mystery.

February 12, 1836: William B. Travis took over command in Neill's absence and in a letter to the governor he said, ". . . we have not more than 150 men here and they are in a very discouraged state." This is Travis' first use of the 150 figure but in view of the phrase "no more than," he seems to be using it as an estimate.[16]

February 15, 1836: William B. Travis wrote a letter to the governor introducing Erastus "Deaf" Smith.[17] While the letter offers no information as to totals, it does supply a clue as to the disposition of one of the sick or wounded men. Smith was shot at the storming of Bexar more than two months earlier and is still not recuperated. The purpose of the introduction is to help Smith appeal to the government for a pension to provide for his family. The significance here is that at least one of the wounded was still in the Alamo garrison on this date and not fit for service. It may also be significant that Smith's name was not included on Neill's muster roll and yet he was still in the garrison. It is possible that other of the wounded men were simply not counted on any official rolls. Apparently "Deaf" Smith eventually recovered because he played a critical role at the battle of San Jacinto.

February 23, 1836: The Mexican army arrived unexpectedly in San Antonio. William B. Travis dashed off a quick call for help in which he said, "We have 150 men and are determined to defend the Alamo to the last."[18] It is very probable this reference has been used extensively to predict the ultimate number of men who died since Travis' figure was picked up and widely reported. Unfortunately, the number is not correct. In another less famous letter of the same date, signed by Travis and James Bowie, they said, "We have 146 men who are determined never to retreat."[19] The use of an exact number seems to indicate that is the absolute total, although we still have no way of knowing if some sick or wounded might not have been counted. Part of the discrepancy can be explained by the fact that three messengers are known to have left on February 23. Perhaps a fourth unknown person also left to bring the actual total to 146.

March 3, 1836: In his last few items of correspondence, Travis gave us some confirmations and contradictions. In one long letter, he said nothing of a total amount of men, but he did confirm that the only help he received was 32 men from Gonzales and James Butler Bonham, a total of 33 which is a popular figure. In another letter, under date of March 3, Travis said some strange things about numbers. At one point he said, "I am still here, in fine spirits, and well to do, with 145 men."[20] It looks as if Travis is saying the total garrison is 145, which might mean one more courier left to reduce the 146 total. The problem is what about the 32 from Gonzales? In the same letter, Travis reconfirms their arrival but does not seem to be saying that the 32 should be added to the 145. Could that possibly mean that more than 30 men had become inefficient? Probably not, since it has been well documented that no one in the Alamo was seriously wounded before the final assault. More than likely, Travis was either tired or in a hurry and simply did not report the total count correctly.

The 146 count Travis and Bowie used on February 23 is probably very close to being accurate. Of course, such a number throws off the estimates as established in the very beginning. If there were only 146 men on the 23rd, and only 33 more arrived, then the total available number would be 179 and not 183. But that's not the end of the story. Years of research has produced the strong likelihood that eight additional messengers (or perhaps more) left after the siege began and did not return. One messenger, John Smith, left on February 23, returned, and left again on March 3. If the eight men are subtracted from the 179, then the total of available men is 171 or 12 men below the popular 183.

The alcalde of San Antonio, Francisco Ruiz, is undoubtedly a source for much of the popularity of the 183 figure. He was responsible for burning the bodies, and in his report he stated, "The men burnt were one hundred and eighty two. I was an eyewitness. . . ." Since it is widely believed that one Alamo defender was allowed to be buried, we have what appears to be a reliable total of 183 which would seem to leave us with an unexplained 12 men. Is it possible the 12 were sick or wounded and had not been counted previously? That would be one explanation.

There are, of course, other accounts of the fall that purport to relay the number of Texans who died. The estimates of Mexican participants range from the popular 182 to 250, 257, and all the way to the ridiculous 600 reported by Santa Anna. One of the most interesting counts of Alamo victims came from Jose Enrique de la Pena. He wrote:

> According to documents found among these men
> [Alamo victims] and to subsequent information,
> the force within the Alamo consisted of 182 men;
> but according to the number counted by us it was
> 253. Doubtless the total did not exceed either of
> these two, and in any case the number is less
> than that referred to by the commander in chief
> in his communique. . . .[21]

In the notes supporting the above entry in his narrative,
Pena explained that the Texas force consisted of "150
volunteers, 32 inhabitants from the township of Gonzales
who had entered the fort two days before the assault
under cover of darkness, and about 20 or so townspeople
or merchants from the township of Bejar."[22] Obviously
Pena had access to some sort of documents (although what
documents is unclear) that broke down the force by the 150
claimed by Travis to have been in the fortress when the
Mexicans attacked and the thirty-two Gonzales volunteers
who arrived later. The intriguing part of the Pena note is
the "20 or so townspeople or merchants" from Bexar. We
do not know if the twenty merchants participated in the
defense of the mission and subsequently died with the rest
of the men or if they were spared as non-combatants. We
do not have the source of Pena's information about the
merchants but no other account of the Alamo saga includes
any reference that twenty merchants were spared by Santa
Anna. If Pena is accurate with the information, which is
open to much speculation, then the total force defending
the mission would have been 202 or more.

One unknown Mexican, writing to his "brothers of the
heart" as he watched the funeral pyre burn, said, "257
corpses without counting those who fell in the previous
thirteen days, or those who vainly sought safety in
flight."[23] The possibility of some of the Texans' taking
flight at battle's end does present additional possibilities
concerning our count. It is probable Santa Anna desired to
have the Alamo cleared of the dead immediately and thus
ordered the funeral pyre. However, if some of the Texans
did break and run in a desperate attempt to escape, they
would have been killed somewhere out on the prairie and
perhaps their bodies were left to rot where they fell. We

have clues that some of the Texans did take flight, but we have no idea how many or whether or not their bodies were burned. It seems possible, however, that their remains were not included in the Ruiz account of those burned which could open up entirely new speculations as to the number killed.

It seems possible that 200 or more Texans might have perished. Some of the Mexicans did say 250 and 257, which sound high. But then Susanna Dickinson, one of the few Texas survivors, once claimed in an 1881 newspaper interview that the garrison amounted to about 160 sound men.[24] In 1876, in a statement to the adjutant general of Texas, she claimed that, "Among the besieged were 50 or 60 wounded ones from Cos's fight."[25] Putting these two reports together, Susanna seems to be saying there were 160 able bodied men *plus* 50 or 60 wounded men, for a total garrison of between 210 and 220 men. While it is doubtful Susanna's total figures are all that accurate, it is interesting to note that if the figures cited in the above chronology are all exclusive of the sick and wounded, then the total would soar to almost 210 if the sick and wounded

Susanna Dickinson, one of the Alamo survivors, shown in an 1881 photograph taken during her one and only visit to the shrine where she was widowed for the first time forty-five years earlier. *(Courtesy The Archives Division of the Texas State Library.)*

were added in. It is also interesting to note that if three additional Alamo messengers, who are thought to have left on unknown dates, were subtracted from the previously adjusted total of 171, then the balance of 168 is surprisingly close to Susanna's "about 160." Also, one Alamo messenger, John Sutherland, maintained in an interview that there were 206 men in the Alamo,[26] which is close to the total arrived at by adding Susanna's numbers and very close to Pena's total if the twenty merchants were considered combatants.

Some historians scoff at the notion that perhaps more than 200 men were in the Alamo. The usual reasoning behind their position is that the relatives of that many men did not come forward to claim the land due their fallen kin. Such a position seems to be foolish because many, if not most, of the men in Texas in 1836 were actually soldiers of fortune. Many easily could have been present without their families having the slightest clue as to their whereabouts, and thus the relatives had no reason to file a claim or any proof if they did file.

Historians and researchers will continue to scour old records, documents, family bibles and the like seeking those precious scraps of information that might prove or disprove this or that man was or was not in the Alamo. At this late date it would appear the chances of making significant inroads into the problem are slim indeed. But historians are a dedicated bunch, and they will surely keep trying. Most will continue to believe that 180-odd men died that Sunday morning. Some will concede the number could have been over 200. Still others may come up with their own projections. We will surely never know the real truth.

It is tempting to predict that the old saying "the only thing that is certain is that nothing is certain" would apply to the question of how many men died in the Alamo. But that's not exactly true. We know that on March 6, 1836, the Alamo fell and the mystery of how many men died there was launched. It is a guaranteed certain fact that the mystery continues in free flight to this day.

The Thorny Problem of Mr. Rose

In the early 1870s, William P. Zuber rocked the foundation of accepted Alamo history. Prior to that time it was generally believed that, with the exception of a few couriers, all the men who had been in the Alamo at the time the siege began had remained in the fortress and died fighting. It was not an altogether unreasonable assumption since no one had come forward to offer evidence to the contrary. That hypothesis began to change when the 1873 edition of the *Texas Almanac* hit the streets.

The *Texas Almanac* that year included a wildly provocative story, authored by Zuber, which detailed the escape of one Moses [or Louis] Rose from the Alamo nine days after the siege began. There was no pretense that Rose might have been a courier or had some other legitimate reason for leaving. It was simply reported that he chose to leave because he was not ready to die. Needless to say, the story was a historical bombshell and the reverberations are still felt today.

In capsule form, here is the Zuber story. Supposedly, one Moses Rose arrived at the home of Zuber's parents, some time after the fall of the Alamo, with a fabulous tale of how he had made good his escape from the Alamo on March 3. According to Rose, on that date the Mexican guns suddenly fell silent, and Travis concluded the end was near and all hope was lost. Accordingly, he assembled the men and told them their certain fate was death. Though he was committed to stand and fight, Travis offered any man who was so inclined the chance to attempt escape. He then drew a line in the Texas dirt with his sabre and invited any who would stand with him to cross the line. Every man, save Rose, crossed the line. Even Rose's friend James Bowie, deathly ill at the time, had his cot carried across the line.

Shortly thereafter, on the afternoon of the third, Rose scaled the wall. From that vantage point he could see that "from the wall to a considerable distance beyond the ground was literally covered with slaughtered Mexicans and pools of blood." He proceeded to vault to the ground where his wallet [suitcase] of dirty clothes sprang open and some became covered with blood. Regaining his breath, Rose made his way through town, down to the San Antonio river, and completed his escape. After some weeks of terrible hardships, he arrived at the home of his old friends, the Zubers, where he stayed for several days recovering from wounds he received courtesy of a multitude of cactus stickers encountered while trying to make his way across the Texas prairie in the darkness of night.

While recuperating, Rose told and retold his story. Zuber's parents listened and were so enthralled with what he said, especially the part about the speech, that the words became indelibly inscribed on their memories. The Zubers were so impressed with Rose and his story that they often repeated what he said among themselves and to their son William. Apparently, the story was retold enough that thirty-five years later, when Zuber decided to commit the saga to writing, he was able to remember every detail.[1]

It goes almost without saying that, as a group, historians pounced on the tale like a flock of ducks on a defenseless June bug. For some, the pouncing has yet to cease. Since the story was so revolutionary, the first order of business was to examine Zuber very closely to be sure he was not the type that might attempt a terrific hoax. Apparently he was not. Zuber, in fact, was active in the Texas revolution himself. He was on his way to the Alamo when that fortress fell, so he volunteered to fight with Sam Houston and, on the day of San Jacinto, he was with a rear guard protecting the army baggage. He later fought against the Indians and then went on to become somewhat of a

At the extreme left is William P. Zuber, the man who gave the world the story of Travis and the line. Zuber, who also fought in the war for independence, is shown at a 1901 meeting of Texas Veterans. Although Zuber did not participate in the battle of San Jacinto, since he was part of the rear guard at Harrisburg, he was the last surviving member of the army at the time of his death in 1913. *(Courtesy The Archives Division of the Texas State Library.)*

legitimate historian. He was a charter member of the Texas Historical Association and authored a very interesting, although not altogether accurate, book entitled *Eighty Years in Texas*. Those credentials do not seem to indicate Zuber was of the mold to try to fool the world with a pack of lies. He, himself, said he would not do so, even to save his life.[2]

Still the historians scoffed at Zuber and his story. If it was true, they wondered, why had he waited thirty-five years to make it public? Frankly, his explanation of the long delay was not sufficient to satisfy many serious historians. According to Zuber, prior to writing the story he had assumed he could not remember enough details to accomplish the task. But then what amounted to a miracle occurred. Zuber reported:

> In 1871, after much reading of early events in Texas—mainly in Richardson's Texas Almanac—I experienced a phenomenal refreshment of my memory of what I had seen, heard, and read of during my earlier life. Among other things, I recovered scraps of Travis's speech, as Rose had disconnectedly repeated them to my parents, and they had likewise repeated them to me.[3]

A phenomenal refreshment of memory! Is there any wonder the historical community continued to doubt Zuber and his tale? Anyone attempting to use such an explanation today would be laughed out of the state. Zuber probably would have fared much better had he claimed he wanted to get the story in print while his mother was still alive to verify what he said. He did include a statement of authenticity from his mother which supposedly verified that what Zuber said was a faithful representation of the Rose story.[4]

The watchdogs of historical accuracy pressed on. They doubted that after so many years Zuber could have recalled the words of Travis' speech; and frankly, they doubted that Rose himself would have recalled every word. Zuber answered that challenge with the frank admission that he did not propose to have reported the speech literally but rather had constructed it from the bits and pieces of what his parents remembered. He thus admitted he had made up his version of the speech. But, he steadfastly maintained that Travis had made a most dramatic and memorable talk and that Rose had been so impressed he had recalled many of the exact words, though certainly not all the words and probably not in any specific order.[5]

So far, Zuber was perhaps holding his own in the court of historical inquiry. But he had a long row left to hoe. His most difficult problem was proving that Moses Rose had ever been in the Alamo in the first place. Many records of Alamo victims included the name of J. M. Rose or just Rose, but that person was thought to have died in the fortress. There was no record of any other Rose having participated. Zuber tried to answer that challenge by merely surmising someone had made a mistake and that J. M. Rose was really Moses Rose and that he had not died as everyone assumed. That was actually considered possible since many errors are known to have been made in attempting to establish exactly who died in the Alamo. Zuber also maintained that other acquaintances of Moses Rose knew the old man had gone to the Alamo, but he failed to name those mysterious "other" people.

Zuber apparently never had to face what could have been a serious challenge to his position that the Rose assumed to have died was actually Louis Rose. In 1853, Susanna Dickinson, a survivor of the massacre, gave sworn testimony on behalf of the heirs of a Rose who was killed in the Alamo. Susanna testified that she knew a young man about thirty years old named Rose who was in the fortress. She did not recall his given name but said she thought he had come to Texas with Davy Crockett. She claimed Crockett and Rose frequently were housed in her quarters in San Antonio.[6] In 1857 Susanna again gave additional testimony concerning the same Rose. In the second instance she recalled that his given name was James. She also said that, as far as she knew, he was the only man named Rose in the army.[7]

Although the Susanna Dickinson testimony existed at the time Zuber broke his story, it had apparently been so long since she had given the details that no one dusted off the records and challenged Zuber. Given the spunk the man later demonstrated, he probably would have assumed that Susanna was simply wrong about there being only one Rose and let it go at that. Of course, one interesting point often overlooked is that Susanna Dickinson lived all her adult life in Texas and did not die until 1883, ten years after the Rose story broke. Since Zuber was an active historian long before Susanna passed away, it seems odd Zuber never sought her out for verification of his story.

Even without the challenge of the Dickinson testimony, the historical community never seemed to accept anything Zuber said as proof his Rose was in the Alamo. Apparently those historians, and Zuber as well, overlooked a sliver of evidence that has existed since two weeks after the fall of the Alamo. Incredibly, the evidence is contained in the March 24, 1836 issue of the *Telegraph and Texas Register* which was surely one of the most read issues of that publication because it contained the first report on the names of Alamo victims.

According to the editors of the *Telegraph*, they obtained their preliminary list of victims from John Smith, the courier who carried Travis' last message out of the Alamo, and from a Mr. Navon who was probably Gerald Navan, thought by many to have also been an Alamo courier.[8] The list contained only 115 names and the information was not complete. However, one name on the list was "Rose, of Nacogdoches." It would appear that twelve days after the final battle, two men who had been in the Alamo reported that a former resident of Nacogdoches named Rose was one of the victims. No other Rose is included on the list.

The significance of the information in the *Telegraph* is that the James (or J. M.) Rose mentioned by Susanna Dickinson was not from Nacogdoches; he was from Ohio and probably came to Texas to fight in the war for independence and joined the Crockett party in San Antonio.[9] It would appear that Susanna did not know of Moses Rose and that John Smith did not know of James Rose. Given the trying times Mrs. Dickinson and Mr. Smith endured, the fact that neither would have known all the men in the fortress does not seem improbable. But for William Zuber it might have been significant that men who had lived in Texas for some time reported that one of their Nacogdoches neighbors named Rose died in the Alamo. Zuber apparently never picked up on what may be a valuable clue. Historians also ignored the apparent evidence because they continued to scoff at the notion that Moses Rose had been in the Alamo. Without sufficient, verifiable evidence of Rose's presence in the fortress, Zuber's case was greatly damaged. Historians, acting every bit the part of a school of sharks, moved in for the kill and unloaded a barrage of doubts about the validity of poor old Zuber's story.

There was the major problem of the date on which Rose said he left the mission after Travis had given his speech. Alamo scholars have always pointed out that there was no evidence to suggest that, on the afternoon of the third of March, there were piles of dead Mexicans and pools of blood outside the Alamo walls. In addition, Travis had written a letter on that date in which he did not *seem* to indicate he was without hope; certainly he was not to the point of "throwing in the towel" and offering the men the option to escape.[10] Finally, there was the complication that no Alamo survivor who was in the fortress on March 3 ever mentioned the line or the speech *before* the Rose story was published.

Zuber, apparently somewhat of a fighter in his own right, was not prepared to sit still in the face of such criticism and innuendos about the credibility of his story. In 1901, he struck back with a lengthy letter published in the *Southwestern Historical Quarterly*. His intention was to explain away each argument against the story but, unfortunately for Mr. Zuber, he only succeeded in making matters worse.[11]

As an example, in his rebuttal Zuber went to great lengths to explain why John Smith, the courier known to have left the Alamo on March 3 with Travis' dispatch, had never mentioned either the line or the speech. Zuber conceded that had Smith left after dark in the evening of the third, as was generally believed, and never mentioned the speech, that would be proof Rose lied. But, Zuber concluded that Smith had left sometime after midnight in the darkness of the *morning* and thus was long gone when the speech was made in the afternoon. Apparently, Zuber never bothered to read a copy of the Travis letter, or he would have known it was clearly stated that James Bonham had arrived at 11:00 a.m. the morning of the third. How could Smith have left before sunrise carrying a letter that announced Bonham's arrival at 11:00 a.m.? If we listen closely, we may still be able to hear the historians laughing at such a notion.

For a lot of people, this complication might have been a deathblow to their story. But not for Zuber, not by a long shot. When this seemingly monumental discrepancy was pointed out to him, Zuber returned a volley to explain away the controversy. As to the matter of Travis' mentioning Bonham's arriving at 11:00 o'clock in the morning, Zuber concluded that Travis was tired and pressed for time and that he simply made a mistake. According to Zuber, Travis probably meant "yesterday morning, last evening or tonight" He also concluded that the error was "surely not an extraordinary one."[12]

To support his contention, Zuber went into significant detail explaining that the courier Smith could not have left after dark on the third and arrived in Washington, Texas after sunrise on the morning of the sixth. To accomplish that, a rider would have had to cover 180 miles in 60 hours without a change of horses. Zuber concluded such a ride was not possible; therefore Smith must have left early in the morning of the third which proved Travis erred and explained why Smith never said anything about the line— he was long gone when the incident occurred. That explanation probably did not hold much water, because knowledgeable horsemen advise that 180 miles in sixty hours would not have been impossible on a range-trained horse. A difficult ride perhaps, but not impossible.[13]

As to the prospects of dead Mexican soldiers being outside the walls on March 3, Zuber offered some obscure story about John Smith's saying as much when he reached the convention to present Travis' letter. Supposedly, some members of the convention heard what Smith said and passed along the details to Anson Jones, who happened to be traveling through town. Jones, a future president of the republic, then continued on his journey and later encountered Zuber, who was, himself, on his way to the Alamo. Jones, according to Zuber, passed along the story of how several times the Mexicans had closed to the outside of the walls, on or before the third, and had been repulsed leaving behind the bodies of the soldiers who had been killed. Although he admitted Jones did not retell such a story when he published his *Republic of Texas*, Zuber, nevertheless, proposed that the story was proof there were dead Mexicans and pools of blood around the fortress on the afternoon of the third. As to why Travis made no mention of such in his letter, Zuber simply concluded that Travis did not have time to write such details. Clearly Zuber was grasping at straws and not catching many.[14]

Zuber's most glaring mistake, in the 1901 story, concerned the departure times of Rose and Smith. He stood fast in the belief that Rose left in the afternoon of the third, as he had told Zuber's parents. In the same paragraph, however, he states that Smith had to leave after midnight to escape the vigilance of the Mexican guards since they "were on strict watch for men from the Alamo." Apparently, Zuber wanted everyone to believe that Smith had to leave under cover of deep darkness to avoid detection and yet Rose could waltz out of the Alamo in the middle of the afternoon and not be detected. As far as can be determined, Zuber never addressed that particular conflict in his story.[15]

Quite understandably, William Zuber's "explanations" were dismissed by the historical community even more quickly than the original story. A stalemate developed with historians continuing to doubt the tale and Zuber sticking by what he felt was the absolute truth, as reported by Rose. Ironically, Zuber did not live to see the impasse begin to break down.

The next major development came in 1939, when R. B. Blake discovered some dramatic evidence in the dusty old files of the Nacogdoches County Courthouse. The records showed that Louis Rose had in fact been in the Alamo and that his testimony had been accepted in at least six land-claim cases on behalf of relatives of Alamo victims. In the case of John Blair, for instance, Rose testified "left him in the Alamo 3 March 1836." That testimony helped Blair's relatives claim the bounty of land that was due to any man who died in the fortress. Unfortunately, William P. Zuber died before the Rose testimony was uncovered so he did not live to see at least part of his story vindicated.[16]

Historians were left scrambling for facts. The cornerstone of their dismissal of the Zuber story had been pulled out from under them. Rose—Louis Rose—was, indeed, in the Alamo and did leave. Could that possibly mean the rest of the story was true? If so, history books would surely have to be rewritten. If it was at all possible, you have to believe that old Zuber was out there somewhere, in spirit only, having a laugh of his own.

When their main line of defense against the validity of the Rose tale went up in the dust raised by Blake reviewing those old records, the historians and scholars were forced to retreat to other less defensible positions. There was still the most puzzling problem of why Susanna Dickinson, who survived the massacre, never mentioned Rose or the Travis line until well after the Zuber's story became widely known. Zuber doubters pointed out correctly that she had, on several occasions, given testimony on behalf of the heirs of men killed in the Alamo and she had spoken only of the Rose known to have died there. The historians also pointed out that when she did talk of the supposed episode, her account always seemed to have been spiced with editorial prompting and occasionally directly contradicted the Zuber tale. What those detractors failed to mention is that Susanna Dickinson was not interviewed by *any* journalist or historian until 1874, one year after the Zuber story broke. Susanna, who was illiterate,[17] never volunteered any information but rather merely responded to questions either from the Land Board, the Adjutant General, or journalists. The fact that she did not talk about the line until after the Zuber story broke appears to be of no consequence since journalists did not get around to interviewing her until after the story appeared in the *Texas Almanac.*

Zuber himself had dismissed the failure of Mrs. Dickinson to mention the event prior to the almanac story with the simple explanation that she was not present when the men were called together. He concluded she was off in some building at the time and just did not see what happened.[18] That explanation also solved the mystery of why her accounts differed from his when she did talk. In Zuber's defense, that may be exactly what happened. See "Oh, Susanna" elsewhere in this volume for more details.

There was, of course, still the problem of the date. Historians stood fast in their belief, based primarily on Travis' letter of the third, that the colonel had not lost all hope on that date. There was also no acceptable proof whatsoever that dead Mexicans were piled up around the compound, except on the morning of the sixth. Another impasse seemed to have developed.

The impasse took a slight turn in 1961, when Walter Lord offered a sort of explanation in *A Time to Stand*. Lord, who did a monumental amount of primary research for his book, reviewed some then unpublished testimony by Susanna Dickinson and seemed to conclude that Rose had simply erred when he said the third and that he actually meant the fifth. It seemed that Lord was saying if we could allow Rose the latitude of being wrong about the date, then perhaps, just perhaps, the Zuber tale had some validity. Even though Lord's explanation, under close examination, seems to have some holes (see "Oh, Susanna") it still remained that at last a respected historian was accepting some of the Zuber story.[19]

Since publication of *A Time to Stand*, there has been no great unearthing of primary information of the caliber that Blake found in those dusty old records. But one tiny and perhaps flimsy scrap of evidence has come to light that might substantiate a portion of the Rose story. That evidence is in the form of a letter purportedly written by one of the defenders, Issac Millsaps, on the morning of March third. In part, Millsaps is supposed to have said:

> My Dear, Dear Ones,
> We are in the fortress of the Alamo a ruined church that has most fell down. The Mexicans are here in large numbers they have kept up a constant fire since we got here. All our boys are well & Capt. Martin is in good spirits. Early this morning I watched the Mexicans drilling just out of range they were marching up and down with such order. They have bright red and blue uniforms and many canons. Some here at this place believe that the main army has not come up yet. I think they are all here even Santanna. Col. Bowie is down sick and had to be to bed I saw him yesterday & he is still ready to fight. He didn't know me from last spring but did remember Wash. He tells me that help will be here soon & it makes us feel good. We have beef and corn to eat but no coffee, bag I had fell off on the way here so it was spilt. I have not seen Travis but 2 times since here he told us all this morning that Fanning was going to be here early

with many men and there would be a good fight.
He stays on the wall some but mostly to his room
I hope help comes soon cause we can't fight them
all. Some says he is going to talk some tonight &
group us better for Defence. If we fail here get to
the river with the children all Texas will be before
the enemy we get so little news here we know
nothing. There is no discontent in our boys some
are tired from loss of sleep and rest. The
Mexicans are shooting every few minutes but
most of the shots fall inside & no harm. I don't
know what else to say they is calling for all
letters, kiss the dear children for me be well &
God protects us all.

Isaac

If any men come through there tell them to hurry
with powder for it is short I hope you get this &
know—I love you all.[20]

Despite the poor English, Millsaps does manage to give
us the apparent rumor that Travis planned to speak to the
men again on March 3. Yes, this is flimsy evidence and
certainly cannot be considered proof. But, it is not hard to
imagine that if Travis was planning to talk about defense of
the mission and if he had decided all was lost, it would
have been a perfect time to offer any who wanted to
chance it the opportunity to leave. This one letter is the
only evidence that Travis may indeed have talked to the
men on the third as Rose and, consequently, Zuber
claimed. Unfortunately, the evidence is tainted.

In the March 1989 issue of *Texas Monthly* magazine, in
an article entitled "Highly Suspect," writer Gregory Curtis
said of the Millsaps letter, "in my opinion it is a forgery."
Curtis reported that respected Alamo historian Walter Lord
and noted document dealer Mary Hamilton both dismissed
the document as a forgery as early as 1964. Curtis also
quoted Edward G. Holley of the University of Houston
library, which owns the original document, as saying "I
always had doubts about that letter." Apparently Holley's
doubt showed through whenever he wrote about the letter

because he referred to it as "believed" to have been written from the Alamo.

There are several points about the Millsaps letter which do seem suspicious. The use of the salutation "My dear, dear ones" was not, as Curtis correctly pointed out, in general use until about the time of the Civil War which was twenty-four years after the fall of the Alamo. Even more suspect is that the letter is signed simply "Isaac" and in the revolutionary days of Texas it was very rare indeed for a writer to sign documents with only the first name. Curtis also offered some graphic evidence that the handwriting used in the Millsaps letter appears similar to that of the infamous forger John Laflin who was known to have been operating in Texas about the time the letter appeared.

Curtis also found the supposed Millsaps description of the Alamo as a "ruined church" to be "an extremely unlikely description. . . ." He pointed out that what we know as the Alamo was, in 1836, a small chapel in a very large mission compound. Curtis even found fault with the Millsaps description of the Mexican soldiers being attired in bright red and blue uniforms because it is generally believed that most of Santa Anna's troops were peasant soldiers who wore white sackcloth.

Perhaps the most damaging evidence against the letter's authenticity was not in the Curtis article. According to Michael Green, archivist of the Texas state library, the signature on the "supposed" Millsaps letter does not *appear* to match the one other known Millsaps signature. Green also advised that there is a difference in the spelling used for the name in the two signatures. In the face of all the evidence, Bernice Strong of the Daughters of the Republic of Texas library at the Alamo said she was "afraid" the Millsaps letter was not authentic. Her fear may be justified.

It is possible to argue the controversial points of the letter. Even though the salutation was not in general use, Millsaps could have invented it out of a desire to show deep affection for his blind wife and seven kids. Perhaps Isaac only signed his first name in haste to be sure the letter was finished when the courier left (although he did take time to add a postscript.) A lot of people have similar handwriting so the similarities between Millsaps and forger Laflin may be coincidence. Variances in style and even in the spelling used in signatures on the Texas frontier are not unheard of. The Alamo was, indeed, a ruined church and at least some of the Mexican soldiers did wear red and white uniforms.

As Curtis pointed out, we may never know the truth until someone springs for $5,000 to have scientific tests run that would settle the issue once and for all. However, as far as the Zuber/Rose story is concerned, the authenticity of the letter is actually of little consequence. Should the letter be proven genuine, the information provided in the document might then be construed as proof that Travis did plan to speak to the men on March 3. Should the letter be proved a skillful fake, that information would not damage the Zuber contention in any way.

At this late date, the Zuber/Rose controversy rages on. Those persons interested enough to have an opinion generally fall into one of two camps. The doubting historians do not think the episode ever happened. Hollywood directors and screen writers, along with patriotic, legend-loving Texans, are generally of the opinion that, unless someone can prove it did not happen, they are going to believe it did. The issue will probably never be resolved to the satisfaction of all.

Any writer of Texas history who is brave enough to address the Rose issue is almost duty-bound to advance an opinion. A great many of those writers seem to run up the white flag and escape the issue by concluding that something may have happened but it probably did not. There shall be no white flag flown here.

The largest single problem with the entire Rose affair is the apparent desire of most people to prove the story is either all true or all false. Opponents will cite one or two points thought to be incorrect or suspicious as evidence that the entire story is fake. Zuber, on the other hand, seemed obsessed to prove everything Rose said was fact. From a realistic and logical standpoint, the proposition that Rose must be either all right or all wrong is utterly ridiculous. There are several accounts of the fall of the Alamo, written by persons who had personal knowledge of the events, which contain significant mistakes and omissions. Take the case of Susanna Dickinson, for one. She gave so much conflicting information, that, if we did not know she was really there, we might dismiss her stories as the ramblings of a fool. But we know she *was* there so she is afforded certain latitude due to the frailness of memory. Perhaps the same courtesy should be afforded to Rose and, in turn, to Zuber, who did not write the story for more than thirty-five years.

In actual practice, the Rose story is like a historical jigsaw puzzle. To get the true picture, we must determine which pieces of the Rose story can be accepted as fact and then fit them into their proper order. The first piece of the puzzle is determining that Louis Rose was in the Alamo in the first place. R. B. Blake, the historian who discovered the old records which showed Rose's testimony in the land cases, also wrote a chapter entitled "A Vindication of Rose and His Story" for the book *In the Shadow of History*. In that story, Blake went to great pain to demonstrate that Land Board Commissioners were ever on the lookout for frauds and accepted testimony only from persons known to them and known to be of sufficient good character. Rose's testimony was accepted in sixteen cases and never once rejected, so the commissioners were satisfied that he was in the Alamo. Exactly how Rose established that fact before the commissioners has been lost, but since they accepted his word, it seems safe to assume they had some verification. We now have one piece of our puzzle in place.

The next problem is the matter of the Mexican cease-fire. Rose said it occured on March 3, but other reliable evidence indicates it was on the fifth, which means Rose either lied or was mistaken. Either way, for our puzzle we have to put the cease-fire on March 5.

Now we have the problem of when Rose left. He said it was after the cease-fire, which means sometime in the night of the fifth or in the early morning of the sixth. However, he also said that when he left there were considerable Mexican casualties and pools of blood around the fortress. He even said that his suitcase sprang open and his clothes became soaked with spilled Mexican blood, and Zuber's mother confirmed that she saw the blood. The only possible explanation for that happening is that Louis Rose left early in the morning of March 6, after the final assault began. Perhaps the puzzle is beginning to take shape.

The next piece of the puzzle that must be fitted into place is the matter of Travis' speech. It would appear that Travis did make some sort of stirring speech before the men. Zuber was too adamant in his quest to have history believe it happened. Apparently, Rose was also sufficiently moved to speak often of what Travis had said. He was also very poorly educated and thus it is doubtful he could have invented the speech. Then there is the possible reference to a speech, or talk, in the Millsaps letter. Admittedly, such is not concrete proof, but from this far-removed vantage point it does seem a safe assumption that Travis gave a speech. Remember, he was a lawyer and, judging from his letters, was given to patriotic oration. The question is, when did it occur?

Rose said he left after the speech on March 3, which, according to our puzzle, was a lie because he would not have known of the cease-fire or the Mexican casualties. Does it necessarily follow that Travis gave the speech on the fifth and not the third? Perhaps.

If Travis's speech occured on March 5, that would actually go a long way toward resolving many Zuber challengers. It would perhaps explain why none of the couriers saw the event, and if the talk was late in the afternoon or early evening, it might explain why Susanna Dickinson did not see it and why her husband never mentioned it to her. But there is still the nagging problem of why Rose said the speech was on the third.

Apparently there are three possibilities concerning the date of the speech. Rose could have simply been mistaken, or he could have lied. If he lied, why did he choose the third? Why not the second or the fourth or any other date? There is also the possibility that Rose told the truth about the date of the speech and lied about when he left.

There is some reason to believe that Travis did give his speech on March 3. He would have deduced by the afternoon of that date—based on the news Fannin was not coming but many more Mexicans were—that all hope was probably lost.[21] If, as the supposed Millsaps letter suggests, he planned to talk to the men anyway on that date, it would have been the perfect opportunity to give the troops the choice of staying or leaving. It is also possible Travis offered the men the chance to leave anytime they saw fit.

So why might Rose have lied? To examine that problem, we must look at a possibility often ignored by historians— namely, that old Rose was a coward of the worst kind.

From the pieces of our puzzle already in place, we can surmise that Rose left after the final assault began and yet he told a vastly different story. One possible, if not probable, explanation is that when the final assault began, Rose's true color began to show and he decided to run rather than defend the mission.

Rose himself actually gives us a clue of his cowardice. He clearly states, and Zuber's parents confirmed, that when he left the Alamo, he took his suitcase with him and some of his clothes became blood soaked. Since Rose must have left after the final attack began, it appears that while the other men took up their arms to fight, Rose took up his suitcase for flight. If he had engaged in any of the fighting, the odds that he would have had time to retrieve his suitcase before leaving seem very remote.

Cowards, as a general rule, are not prone to getting up on a soapbox and admitting their inclination to the general populace. They usually choose instead some provocative excuse or strange rationale for their actions. If Rose did turn tail and run at the moment of truth, he surely would not have admitted that. He could not ignore the matter altogether because, as Zuber said, other people knew he had been in the Alamo. He could not claim he left in the heat of battle, as he probably did, because how would he explain the suitcase?

What he would have done is come up with some story to explain his actions. He would have needed a perfect excuse for leaving; and if Travis did give a speech on March 3 and offered the men the chance to leave, presto, Rose would have had his excuse. Remember, we have only Rose's word that he did *not* cross the line. For all we know, Rose may have crossed with everyone else and then changed his story later to fit his purpose. Even though any act of leaving might be construed as cowardice, the pitiful Rose may have deduced that leaving with Travis' permission would certainly sound better than abandoning the fort while it was under attack.

Based on the cowardice theory, it would appear the possibility that Rose got the date of the speech wrong is remote. If the Travis talk had occurred on March 5, there would have been no reason for Rose to lie. He could have simply stated he left the evening before the assault on the morning of the sixth. But if the speech happened on the third, that would have given him the excuse of having left three days before the assault, which does not smack so solidly of cowardice. Since Rose was illiterate, the fact that his story is somewhat disconnected is not surprising. In all probability, he would have never dreamed the Alamo would attain such historical significance and that his story would one day come under such scrutiny. The man was probably just trying to make himself look a little better in the eyes of his friends and acquaintances.

It would appear that all the available pieces of the puzzle are now in place and perhaps we can see the picture of what probably happened:

> On March 3, Travis concluded that no help was coming. Because of the newly arrived Mexican reinforcements including the commander in chief, Santa Anna, he may have deduced the end was near and assumed the men would have reached the same conclusion. Accordingly, on that date he called the men together and gave them advice on the defense of the mission. Then he explained the true situation and offered the men the chance to leave and no one, including Rose, chose that option. It was a brief, emotional ceremony and neither the couriers nor Susanna Dickinson saw or heard what transpired.
>
> On the morning of March 6, Louis Rose awoke to find the mission under full attack. In an instant, he chose to run rather than fight. He grabbed his suitcase and headed for the wall. He found a spot where the fighting had subsided and over he went. His suitcase broke open on impact so he quickly scooped up his bloody clothes and then miraculously disappeared into the early morning darkness. His fluency in Spanish and swarthy looks helped him masquerade as a Mexican, and he made good his escape. To disguise his act of cowardice, he changed the date of his leaving to coincide with Travis' offer of the chance to leave. He made his way to the home of his old friends, the Zubers, and told his great lie over and over to be certain

they believed it. They in turn told all the details to their son William, who thirty-five years later reduced it to writing to preserve the information for history. Zuber, in his zest to give the world the story of Travis' speech, inadvertently helped perpetuate the memory of the only coward of the Alamo.

This picture of what may be the real story of Rose's escape from the Alamo is certainly open to discussion. It is based on a logical interpretation of what few facts are known and thus everything is open to scrutiny and, perhaps, revision. But it must be noted that if we are to acknowledge the probability that the Zuber tale is not a total fabrication, then this version, or something very similar, is the only way all the questions about Rose and his tale of escape can be reasonably accepted. The only question that remains is: Did Travis draw the famous line in the dirt?

Travis and the Grand Canyon Line

When William P. Zuber exploded his historical bombshell about Louis Rose escaping from the Alamo, he also created one of the most endearing legends in the annals of heroism. The story of William B. Travis dramatically scratching a line into the Texas dirt with the tip of his sabre and then inviting all who wanted to stand and fight with him to step across is one of the most cherished legends in Texas history. And yet, many doubt it ever happened.

We have only the word of Zuber to authenticate the story, and thus many historians refuse to believe it. Not one of the other persons who survived the massacre ever mentioned the line or the speech before publication of the Zuber story. Does that mean Travis didn't draw it? In all probably, we will never know for sure one way or the other. But that's not the end of the story.

In the late 1870s, Zuber was under so much fire about the story that he wrote a letter to the adjutant general to try to clarify his position. He admitted he had made up the Travis speech but claimed he used words essentially the same as those Rose had reported. In that same letter Zuber also said, "I found a deficiency in the material of the speech, which from my knowledge of the man, I thought I could supply. I accordingly threw in one paragraph which I firmly believe to be characteristic of Travis, and without which the speech would have been incomplete. I distinguished said paragraph, by inserting it between brackets: & it was excepted in my mother's certificate. But, both the distinction & the exception, were omitted by the printer. That one paragraph contains every word of fiction in my article in the Almanac."[1]

Although Zuber never said the paragraph he "threw in" concerned the line, that is the conclusion reached by many historians. The sad part of the story is that if Zuber did bracket his "thrown in" paragraph, then the printer of the *Texas Almanac* could have saved everyone a lot of grief by including the brackets when the story was printed. It did not happen. The current editor of the Almanac also advises that the old records of the publication are not to be had, so we cannot go to the actual source and learn what paragraph was bracketed. We are left with conjecture, but it does appear that those "many historians" who believe the extra paragraph concerned the line may be off their historical base.

In the Zuber story can be found the following paragraph: "Col. Travis then drew his sword, and with its point traced a line upon the ground, extending from the right to the left of the file. Then, resuming his position in front of the centre, he said, 'I now want every man who is determined to stay here and die with me to come across this line. Who will be the first? March!' "[2]

If that were to have been Zuber's "thrown in" fictional paragraph, it would surely mean the story of the line is fictional. Many historians believe it is, indeed, "the" paragraph that was added, but there is a glaring problem with that logic. Zuber clearly says he threw in *one* paragraph— one; not two or three or a few or anything else—just one. The problem is, in his story, he mentions the line in three successive paragraphs. In the one immediately following the drawing of the line, he says, "The first respondent was Tapley Holland, who leaped the line at a bound. . . ." and "Every sick man who could walk arose from his bunk and tottered across the line." In the next paragraph Zuber says of Rose, "He stood till every man but himself had crossed the line." Without any doubt, the line is an integral part of three paragraphs. It should also be noted that Zuber wrote his letter about the one paragraph after the story was published in the almanac so even if his original manuscript

An early drawing depicting William B. Travis scratching a line in the Texas dirt and inviting all the men who wanted to fight to cross the line and stand with him. Legend has it only one man, Moses Rose, did not cross. *(Courtesy The DRT Library at the Alamo.)*

had the entire line episode lumped into one large paragraph he would have known it was changed for publication and surely would have mentioned the change.

Would not common horse sense seem to dictate that, if Zuber had been admitting he had "thrown in" the story of the line, he would have said something like "I threw in a few paragraphs" or "I threw in one episode"? He said it was one paragraph and one paragraph only.

There is another, more obscure point that perhaps has to be made concerning Zuber's admission of the fictional paragraph. He says he added the paragraph because "without which the speech would have been incomplete." It would seem that drawing the line and inviting the men to cross would be more of an extension to rather than a part of the speech. With very little creative effort it would be possible to produce a very patriotic speech that did not culminate with the drawing of a line.

The question now becomes what paragraph was added if it was not the one about the line. There appears to be but one choice. Consider the following three-paragraph excerpt from the Zuber story:

But I leave every man to his choice. Should any man prefer to surrender, and be tied and shot; or attempt an escape through the Mexican ranks, and be killed before he can run a hundred yards, he is at liberty to do so.

My own choice is to stay in this fort, and die for my country, fighting as long as breath shall remain in my body. This I shall do, even if you leave me alone. Do as you think best — but no man can die with me without affording me comfort in the moment of death.

Col. Travis then drew his sword, and with its point traced a line upon the ground, extending from the right to the left of the file. Then, resuming his position in front of the centre, he said, "I now want every man who is determined to stay here and die with me to come across this line. Who will be the first? March!"

Now, the same excerpt without the middle paragraph:

But I leave every man to his choice. Should any man prefer to surrender, and be tied and shot; or attempt an escape through the Mexican ranks, and be killed before he can run a hundred yards, he is at liberty to do so.

Col. Travis then drew his sword, and with its point traced a line upon the ground, extending from the right to the left of the file. Then, resuming his position in front of the centre, he said, "I now want every man who is determined to stay here and die with me to come across this line. Who will be the first? March!"

This is graphic proof that the middle paragraph could easily have been left out and the story would still make sense. The first paragraph could not be omitted since that is where Travis gives the men the option of trying an escape. The third paragraph could not be omitted because the two following paragraphs also discuss the line. From the entire speech, it appears only the middle paragraph in this example could have been "thrown in." In addition, it must be noted that the suspect paragraph does, indeed, seem to complete the speech, just as Zuber said. It seems to follow that Zuber's great admission of the "thrown in" paragraph had nothing to do with the line.

We still do not have any solid proof as to whether or not Rose was lying about the line incident, but it seems a bit farfetched to think he would have gone to the trouble to invent the line, the name of the first man to cross, the story of Bowie being carried across, and all the rest. Why would he bother? All he had to say was Travis offered the chance to escape and he took it. Period, end of tale. But he did say so much more.

There is one serious complication in the scenario presented here about which paragraph was invented. If, as theorized, Zuber fabricated the part about Travis saying he was committed to staying even if he had to do so alone, does it necessarily follow that Travis was not committed to staying? Most certainly not! Everything Travis wrote from the Alamo indicated he personally was committed to manning his post until the bitter end. Zuber, being a student of Texas history as he said, must have known of Travis' commitment. Therefore, if Rose omitted any reference to Travis' commitment, it seems totally logical that Zuber would have added a paragraph that he firmly believed to be characteristic of Travis, and "without which the speech would have been incomplete."

There can be little doubt that the largest single challenge to the possibility of Travis drawing the line and offering the men the chance to escape on March 3 is the belief that the acting commander of the Alamo had not lost all hope on that date and thus would not have made the escape offer. The evidence cited by historians supporting that view is always the letter Travis wrote on the third.

COMMANDANCY OF THE ALAMO, BEJAR: In the present confusion of the political authorities of the country, and in the absence of the commander-in-chief, I beg leave to communicate to you the situation of this garrison. You have doubtless already seen my official report of the action of the 25th ult., made on that day to General Sam Houston, together with the various communications heretofore sent by express. I shall, therefore, confine myself to what has transpired since that date.

From the 25th to the present date, the enemy have kept up a bombardment from two howitzers (one a five and a half inch, and the other an eight inch) and a heavy cannonade from two long nine-pounders, mounted on a battery on the opposite side of the river, at a distance of four hundreds yards from our walls. During this period the enemy has been busily employed in encircling us with entrenchments on all sides, at the following distance, to wit—in Bexar, four hundred yards west; in Lavilleta, three hundred yards south; at the powder-house, one thousand yards east by south; on the ditch, eight hundred yards north. Notwithstanding all this, a company of thirty-two men from Gonzales, made their way into us on the morning of the 1st. inst, at three o'clock, and Col. J. B. Bonham (a courier from Gonzales) got in this morning at eleven o'clock without molestation. I have so fortified this place, that the walls are generally proof against cannon-balls; and I shall continue to entrench on the inside, and strengthen the walls by throwing up dirt. At least two hundred shells have fallen inside our works without having injured a single man; indeed, we have been so fortunate as not to lose a man from any cause, and we have killed many of the enemy. The spirits of my men are still high, although they have had much to depress them. We have contended for ten days against an enemy whose numbers are variously estimated at from fifteen hundred to six thousand, with Gen. Ramirez Sezma and Col. Bartres, the aid-de-camp of Santa Anna, at their head. A report was circulated that Santa Anna himself was with the enemy, but I think it was false. A reinforcement of one thousand men is now entering Bexar from the west, and I think it more than probable that Santa Anna is now in town, from the rejoicing we hear. Col. Fannin is said to be on the march to this place with reinforcements; but I fear it is is not true, as I have repeatedly sent to him for aid without receiving any. Col Bonham, my special messenger, arrived at Labahia fourteen days ago, with a request for aid; and on the arrival of the enemy in Bexar ten days ago, I sent an express to Col F. which arrived at Goliad on the next day, urging him to send us reinforcements—none have arrived. I look to the colonies alone for aid; unless it arrives soon, I shall have to fight the enemy on his own terms. I will, however, do the best I can under the circumstances, and I feel confident that the determined valour and desperate courage, heretofore evinced by my men, will not fail them in the last struggle, and although they may be sacrificed to the vengeance of a Gothic enemy, the victory will cost the enemy so dear, that it will be worse for him than a defeat. I hope your honorable body will hasten on reinforcements, ammunition, and provisions to our aid, as soon as possible. We have provisions for twenty days for the men we have; our supply of ammunition is limited. At least five hundred pounds of cannon powder, and two hundred rounds of six, nine, twelve, and eighteen pound balls—ten kegs of rifle powder, and a supply of lead, should be sent to this place without delay, under a sufficient guard.

If these things are promptly sent, and large reinforcements are hastened to this frontier, this neighborhood will be the great and decisive battle ground. The power of Santa Anna is to be met here or in the colonies; we had better meet them here, than to suffer a war of desolation to rage our settlements. A blood red banner waves from the church of Bexar, and in the camp above us, in token that the war is one of vengeance against rebels; they have declared us as such, and demanded that we should surrender at discretion or this garrison should be put to the sword. Their threats have had no influence on me or my men, but to make all fight with desperation, and that high-souled courage which characterizes the patriot, who is willing to die in defense of his country's liberty and his own honour.

The citizens of this municipality are all our enemies except those who have joined us heretofore; we have but three Mexicans now in the fort; those who have not joined us in this extremity, should be declared public enemies, and their property should aid in paying the expenses of the war.

The bearer of this will give you your honorable body, a statement more in detail, should he escape through the enemy's lines. ***God and Texas ! — Victory or Death ! !***

P.S. The enemy's troops are still arriving, and the reinforcements will probably amount to two or three thousand.

Frankly, a scholarly review of this letter would seem to render the notion that it was proof Travis had not lost all hope as pure hogwash. If anything, quite the opposite seems to be the case.

It is a fact that Travis did offer some encouraging words in his letter. At one point he says, "The spirits of the men are still high, although they have had much to depress them." In another place he says, "I hope your honorable body [the convention] will hasten on reinforcements, ammunition, and provisions to our aid, as soon as possible." He then identified some of the items he needed most, such as the powder and cannon balls, and predicted that if "large reinforcements are hastened to this frontier, this neighborhood will be the great and decisive battle-ground."[3] It is not hard to find historians who will offer the opinion that any man requesting supplies and reinforcements had not given up all hope.

The letter of March 3, 1836 is, however, an interesting document in that, while showing some optimism and want of supplies, also shows great despair. Travis "fears" Fannin is not coming, and is left to look to the colonies for help, a slim prospect indeed. The most unusual part of the letter is that it appears Mexican reinforcements began to arrive *while Travis was writing*. Note that at one point he says he thinks rumors of Santa Anna's being in command are false. Then, in the next line he says reinforcements are just now arriving and suddenly he thinks Santa Anna has arrived. He even concludes his letter with a postscript that reinforcements are still arriving.

Consider the facts of March 3. In the morning, according to the Millsaps letter quoted in "The Thorny Problem of Mr. Rose," Travis told the men Fannin was coming and soon. Then James Butler Bonham arrived about 11:00 a.m. with the news Fannin probably was not coming. Travis would then have known, as he said, his only chance for help was from the convention meeting 180 miles away in Washington. He also would have known a courier would require three or four days to reach Washington. Even if reinforcements were available and left immediately, they would require at least that much time (and probably more) to come to the aid of the garrison. The question then becomes whether Travis had enough optimism to believe he could hold out for more than a week. Perhaps he had such optimism when he began the letter, but given his precarious position, surely the arrival of two or three thousand reinforcements for the enemy would have changed his mind.

It seems very possible that any optimism Travis may have clung to early on the third would have been drained by the news of Fannin and the arrival of the additional Mexican troops. More than likely, after Travis finished his letter and had time to survey fully what was happening, he came to the conclusion that the dreaded final assault was imminent. He probably concluded that the Mexicans had been waiting for Santa Anna and more troops to arrive before attacking. But now, on the third, in Travis' mind, the stage was set. He probably expected the final assault for the following day, surely within a day or so. That tracks exactly with what Travis said in his last speech, according to Rose. It seems logical that the acting commander might well have surmised the end was near and he decided to give the men their choice of staying or going.

Another point concerning Travis' correspondence which is sometimes overlooked is that on the third, the same day some historians claim he had not lost all hope, Travis also wrote another letter to David Ayers. He said:

> Take care of my little boy. If the country should
> be saved, I may make for him a splendid fortune;
> but if the country be lost and I should perish, he
> will have nothing but the proud recollection that
> he is the son of a man who died for his country.[4]

This letter contains the only written reference Travis
made about his son from the Alamo and the words
certainly do not sound as if they came from a man who
was overly optimistic. On the other hand, if Travis had
decided the end was near, such a touching letter would be
consistent with the views of a man who expected his
chances of survival had become slim.

If Travis had determined to give the men the chance to
escape, at their option, it seems to follow that he would
have done so on March 3, the day he must have decided,
after writing the letter, that their fate was sealed. Even if
he did not expect the assault the very next day, he had to
know it was coming soon, and any chance for an escape
would probably be gone by the morning of the fourth.
Thus, he gave the speech and offered the men their choice.
Based on the letter, that interpretation is just as reasonable
as the one alluding to Travis still being optimistic on the
third, perhaps even more so.

So what did Travis say in his famous speech? We will
never know. Oh, yes, Zuber gave us his reconstructed
version, but it is so full of incorrect information that little
credence can be given to it. At one point Travis supposedly
told the men that Fannin probably was not coming and
that none of his couriers had returned. We know that just a
few hours before the probable speech, Bonham had indeed
returned.

Several paragraphs, perhaps an entire story, could
doubtlessly be devoted to cutting the validity of the speech
to ribbons, but what would be the point? Zuber, after all,
admitted that he constructed the speech from bits and
pieces of what his parents said Rose had told them. He
was relying on a phenomenal refreshment of memory that
may not have been so fresh. Zuber's point, however, was
to make sure the world had some record that Travis did
give an inspirational and patriotic speech to the men. He
never pretended to have presented the exact speech, so

why challenge what he said? Based on all the evidence, it appears Zuber was probably correct and Travis did give some sort of an inspirational speech that induced the men to stay. That might be enough said if it were not for the problem of the line in the dirt.

It is a fact that there is absolutely no proof that Travis drew the line. But as a host of loyal Texans will quickly point out, there is also no proof that he did not draw it. The irony of the line controversy is that Zuber, the man who gave us the story of Rose and the line, never saw fit to defend the line portion of the story. He did his best to prove many other elements of the story, but his objective was to get the historical community to accept that Travis made the speech. For Zuber, the line was incidental (which proves he could have never made it in Hollywood as a director).

One point is worthy of mention concerning the line. With our 20-20 historical hindsight, we consider the line in the dirt episode heroic and marvel at the patriotism and bravery of the men. Dramatic portrayals on television and in the movies have helped us create images that are perhaps larger than life. It seems more likely that, in reality, after the reinforcements and Santa Anna arrived, Travis simply called the men together, quickly explained the situation and what he perceived to be their true predicament. It quite possibly was a private, somber moment between Travis and the men, not one intended to be publicized or glorified. It is also unlikely that *all* the men would have been included since some of the troops would have remained on the walls as lookouts, and there were almost certainly more sick men than just James Bowie. Time has a way of embellishing the romance of heroism, and there is no reason to suspect that such is not the case concerning Travis and his line in the dirt.

For modern Texans, the line is anything but incidental. Unfortunately, we are left with the prospect of either believing the story or not. There is no middle ground. The natural inclination for Texans is to believe it. We know Rose was in the Alamo and did escape because he was not ready to die. Some of the facts in the story may have been juggled to accommodate Rose's personal motive, but there appears no reason to fabricate the line episode since that would have served no purpose. It would seem that if the line story were omitted, then the entire Rose story would have to be discounted as well. Based on the evidence we have, it would not appear prudent to throw out the entire Rose episode. Therefore, if we believe any of the story, we should accept the line portion.

Noted and much loved Texas historian J. Frank Dobie once addressed the issue of the Travis line in a chapter for *In the Shadow of History*. One very significant passage from that book is worthy of repeating. Dobie said:

> It is a line that not all the piety nor wit of research will ever blot out. It is a Grand Canyon cut into the bedrock of human emotions and heroical impulses. It may be expurgated from histories, but it can no more be expunged from popular imagination than the damned spots on Lady MacBeth's hands. Teachers of children dramatize it in school rooms; orators on holidays silver it and guild it; the tellers of historical anecdotes—and there are many of them in Texas—sitting around hotel lobbies speculate on it and say, "Well, we'll believe it whether it's true or not."[5]

Dobie concluded, "I think Travis made the speech,"[6] which meant he also drew the line. I also think Travis made a speech and drew the line. Although the temptation would be great, I would not make such a statement simply because I am a loyal and devout Texan. I believe that what little evidence we have, coupled with logical adjustments to the Rose story, produces sufficient reason to accept the essence of the Zuber tale and, consequently, the line incident. Without proof that Travis did not draw the line, believing the story would seem to be requisite to being a loyal Texan.

Oh, Susanna

Just before dawn on the morning of March 6, 1836, Captain Almaron Dickinson burst into the garrison room where his wife Susanna and fifteen-month-old daughter Angelina were hiding. "My God, Susanna," he yelled, "the Mexicans are inside the walls. All is lost. If they spare your life, take care of my child." With that simple oath, the Captain closed the door behind him and dashed off into history as one of the men who died defending the Alamo.[1]

Susanna Dickinson also took her place in history that eventful morning. Although slightly wounded, she was indeed spared thanks to the intervention of General Santa Anna himself. In fact, the general took such a liking to Susanna and her baby that he even offered to send them to Mexico City where she could live a life of luxury and the baby could be raised as the general's own child. Mrs. Dickinson declined that offer, and the general opted to let Susanna carry the message to all of Texas that the Alamo had fallen.[2]

Susanna and her baby were sent forth with only a slave for protection. On March 13, the rag-tag little group was discovered near Gonzales by the famous Texas spy Erastus "Deaf" Smith (the same man who would later burn Vince's Bridge near the San Jacinto battlefield and cut off any possible retreat of Santa Anna after the battle). Smith shepherded the group on to Gonzales where Sam Houston was waiting, and Susanna confirmed the horrible rumor. The Alamo had fallen.

Mrs. Dickinson could have told us so much more. She could have given future generations intimate details from the last thirteen days of the lives of so many men. Perhaps she could have given us an undisputable count of the number of men who died and possibly all their names. She might have enlightened us with details about how Travis handled the men and how they felt about him. She could have given us specifics on how many men were unable to fight due to previous wounds, which flags flew over the fortress, a description of the small flag Travis carried with him, and full details on exactly how many men arrived with Davy Crockett. Oh, Susanna, she could have given us so much information that perhaps the Alamo saga would not be the romantic mystery it is today. But she never did.

Apparently, Susanna, who was unable to read or write, never understood or fully appreciated her unique position in history. Perhaps she was intimidated by her poor education and lacked the confidence to boldly step forward and assume her rightful place in history. Or perhaps she was too busy trying to survive in the harsh new land called Texas.

By today's standards, one of the strangest aspects of Susanna's involvement in the Alamo saga is that no journalist or historian approached her for an interview until 1874, thirty-eight years after the fact.[3] If the Alamo had fallen yesterday, by today there would be so many reporters circling around Susanna that she could not stir 'em with a stick. It is possible journalists did approach her earlier and were turned away, but if so, they left no record of the rebuff.

Once Mrs. Dickinson did start talking to formal journalists, her lack of education became a liability to future historians. Most of her interviews virtually reek of editorial prompting and, in some cases, out-and-out fiction that probably was supplied by the writer to fill in holes where necessary. Given her education level and the fact that she was relying on thirty-eight-year-old memories, there is little doubt that much of the substance of Susanna's interviews can be ignored by serious students of history.

Susanna was not exactly silent for all those years. There is some evidence that she discussed her Alamo involvement shortly after the fall but apparently not in any formal interviews for publication. She also helped, on several occasions, with the claims of relatives and descendents of men thought to have died in the Alamo. In the case of James R. Rose, Susanna gave testimony twice.[4] But it is not James Rose whom historians are particularly interested in. The Rose everyone wanted to know about was Louis, the man Walter Zuber said escaped from the Alamo and brought the story of Travis' speech and the line in the dirt.

Many opponents of the Zuber story are quick to point out that before the Zuber story broke in the *Texas Almanac* of 1873, Susanna had said nothing about a Travis speech or a line in the dirt. But those same historians ignore that Susanna had not said much at all prior to that time. Zuber dismissed such arguments by concluding that Susanna simply did not see what happened and thus had no knowledge of the event.

When Susanna did start talking about the incident, her information was not considered reliable. In one account she reported the event as happening on the first day instead of on the tenth day. In an 1881 interview with a reporter from the *San Antonio Express*, she gave her worst account of the incident. She said:

> . . . Travis called his well men and drew a line with his sword and said: "My soldiers, I am going to meet the fate that becomes me. Those who will stand by me let them remain, but those who desire to go; let them go—and who crosses the line that I have drawn—shall go.'" I came to the door of the room I had [the Baptistry] and watched them. It was a most impressive scene.[5]

Anyone who has studied Texas history knows that the men who crossed the line were the ones who stayed and any not willing to cross were to leave, exactly reverse of the way Susanna told the story. Also, since the line incident most certainly happened in the Alamo yard, it would have been very difficult to see the happenings from the door of the baptistry, which was in the chapel far to the rear of the fortress. Oh, Susanna, what have you done to us!

Historians continued to argue the point and probably always will. In 1961, when Walter Lord published his wonderful and well-researched *A Time to Stand*, he addressed the issue of Susanna and the line. In doing his extensive research for the book, Lord uncovered a previously unpublished statement that Mrs. Dickinson had given before the state adjutant general who was trying to establish the definitive list of Alamo victims. The part of her statement of September 23, 1876, that pertains to the Rose story follows, and the part cited by Lord is in italics:

> *On the evening previous to the massacre, Colonel Travis asked the command that if any desired to escape, now was the time, to let it be known & to step out of the ranks. But one stepped out. His name to the best of my recollection was Ross. The next morning he was missing.* — During the final engagement our Milton, jumped over the ramparts & was killed —
>
> Col. Almonte (Mexican) told me that the man who had deserted the evening before had also been killed & that if I wished to satisfy myself of the fact that I could see the body, still lying there, which I declined.[6]

In Lord's opinion, this account by Mrs. Dickinson, more than all the others, seemed to have a ring of truth and the words did not appear to be prompted or contrived. But there were still problems. The testimony was given three years after the Zuber story, which means she could have gotten her basic facts from the *Texas Almanac*. Lord concluded, however, that the time, in this particular instance, was not damaging. Then there was the matter of the name—Ross, not Rose—but that was dismissed because the name given was the product of a memory forty years removed from the actual event and because there is no record of a Ross having been in the Alamo.[7]

The biggest problem was the date. Mrs. Dickinson mentioned the evening previous to the assault which would have been March 5, not the third as Rose had said. Walter Lord solved this issue simply by allowing Rose to have been wrong about the date, and by declaring it had actually been March 5 when he left. Finally, a well-respected historian seemed to be conceding that there was some sort of confirmation that Travis did make an offer to the men to leave. Unfortunately, under a historical microscope, Mrs. Dickinson's statement of September 1876 seems totally preposterous.

She said the offer was made on the night before the massacre and, of Rose, "The next morning he was missing." Now, we know the Mexicans attacked well before dawn on the sixth and, in fact, the deed was done by first light. If Susanna's statement is to be believed, we must also accept the fact that someone was up very early counting men and checking roll on the morning of the sixth. The Alamo compound was a huge affair, perhaps as large as a city block, with men scattered everywhere. To check on the whereabouts of more than 180 men, in the darkness, would have required some time, perhaps more than an hour. It seems highly unlikely that anyone in the Alamo was up and checking names at 4:00 or 4:30 in the morning, especially if he thought the end was near.

Even if we stretch our imagination and accept the possibility that someone was up early counting men, that person surely would have become involved in the attack when it began. So how would the information have gotten back to Mrs. Dickinson that "Ross" was missing? It's hard to envision one of the defenders breaking off his fight to dash to the chapel and report, "Oh, Susanna, by the way, Ross is missing." Such a possibility seems far too remote to be given much consideration, so it seems to follow that whatever Travis did, he did prior to March 5.

Then there is also the problem of Almonte telling Susanna that the man who deserted had been killed and she was welcome to see the body if she liked. Lord ignored that comment, and perhaps it does not apply. But if accepted, it would certainly mean someone tried to get away the evening before the attack and did not make it. Many historians now accept that at least one messenger left on the evening of the fifth so perhaps there were two who left the Alamo that night and one did not survive.

Critics of Zuber's tale in the almanac will try to discount the possibility that the event happened prior to the fifth because then surely Susanna's husband Almaron would have mentioned the incident. Perhaps or perhaps not.

Portrait of Susanna Dickinson taken years after fall of the Alamo. Susanna, who lost all she owned to the Mexican army, led a difficult life for many years following the fall of the Alamo. After several unsuccessful marriages, she finally married John W. Hannig in 1857 and lived a quiet life in Austin, Texas until her death in 1883. *(Courtesy The Daughters of the Republic of Texas Library at the Alamo.)*

Portrait of Angelina Dickinson, the daughter of Susanna who, as an infant, survived the final assault and came to be known as the "Babe of the Alamo." This picture has often mistakenly been portrayed to be a young Susanna Dickinson. However, when Susanna was the approximate age her daughter appears to be in this picture, photography had not yet been invented. *(Courtesy The Daughters of the Republic of Texas Library at the Alamo.)*

Given that the Alamo saga was played at a time when chivalry had not yet died, it seems probable that if Travis had concluded the end was near, he would not have wanted to alarm the women and children and thus probably made his offer privately to his men. Captain Dickinson, a gentleman from the Old South,[8] might have perceived correctly that his little family was caught in a situation from which there was no escape. He surely could not have risked trying to break through the Mexican lines with a wife and baby, and he just as surely would not leave them. They were stuck, so why add to his wife's anguish? It is also remotely possible that Dickinson never had the chance to talk to his wife after the speech was given. He may very well have been too busy on the walls.

So what of Mrs. Dickinson's accounts of the line incident? More than likely they were the product of editorial prompting. During the siege, Susanna was probably busy tending to the wounded men, caring for her fifteen-month-old baby, or dodging Mexican cannonballs and simply did not see what happened. Score one for Zuber.

Regardless of what Susanna did or did not see during her time in the Alamo, it seems her life took a dramatic turn for the worse after the fall. Not only did she lose her husband and all her worldly possessions in San Antonio, but she also lost her house in Gonzales when Sam Houston ordered the town burned. Seven months after the fall of the Alamo, when the Republic of Texas was beginning to take political shape, Mrs. Dickinson attempted to get reimbursed by the government for personal belongings she lost when the Mexicans retook the Alamo. On October 12, 1836, Susanna submitted her first bill[9] as follows:

3 feather beds $40.00 each	$120.00
A large quantity of bedding	100.00
A larger stand of curtings	25.00
large tables	10.00
Kitchen furniture	50.00
clothing	100.00
	$405.00

The second bill, undated but probably submitted on the same day, included much more personal detail, as follows:

Household furniture as per previous bill	405.00
50 pieces of china @ 1.00 each	50.00
1 set silver tea spoons	8.00
8 pieces glass @ 1.00 each	8.00
1 large tea board	5.00
1 small tea board	2.00
7 chairs @ $2.00 each	14.00
1 ten gal brass kettle	10.00
1 large dining table	12.00
1 dressing table	6.00
2 trunks of clothing	150.00
2 bolts of linen	24.00
cash	150.00
18 head of cattle among which was 5 cows and calves & 2 yoke of oxen	120.00
1 chest _____ housetools	200.00
Total amount	1164.00

Each item in the second bill was marked "March 6" and she concluded that all items were "Taken by the Mexicans."[10] To substantiate her claim, Susanna solicited the aid of Colonel James C. Neill, who had been in command of the Alamo until his departure on February 11, 1836. Neill submitted three statements,[11] two concerning the validity of the service of Almaron Dickinson and one concerning Susanna's claim which said:

Columbia Oct 13th 1836
I do hereby certify that the account rendered by Susanna Dickinson for losses sustained in the Alamo is correct and not embracing all her loses.

Yours Respectfully,
J. C. Neill Col of
Artillery & Comd
of the Alamo and
_____ fort & was
to the losses of the applicant

Despite the verification of Colonel Neill, Susanna's claim was disallowed. Another plea on behalf of the widow was made for a donation of $500 to help raise Angelina, the "Babe of the Alamo," but that too was denied on the grounds that it might become a precedent and the Texas government could be called on to help support all the widows and children of the men who fell in the Alamo (or all future wars, for that matter).[12] That must have been a scary prospect to the early fathers of Texas. One Alamo defender, Issac Millsaps, had a blind wife and seven kids, so it is not hard to envision that all the dependents of fallen soldiers combined could have put together claims that would have bankrupted Texas before it got started.

The shaky, destitute government of the Republic of Texas was simply not in any position to risk such a financial undertaking. Years later when Susanna again appealed for aid, she claimed her Gonzales house was worth $1,500 and that she had lost everything she owned in the Alamo. Yet, in her plea for help, she stated that she "had not received a penny from the public treasury to compensate, as far as money can compensate, for the service of her deceased husband and the sacrifice of all her property."[13] For all we know, Susanna might not have talked about the Alamo in the early days because she carried a grudge against the state for not having been reimbursed for all her losses.

Details of Susanna's life after the Alamo are often sketchy but it appears she migrated first to the Houston area. On November 27, 1837, she married John Williams,[14] but it was apparently not a marriage made in heaven. Less than a year later, Susanna was in court trying for a divorce based on the claim of cruelty and barbarity. There was also some evidence that Williams beat and abused Susanna, even caused an abortion, and that he beat Angelina. On March 24, 1838, one of the earliest divorces granted in the Republic of Texas gave Susanna her freedom.[15]

Rumors persist to this day that Susanna was close to Pamela Mann, one of the most outrageous ladies of early Texas. It has been said of Mrs. Mann that when Sam Houston tried to confiscate her oxen during the revolution, that Pamela tracked down the beasts and drove 'em home singlehandedly, something most women might not be able to do. In addition to being a hotel proprietor, Pamela was also quite a character having been charged at one time or another with larceny, counterfeiting, immorality, and even assault to murder. If Susanna was her friend (and we have no absolute proof) then she was certainly keeping dubious company.[16]

We do know that five days before Christmas of 1838, Susanna exchanged vows with Francis P. Herring and got herself a third husband. She did not have him long. On September 15, 1843, Herring, formerly of Georgia, died of what was publicly called digestive fever. Privately, it was rumored Herring died because he preferred drinking something other than water. It would seem Susanna did not have a knack for picking husbands, but she was destined to keep trying.[17]

On December 15, 1847, Peter Bellows became Susanna's fourth husband.[18] Ten years later the marriage came crashing down amid tantalizing intrigue. In the spring of 1857, Bellows sued Susanna for a divorce on the grounds she had "voluntarily left his bed and board and on the first of October, 1854, she had taken up residence in a house of ill fame and was in the constant habit of committing adultery with various unknown persons." Susanna did not show up at the trial to present her defense, so when the case went to the jury on June 15, it did not take the members long to find for Bellows, grant the divorce, and order Susanna to pay $14.90 in costs.[19] When the sheriff tried to attach Susanna's property, he found she had already removed everything and was long gone in search of a new life in Lockhart.

Susanna's life finally did take a turn for the better in Lockhart. Not long after her arrival, she married a cabinet-maker named Joseph William Hannig. Apparently Susanna finally had a man she could trust. She transferred her property to him and even sold land in an old Mexican grant given to Almaron Dickinson for money to help Hannig set himself up in business.[20]

The Hannigs relocated to Austin in 1858 and continued to prosper. The family business grew, and the couple lived in a fine stone house on Pine Street just off Red River Street. William Hannig was a respected businessman and even got himself elected an Austin city alderman. Susanna lived a quiet life and passed the time with friends. One person she enjoyed seeing was Robert W. Crockett, Davy's grandson who visited her in 1878.[21] That same year she was guest of honor when the stage play *Davy Crockett* was performed in the Austin Opera House.

Although Susanna lived all her adult life in Texas and a considerable part in Austin just seventy miles from San Antonio, it was not until 1881—forty-five years after the fall of the Alamo—that she visited the shrine. On April 27 of that year, Susanna led a party of dignitaries, which included a reporter from the *San Antonio Express* through the ruins.[22] It is difficult not to envision some tears slipping down the now elderly lady's cheek as she must have relived so many painful memories.

Two years after her second and final Alamo pilgrimage, Susanna's health failed; and on October 7, 1883, in her sixty-eighth year, she slipped away, and the voice of the Alamo messenger was silenced.[23] Perhaps the largest paradox in the life of Susanna Dickinson Hannig is that, had she been better educated and possessed of a keen eye for observation and an appreciation of history, she undoubtedly could have lived a wonderful life traveling the country—even the world—lecturing on the fall of the Alamo. On the other hand, a well-educated, keen-eyed Susanna almost certainly would have filled in so many of the holes in the Alamo saga that historical study of that event would be far less appealing. Oh, Susanna, how we historians salute you for leaving us those holes!

Alamo Misconceptions

In *A Time to Stand*, Walter Lord said, "The Alamo has intrigued writers for more than 125 years, but the contradictions and gaps in the story remain as exasperating as ever. In the end, the only solution was to go back to the original sources and start all over again. . . ."[1] Now more than 150 years have elapsed since the Alamo fell. Writers still face many of the same contradictions, although Lord did much to close many of the gaps.

Neither Lord nor anyone else will ever erase all the contradictions. As the story unfolded in 1836, the saga of the Alamo captured the interest of Texans, Americans, and people around the world. Everyone was hungry for information, and journalists scrambled to provide details, any details. In the absence of a sophisticated news network on which to rely, many journalists turned to any available source. Letters from supposed eyewitnesses found their way into print even though the information was little more than a guess and often not a good guess.

As the incorrect information spread, it was read, believed, and repeated. Over the years, copious misinformation became accepted as fact and, in many quarters, continues to be believed today. To resolve many of these misconceptions, it is necessary to follow the lead of Walter Lord and go back to the sources.

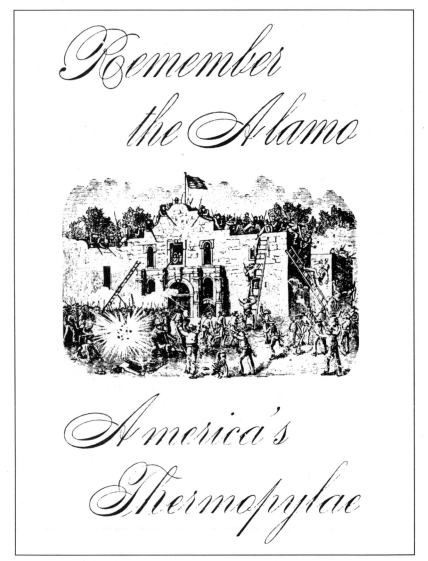

These three early woodcuts show misconceptions about the Alamo attack. **Above** The cover of an 1886 play by Hiram McClane incorrectly depicts the Mexicans using ladders to scale the front wall of the chapel. All three drawings incorrectly show the rounded top of the chapel which was built in 1845 by U. S. Army troops. **Right** An illustration from *Texas: Imperial State of America*, which was a souvenir from the Texas pavilion at the 1904 St. Louis World's Fair. In this drawing the Mexicans are using ladders to scale a wall they could have easily jumped had it actually been that small. (*Author's collection.*)

Left A woodcut from *A Texas Scrap-Book*, compiled in 1875 by D. W. C. Baker shows Mexican soldiers scaling the wall opposite the chapel which was inside the compound.

How Many Mexicans?

Many Texans, perhaps most, would have you believe that the Mexican force opposing the Alamo was at least 6,000 and probably more like 10,000. Of course, for Texans, increasing the number of enemy troops is a bit self-serving, since the more enemy soldiers there were, the more impressive is the fact that so few Texans were able to hold them at bay for thirteen days.

Like many other aspects of the Alamo saga, determining the size of the Mexican force was complicated by wild rumors that flew around the country almost from the time Santa Anna began assembling his army in Mexico. One major problem of estimating the size of the force that went to San Antonio is that many people may have assumed the entire Mexican army, which probably numbered about 6,000 men, was sent to attack the Alamo. Not true. A large part of the force was sent to track down and destroy Fannin's command. Many estimates concerning the Alamo almost certainly did not take into account the fact that Santa Anna received considerable reinforcements after the fall, and those troops were not present for the assault on the fortress.

The unreliability of the numbers probably stems from erroneous reports during the early days of 1836. A. Briscoe, after the fall of the fortress, wrote to a northern newspaper and estimated the Mexican force at 8,000 men, although he added "it may be more or less."[2] Undoubtedly, many assumed more and estimated 10,000 as the number. On February 20, 1836, Tom Find, loyal to the Mexican cause, reported Santa Anna was marching into Texas with 8,000 to 12,000 men.[3] On March 11, Fannin reported, "Santa Anna with 5,000 men are in Bejar."[4] Four of Fannin's men, John Cross, John Brooks, Thomas Rees and B. H. Duval all said, in letters written after the fall, that Santa Anna had 6,000 men.[5] Those letters were certainly read and believed.

Strangely enough, many estimates ignored the evidence supplied by the men in the Alamo. On February 12, 1836, William B. Travis reported Santa Anna was at Saltillo with 2,500 men.[6] Green B. Jameson reported that he had heard 1,500 men or so were on their way to San Antonio.[7] In Travis' famous letter "To all the people in the world," he said he was "besieged by a thousand or more."[8] In his last major communication, Travis said "We have contended for ten days against a force variously estimated at from fifteen hundred to six thousand . . . " He added a postscript "The enemy's troops are still arriving, and the reinforcements will probably amount to two or three thousand."[9] Many people also ignored Sam Houston's contribution. In his famous army orders of March 2, 1836, the general said the attacking force numbered about 2,000.[10] When he first heard of the fall (from information courtesy of suspected Mexican spies) Houston learned the Mexican force numbered about 2,300.[11] Despite wide publicity given to Houston's figures, much of the world still came to believe the attacking force was 10,000, perhaps because the inflated figure made a much better story than 2,000 or 3,000.

Historians are a more dedicated bunch than the general public, and they are never satisfied with approximate numbers or wild guesses. One of the earliest persons to study the Alamo was Reuben Potter, a customs officer in Matamoros, Mexico, at the time the Alamo fell. Potter personally discussed the Alamo with many Mexican soldiers who had participated in the event, and some of what he heard helped him develop a lifelong interest in discovering more about the historical event. One of Potter's objectives was to determine the size of the Mexican force.

Even though Reuben admitted that he had "no direct data," he nonetheless forged ahead. After considerable effort, Potter concluded, "They [the Mexicans] may possibly have numbered 3,000 men; but from the best information and inference I have been able to gather, I believe that their aggregate did not exceed and may have fallen short of 2,500."[12]

Numerous historical investigators since Potter have spent considerable time looking into the number issue. Some have spent days on days searching through ancient military records—what Potter might have called direct data—trying to determine the exact number. Almost all of the most learned and respected historians have concluded that the Mexican force was somewhere between 2,300 and 2,500, and that estimate has become the accepted norm. Interestingly enough, that number is not only in line with Potter's estimate, but it also coincides with what Sam Houston was told just five days after the massacre.

Of course, determining the size of the total force is just half the chore. There still remains the problem of determining how many Mexicans the Texans were able to dispose of during the battle. Some Texas die-hards steadfastly maintain that the Texans took 2,000 or 3,000 Mexicans with them when they died, but the most popular figure bantered around by casual observers to Texas history is that 1,000 Mexicans were put out of service during the battle. Surprisingly enough, that figure is not as absurd as the 10,000 figure for the total force.

One of the problems in determining Mexican casualties is that the Mexicans themselves gave conflicting information. In his official report after the battle, Santa Anna claimed his losses were 70 killed and 300 wounded;[13] Gen. Andrade said 311 total killed and wounded; Col. Almonte's estimate was similar with 65 killed and 223 wounded; Col. de la Pena's figures were also close at 60 dead and 253 wounded; Ramon Caro said simply 400 were killed, but Sgt. Becerra claimed 2,000 were killed; Pablo Diaz, a witness to the battle, said Mexican losses were 6,000 out of 10,000. Susanna Dickinson, who survived the battle, said Mexican casualties totaled 1,600; and another Texan, Dr. J. H. Barnard, who was assigned to tend the wounded in the Alamo after being spared in the Goliad massacre, said 300 to 400 were either killed or died from wounds and another 200 to 300 were wounded and survived.[14]

In the face of such contradictions, many historians returned to Potter for guidance. He had talked to many of the actual participants about casualties and reported most of the estimates were between 400 and 600. Believing that a field of slaughter often might lead to exaggeration, he discounted the 600 and settled instead for an approximate number of 500. Most historians today seem satisfied with an approximation of between 500 and 600.

For those Texans who still cling to the theory of 10,000 participants and 1,000 casualties, news that the actual numbers are probably 2,400 and 600 might come as a great disappointment. It shouldn't. It is generally believed that of the 2,400 available troops, only about 1,800 participated in the final assault. If 600 were killed or wounded, then Santa Anna lost 33 percent of his attacking force, a staggering percentage. Furthermore, since most of the fighting was over in thirty minutes, the Texans, using crude weapons, would have managed to put out of service more than three times their number in one-half of an hour. If so, the Texans did, indeed, trade their lives for a very dear price in enemy casualties, a cost which prompted some Mexicans to claim the victory was not much different from a defeat in terms of troops lost. That fact alone should provide sufficient cause for pride for any Texan.

They Never Knew it was Santa Anna

On February 24, 1836, William Barret Travis penned his famous letter from the Alamo. It has been called the most patriotic letter ever written in American history. It is also apparently the source of an Alamo misconception.

The first line of Travis' letter reads: "Fellow citizens & compatriots—I am besieged with a thousand or more of the Mexicans under Santa Anna."[15] Because the letter received widespread publicity and was reprinted in numerous publications, generations of Texans have assumed that the men of the Alamo knew they faced Santa Anna. That assumption is probably wrong.

When General Antonio Lopez de Santa Anna first mounted his campaign against Texas, his plan was for a two-prong attack, with General Sesma leading the attack on San Antonio de Bexar. Even though the Texans' intelligence network was weak when compared to the Mexicans', the defenders picked up some hints of Santa Anna's plans and were guided accordingly.

Probably the best evidence that Texans intercepted Santa Anna's plans comes from James Walker Fannin—of all people. In a letter of February 16, 1836, Fannin wrote to Acting Governor James W. Robinson and enclosed documents received from the interior of Mexico pertaining to enemy movement. In part Fannin said:

> It [Santa Anna's plan] is designed to enter our country in three Divisions — One to take Bejar, commanded by General Sesma, Filisola, Cos — one against Goliad under Urrea (recently Gov. of Durango) and Col Garay. The Third under Santa Anna himself, to pass either above Bejar, or

between that post, & Goliad, and proceed directly
into the heart of the Colony & then fortify.[16]

Historians have debated the validity of the intelligence,
but Fannin seemed convinced at the time. Shortly after this
letter was issued, one of Travis' most trusted and relied
upon messengers, James Butler Bonham,[17] arrived in
Goliad with an urgent plea from Travis for Fannin to
march at once to the aid of the San Antonio garrison. It is
unthinkable that Bonham and Fannin would not have
discussed the intelligence and that Bonham would not
have carried the information back to Travis. It is also
probable that Fannin's letter was responsible for the
assumption Sesma was in charge of the Mexicans that
attacked San Antonio.

Since no appreciable intelligence was received in the
Alamo prior to February 24, then the question is, why did
Travis say "under Santa Anna" in his famous letter?
Apparently he used the phrase in the context that *all*
Mexican soldiers were under Santa Anna and Travis was
not differentiating the troops that attacked the Alamo.
Lancelot Smither, who also left the Alamo on February 24,
carried his own message under orders of Travis, and Smither
said of the Mexicans, "Sesma is at the head of them."[18]

Apparently it was the Smither dispatch that first reached
Sam Houston in Washington-on-the-Brazos on March 2.
In his famous army orders issued that day, Houston said,
"War is raging on the frontiers. The Alamo is besieged by
two thousand of the enemy, under General Sesma."[19]
The reference to Sesma and two thousand enemy coincides
with the Lancelot information but contradicts the Travis
letter. Apparently Houston was aware of the Fannin
intelligence and considered the Smither information
as confirmation.

On March 3, 1836, Travis mentioned Sesma in two
different letters. In one he said, ". . . with 500 men more I
will drive Sesma beyond the Rio Grande. . . ."[20] In the
second letter, a very long communication seen by many as
his last-ditch effort for help, Travis gives us proof he did
not think the opposing general was Santa Anna. He said,
"A report was circulated that Santa Anna himself was with
the enemy, but I think it was false."[21]

Later in the same letter, however, Travis may have changed his mind. Apparently, as he was writing, a large contingent of reinforcements arrived in the Mexican camp causing the enemy to break out in wild celebrations. About these developments, Travis said, ". . . I think it more than probable that Santa Anna himself was with the enemy [reinforcements], from the rejoicing we hear."

The key phrase in this sentence is "more than probable." That sounds strong, but it still represents just an educated guess since he did not say he *knew* that Santa Anna had arrived. We can surmise that for ten days Travis surely had watched a Mexican general prance around the battlefield in his splendid uniform and riding a fine mount and assumed it was Sesma. It seems also logical that if Travis assumed Santa Anna had arrived, he would have expected to see another imposing figure on the field of battle after he wrote the letter of the third. We know that would not have been the case since Santa Anna was already there, so it does not appear far-fetched to surmise that Travis probably would have concluded that the celebration had merely been over the arrival of reinforcements and not over the arrival of *El Presidente*.

We will never know exactly what Travis or the other men thought during their final three days. Some of the men, Travis included, may have gone to their grave thinking that the opposing general was Santa Anna, but none of them went knowing for sure they faced the dictator. It is just possible that many of the men of the Alamo died thinking they fought against Sesma.

What Was Their Cause?

When Santa Anna was campaigning for the presidency of Mexico, one part of his platform was that he supported the Mexican constitution of 1824 and would keep it intact. Once elected, however, Santa Anna decided the Mexican people were not sufficiently advanced to live under a democracy, so he scrapped the constitution and installed himself as a military dictator. That act more than any other was responsible for the Texas revolution.

When American colonists began settling in the Mexican state of Texas, they did so according to the rules of the

1824 constitution. When their protections provided under that document were withdrawn, the Texans rebelled. Almost from the beginning of the hostilities, opinion in Texas was split over whether to fight for restoration of the constitution or go whole hog for outright independence. Some notable Texans were originally for restoration of the constitution. That was the position of Stephen F. Austin, the father of Texas, but he changed his mind after visiting the United States and finding sentiment high for independence.[22] Sam Houston originally favored restoring the constitution out of fear that an independence stance might cost Texas the support of loyalist Mexican citizens living in the province of Texas. Other prominent Texans, perhaps including William B. Travis, favored independence all along. So what of the men in the Alamo?

Some claim the men of the Alamo were for restoration of the constitution because they fought and died without ever knowing that independence had been declared. With or without a formal declaration, the evidence suggests the men were for independence. On January 12, 1836, William Carey wrote to family saying, ". . . as the safety of Texas depends mostly upon the keeping of this place they [government officials] certainly will as soon as possible do something for us especially when we expect to declare independence as soon as the convention meets."[23]

Colonel James C. Neill sent a letter dated January 23, 1836, to Governor Smith requesting permission for the men of the garrison to send delegates to the constitutional convention so they could have a voice in the affairs of the day. He declared that his men were, "all in favor of independence."[24] Private M. Hawkins echoed those thoughts on January 24 with ". . . every man here for independence."[25]

In a letter to Governor Henry Smith, dated January 27, 1836, Amos Pollard, surgeon for the Alamo garrison, wrote, ". . . God grant that we may create an independent government."[26] In another letter to the governor, dated February 13, Pollard put the garrison opinion in the form of a threat to the local Mexicans. He said, "Four Mexicans are to represent this jurisdiction in the convention. . . . those representatives shall distinctly understand previously to their leaving that if they vote against independence they will have to be very careful on returning here. . . ."[27]

The garrison engineer, Green B. Jameson, got into the act on February 11 with a letter of his own to the governor. He said, ". . . when I left home it was with a determination to see Texas free & independent, sink or swim, die or perish. And I have sanguine hopes of seeing my determination consummated. . . ."[28]

The best evidence of all comes from William B. Travis himself. In a letter March 3, to his old friend Jesse Grimes, Travis declared, "Let the convention go on and make a declaration of independence, and we will then understand, and the world will understand, what we are fighting for. If independence is not declared, I shall lay down my arms, and so will the men under my command. But under the flag of independence, we are ready to peril our lives a hundred times a day. . . ."[29]

Based on such overwhelming evidence, it would appear any time spent contemplating the possibility that the men of the Alamo were fighting for anything other than independence for Texas would be time wasted.

The Alamo Flag

Visitors to the Texas state capitol often marvel at the magnificent painting by Arthur McArdle depicting the final assault on the Alamo. McArdle spent years researching the Alamo before he committed what he learned to canvas. His painting is considered one of the most accurate, and yet it perpetuates one of the most confusing misconceptions about the Alamo. According to the evidence, the flag that waved proudly over the Alamo mission was not a modified Mexican flag as portrayed by McArdle.

The idea that a Mexican flag flew over the Alamo originated from the assumption that the men were fighting for restitution of the Mexican constitution that Santa Anna had scrapped. Reuben Potter, one of the earliest Alamo historians, presumed that the Alamo defenders wanted restitution of the Mexican constitution, and therefore Potter concluded that the flag was some variation of the Mexican Flag of 1824.[30] Future generations of writers apparently followed Potter's lead, and thus the legend grew and spread. However, as has been demonstrated, the Texans were not fighting for any Mexican constitution.

The possibility that a Mexican flag flew over the Alamo was supported by a quick entry in the diary of Almonte. Writing in his diary of the events of February 23, as the Mexican army approached Bejar, Almonte wrote:

> The enemy, as soon as the march of the division was seen, hoisted the tri-colored flag with the two stars, designed to represent Coahuila and Texas. The President with all his staff advanced to Campo Santo. The enemy lowered the flag and fled and possession was taken of Bexar without firing a shot.[31]

Many historians concluded that the flag was simply removed from the town and hoisted over the Alamo. In his diary entry for March 6, Almonte indicates only one flag was taken from the Alamo, so naturally it has been assumed that flag was the same Mexican banner that had been hoisted over the city.[32] Unfortunately for that theory, there is no confirmation. In fact, given the disposition of the men inside the Alamo, which was overwhelmingly in favor of independence, it seems highly unlikely that a Mexican flag of any kind would have been allowed to fly over the mission. So what about Almonte's statement?

We know what Almonte said about the flag appearing in the town, but what we do not know is who hoisted it. Almonte seems to be saying that as the Mexicans drew close to San Antonio, the flag was seen. The problem is, by the time the enemy was that close, the Texans were inside the Alamo. It seems very doubtful that any Texan would have lingered long enough to raise and then lower a Mexican flag. There is also the problem of a flag with two stars, one each for the Mexican states of Texas and Coahuilla. Perhaps some of the Mexicans who were a part of the garrison might have had sympathy for Coahuilla, but the Texans didn't give a hoot or a holler for anything Mexican. They were after independence for Texas.

So what about the flag in the town? It is possible the loyal Mexican citizens of San Antonio hoisted it. We know Travis did not trust the local citizens;[33] and with the sudden appearance of the army and the retreat of the Texans, those citizens may have tried to send a friendly signal to Santa Anna. If so, then why was the flag lowered? Perhaps those same Mexican citizens realized the flag was not the real Mexican flag but a rebellious variation and therefore lowered it to avoid negative inference. It is also possible that some Texan removed the flag and destroyed it. Whatever the circumstances, it appears probable that the Mexican flag did not fly over the Alamo.

One flag that did wave over that old fortress was the azure blue banner of the New Orleans Greys. That banner was captured during the final battle, and Santa Anna had it sent to Mexico City as proof the Texans were receiving aid from the "United States of the North." In honor of its 1986, sesquicentennial celebration, the state of Texas asked that the flag be returned for public display. The request was denied and the precious flag lies today rotting away in the archives in Mexico City.

Photo of flag of the New Orleans Greys, the only flag known to have been captured when the Alamo fell. The banner has an azure blue background with white letters. (*Courtesy the DRT Library at the Alamo.*)

There is one final Alamo flag mystery. While preparing to lead a detachment of men into San Antonio, William Barret Travis purchased some much needed supplies with his own money.[34] According to documents filed on behalf of the estate of Travis, one of the purchases was a $5.00 flag.[35] The description of that banner has been lost to history, but unless Travis was forced to leave the flag behind in his San Antonio quarters when the men retired into the Alamo, we can be sure that at least two flags were flying over the Alamo on March 6, 1836.

They Died in a Church, Not a Fortress

Many casual observers of Texas history are under the mistaken impression that the Alamo was built as a fortress. Not true. The Alamo was a church.

Mission San Antonio de Valero, originally referred to as Mission San Antonio de Padua and more commonly called the *Alamo*, was established in 1718 by Fray Antonio de Olivares. The name Alamo, Spanish for cottonwood, is thought to have been derived from a stand of trees adjacent to the mission. The present site and that which it occupied in 1836 was selected in 1724, and the cornerstone was laid in 1744. Originally founded as a mission to bring Christianity and education to the Indians in the area, activity in the facility began to wane, and the church abandoned the mission in 1793. The religious use of the church may have ended but the military use was far from over.

Spanish soldiers occupied the mission during Mexico's war of independence and used the facility for a number of years. Once Spain was defeated, Mexican soldiers occupied the mission in 1821 and held it until late 1835 when it was taken by Texans. Of course, Mexico regained control of the mission on March 6, 1836 but their stay was short-lived; and following the victory at San Jacinto, Texans again gained control of the mission where so many heros had died. In the years that followed, the Alamo served as a depot for U.S. cavalry troops, a warehouse, and a retail shop. Finally, shortly after the turn of the century, the Alamo property was purchased and subsequently came under the protection of the Daughters of the Republic of

Texas. Barring the meddlesome interference of some silly politicians, it will probably remain so forever, or as long as there are Texans to appreciate the shrine.

Above A view of U. S. Army wagons being used to transport supplies into the Alamo. **Below** The Alamo being used as a warehouse for the Hugo & Schmeltzer retail operation. *(Courtesy the DRT Library at the Alamo.)*

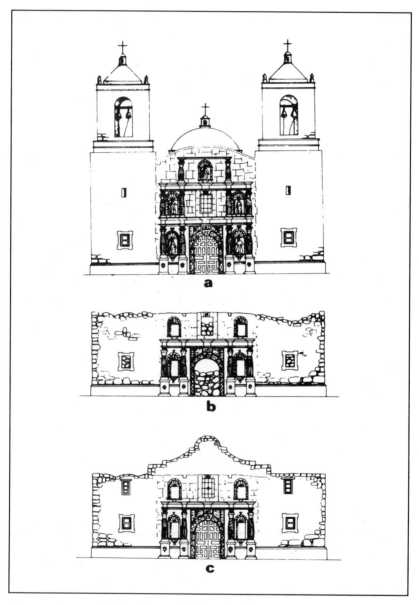

Three views of the Alamo from *Excavations at the Alamo Shrine, 1980,* by Jack D. Eaton. **A.** shows how the chapel front might have looked had it ever been finished. **B.** shows how the chapel front looked at the time of the 1836 battle and **C.** shows the chapel front as it appears today after U. S. Army troops added the rounded center in 1845. *(Courtesy Jack D. Eaton.)*

A reconstruction of the planned (but never finished) design for the front of the chapel as listed in a 1772 inventory. From *Excavations at the Alamo Shrine, 1980* by Jack D. Eaton. *(Courtesy Jack D. Eaton.)*

The notion that the mission was a fortress was derived when the Mexican troops erected earthworks and fortified the place as best they could. With cannons mounted on the walls, the mission may have taken on the appearance of a fortress, but it was still a church. After the Texans took control of the mission, the chore of fortifying the place fell to the garrison engineer, Green B. Jameson. Although trained as a lawyer instead of an engineer, Jameson did his best. In a letter of January 18, 1836, to Sam Houston, Jameson included a plat of the facility, and included the following:

> You can plainly see by the plat that the Alamo was not built by a military people for a fortress, tho it is strong, there is not a redoubt that will command the whole line of the fort, all is in the plain wall and intended to take advantage with a few pieces of artillery, it is a strong place and better that it should remain as it is after completing the half moon batteries than to rebuild it. The men here will not labor and I cannot ask it of them until they are better clad and fed.[36]

Even though Jameson appeared to have chosen his words carefully, he leaves little doubt that the place was no fortress. He seemed to be implying the preference would be to rebuild the place into a proper fort, but owing to the disposition of the men, he would settle for two new half-moon batteries.

The fact that the Alamo was a fortified mission and not a fortress may have contributed to the defeat of the valiant Texans. We know from surviving documents that the original mission was a huge affair with an immense court-yard, perhaps as big as a city block, with various living quarters and barracks on the east and west sides. The chapel was tucked far in the back. We also know that the place was run-down and strewn with litter left behind by the Mexicans. The roof of the chapel had collapsed (if it was ever even completed in the first place) and there was a slight breach in the north wall. But the big problem was size.

The opinion of James C. Neill, commandant of the Alamo, as to the number of troops required to defend the Alamo changed in direct proportion to the rumors of enemy advancements. On January 6, 1836, when no real evidence of enemy activity was to be had, Neill declared in a letter to the governor that he wanted 200 men in the garrison at all times and 300 until the repairs were complete. Apparently the old mission was in such sad shape that an extra 100 men were needed to complete the repairs. On the day Neill wrote that letter he had 104 men.[37]

By January 28, Neill's position and opinions of required force had changed. He had received what he believed to be accurate information (and he was correct) that 2,000 well-equipped, heavily armed Mexicans were marching on his position. He predicted in another letter to the government that "with 600 to 1000 men, I can oppose an effectual resistance."[38] It seems clear that Neill, perhaps with the assistance of Jameson, had concluded that a mission the size of the Alamo would require a considerable force to maintain. On the day Neill wrote this letter, he had 105 men and expected the arrival of William B. Travis with about 25 troops.

The plain truth seems to be that because of the size of the mission, considerably more than 180-odd men were required to hold the Alamo. The fact that the Texans were able to effect a resistance for thirteen days in a run-down old mission is testimony to their resolve. We are left to wonder how long such a small garrison might have sustained themselves in a smaller, better built, proper fortress. Patriotic Texans are also left with one slight thought of some comfort. If the men of the Alamo had to die, at least they were in a church.

Travis and his Uniform

One of the popular misconceptions about the Alamo is that on the morning of March 6, when Travis mounted the north wall to face the Mexicans and death, he did so wearing a splendid military uniform befitting his command. According to the colonel himself, that was not the case.

Thomas F. McKinney, an early Texas merchant and the man from whom Travis had ordered his uniform just before leaving for the Alamo. *(Author's collection.)*

The often reproduced portrait of William B. Travis that was painted by Henry McArdle long after Travis was killed. As a model, McArdle used a photo of Martin D. McHenry of Shelbyville, Kentucky who was said to be a dead ringer for Travis. This painting is probably responsible for the popular notion that Travis wore a splendid uniform. *(Courtesy the DRT Library at the Alamo.)*

In a letter to W. G. Hill on January 21, 1836, Travis wrote, "I have this day sent you orders about contracting with McKinney for our uniforms and equipment. I wish you to attend to it immediately. I spoke to him about my uniform, which I have written to him to purchase. I am ordered off to the defense of San Antonio which is threatened with an attack from the enemy. I shall leave in two days."[39] On the day Travis wrote that letter, he had exactly forty-five days to live.

Judging from the letter of January 21, Travis seemed to have been placing an order for a uniform. Travis left San Felipe two days later and proceeded to the Alamo and an appointment with destiny. Given the mail time lag and long periods of time required for the production of uniforms on the Texas frontier, it seems doubtful that the uniform caught up with Travis before the Mexicans did. Sergeant Felix Nunez, of the Mexican attack force, claimed he appropriated Travis' jacket after the battle and that is was made of homespun Texas jeans.[40]

The misconception about Travis and his uniform almost certainly is derived from the popular photographs of a painting of the lieutenant colonel, apparently in full-dress uniform. The painting is a composite portrait done by H. A. McArdle, who apparently had added the uniform because he thought it befitted the man. Considering Travis' courage and daring, the artist was correct. If fate would allow us to make subtle changes in history, a very nice touch would be to allow Travis the simple luxury of a fine uniform. Given the character of the man, a uniform probably would have made facing an enemy of far superior numbers a bit more palatable.

The Last Messenger

After dark on March 3, 1836, John Smith galloped out of the Alamo on his way to the constitutional convention in Washington-on-the-Brazos, Texas. He carried with him a last desperate plea for help. William B. Travis, reacting to the news that Colonel James W. Fannin, Jr., was not coming to the aid of the garrison, sent an urgent message to the convention requesting aid from the colonies and concluding that unless the aid arrived soon, he would "have to fight the enemy on his terms."[41]

John Smith also galloped into the history books since, for years, he was widely believed to have been the last messenger sent out of the Alamo. Apparently, that notion is another misconception. Three separate letters, all written from Goliad after the fall of the Alamo, suggest that another messenger left sometime after Smith.

The first letter, written March 8, is from Thomas Rees to Gerald Birch. Rees says, in part, "The enemy is at hand & we expect to be attacked every hour they have arrived at St Antonio six thousand troops & have been fighting the American troops for the last fifteen days. We received an express this evening that the Americans have not had a man killed & only three slightly wounded. There is about two hundred that has possession of the fort & will keep possession of it if their ammunition holds out till they can be reinforced."[42]

On March 9, two letters also mentioned a courier. Writing to his father, B. H. Duval said, "By last express, yesterday, from San Antonio we learned that our little band of 200 still maintained their situation in the Alamo. Santa Anna is there himself and has there and in the vicinity at least 6000 troops—Contrary to the expectation of every one he has invaded the Country when least expected."[43] On the same day, John S. Brooks wrote to James Haggerty in New York. He said, "We have again heard from Bexar, Santa Ana has arrived there himself, with 3000 men, making his whole force 4800. He has erected a battery within 400 yards of the Alamo, and every shot goes through it, as the walls are weak. It is feared that Bexar will be taken and that the devoted courage of the brave defenders will be of no avail."[44]

Based on these three letters, it seems almost certain that an Alamo courier arrived on the evening of the 8th. Since the courier had information about the Mexican battery that was erected 400 yards north of the Alamo on the 4th, he must have left after Smith did on the 3rd. Since a spirited ride from San Antonio to Goliad would have taken two or three days, the last courier must have left the garrison on the evening of the 5th, the night before the final assault. Apparently, Travis felt the need for one more desperate attempt to entice Fannin to come to his aid.

So who was this real last messenger from the Alamo? All the evidence points to sixteen-year-old James L. Allen, a native of Kentucky. Allen said he was the messenger and his friends believed him. Following his scouting mission, Allen contributed to the cause of Texas. He was a scout for the famous Texas spy "Deaf" Smith and he later served as a Texas Ranger and fought Indians. Allen served, at various times, as mayor and tax collector of Indianola, Texas, and he fought in the Civil War until captured. Allen died, at age 80, in his home near Yoakum, Texas.

If young James was the last courier (and it appears certain he was) then all the journalists of Texas, and the world, missed a sure bet by never interviewing him. Allen lived until 1901 and never recorded his version of what transpired in the Alamo, and he was there for eleven or twelve days of the siege. Although a few friends recorded some of what Allen said, we can only wonder what specific details Allen could have provided and what mysteries he might have unraveled.

Endnotes

Sam Houston and the Alamo Conspiracy

1. The complete text of Sam Houston's speech before the United States Congress was originally printed in the 1860 issue of the Texas Almanac. It was reprinted in *The Texas Almanac, 1857-1873: A Compendium of Texas History* (Waco: Texian Press, 1967), 254-268 (hereafter cited as *Almanac*).
2. Amelia W. Williams, *A Critical Study of the Siege of the Alamo and of the Personnel of Its Defenders* (Ph.D Thesis, University of Texas, 1931), 356. The thesis was reprinted in condensed form in *Southwestern Historical Quarterly*, (hereafter *SWHQ*) volumes 36 and 37, 1933-1934.
3. E.C. Barker and A.W. Williams, [editors], *The Writings of Sam Houston*, 7 volumes (Austin:The University of Texas Press), 2:322.
4. Ibid, 339-340.
5. William C. Binkley, [editor], *Official Correspondence of the Texas Revolution, 1835-1836*, 2 volumes (New York: D. Appleton-Century Company, 1938), 267-268.
6. H. P. M. Gammel, [compiler and arranger] *The Laws of Texas, 1822-1897*, 10 volumes (Austin: The Gammel Book Company, 1898), 1:847.
7. There are two generally accepted spellings for Dickinson. Many sources, including *The Handbook of Texas*, use Dickenson. However, Susanna's biographer, C. Richard King, used Dickinson so that spelling is used in this book.
8. Henderson Yoakum, *History of Texas From Its First Settlement in 1685 to Its Annexation to the United States in 1846*, 2 vols. (New York: Redfield, 1856), 2:475.
9. Barker and Williams, 319-322.
10. John H. Jenkins, [General Editor], *The Papers of the Texas Revolution, 1835-1836*, 10 volumes (Austin: Presidial Press, 1973), document number 1576. Hereafter, Jenkens documents will be referred to by number.
11. Yoakum, 2:460-470.
12. Binkley, 2:381-383.
13. Charles A. Gulick Jr., [editor], *The Papers of Mirabeau Buonaparte Lamar*, 3 volumes (Austin: Texas State Library, 1930), 3:315-316.
14. Barker and Williams, 4:364-366.
15. Ibid, 4:367-368.
16. Apparently Houston added up the total losses at the Alamo, at San Patricio, and at Auga Dulce Creek.
17. Barker and Williams, 5:17-19.

The Crown Jewel of Texas Legends

1. Barker and Williams, 4:364-366.
2. Enrique de la Pena, *With Santa Anna in Texas*. Translated and edited by Carmen Perry (College Station: Texas A&M University, 1975), 53.
3. Carlos E. Castaneda, *The Mexican Side of the Revolution* (Dallas: P. L. Turner, 1928), 86.
4. John S. Ford Papers, University of Texas Archives, Austin.
5. Many historians consider the accounts of Jose Enrique de la Pena and that of an unknown officer which was translated by George Dolson and later printed in Thomas L. Connelly, [editor], "Did David Crockett Surrender at the Alamo? A Contemporary Letter," *Journal of Southern History*, August 1960, as perhaps the most reliable of the Mexican accounts.
6. In the narrative written from his diary notes, de la Pena explained in detail that once the Mexicans had breached the walls and begun pouring into the Alamo, the defenders sought cover in the rooms around the courtyard. Pena flowered his account somewhat by implying that many of the Texans wanted to surrender and the Mexicans were inclined to agree. However, according to Pena, some of the Texans continued fighting which inspired the Mexicans to do likewise.
7. Binkley, 2:272-275.
8. Jenkins, document number 1784.
9. Adina De Zavala, *History and Legends of the Alamo and Other Missions In and Around San Antonio* (San Antonio: by the author, 1917), 23-25.
10. James C. Neill, Muster Roll, Texas State Library Archives.
11. Of the eight men listed as sick or wounded on Neill's muster roll, four are definitely thought to have died in the Alamo. Two more probably died, and the remaining two may have, but no one can be certain because of the problems often encountered when comparing names on old records.
12. San Antonio *Daily Express*, April 28, 1881, from copies in the Daughters of the Republic of Texas Library at the Alamo.
13. Cos was General Martin Perfecto de Cos, Santa Anna's brother-in-law, who was in command of the Alamo when the Texans attacked in early December of 1835. After five days' fighting, Cos surrendered, and the Texans occupied the Alamo for the first time.
14. Susanna Dickenson's testimony before the State Adjutant General, September 23, 1876. From a typed copy of the testimony in the Texas State Library Archives, Austin.
15. Hobart Huson [editor], *Dr. J. H. Barnard's Journal* (privately published, 1950). This journal also contains some excellent

first-hand information on the massacre of Colonel Fannin and his men at Goliad.
16. Connelly, 368-376.
17. Colonel Juan Nepomuceno Almonte, "The Private Journal of Juan Nepomuceno Almonte," *SWHQ,* 48:23.
18. Williams, *SWHQ,* 37:35-36.
19. The Loranca interview was reprinted in the San Antonio *Daily Express,* January 5, 1878.
20. *Almanac,* 39-40.
21. San Antonio *Daily Express,* May 12 and 19, 1907.
22. Walter Lord, *A Time to Stand* (New York: Harper & Brothers, 1961), 208.
23. Ibid.
24. Ibid.
25. *SWHQ,* 5:1-11.

Crocket vs. Kilgore, Santos, et al.: Davy's Last Fight

1. New Orleans *Post Union,* March 29, 1836.
2. Richard G. Santos, *Santa Anna's Campaign Against Texas* (Waco: Texian Press, 1968), 76.
3. There is some evidence that the Pena book was first published in 1836 but no surviving copy has ever been found. Some historians speculate that because of the inflammatory nature of the material the original copies were suppressed.
4. Pena, 53.
5. Corpus Christi *Times,* July 31, 1974.
6. Connelly, *Journal of Southern History,* August 1960, 371-376.
7. Lord, *A Time to Stand,* 209.
8. There is no record of Santa Anna's tent ever being erected on the field of battle at the Alamo as it was at San Jacinto. By all accounts, Santa Anna made his headquarters in a villa in the town of San Antonio. Even if Santa Anna had a tent erected, it would have been outside the Alamo proper, and thus the captives bodies would not have been found inside the Alamo compound.
9. Almonte, *SWHQ,* 48:23.
10. Helen Hunnicutt, "A Mexican View of the Texas War: Memoirs of a Veteran of the Two Battles of the Alamo," *The Library Chronicle* (Austin: University of Texas Press, vol IV, summer 1951), 63.
11. The most complete study of the men of the Alamo to date can be found in *Roll Call at the Alamo,* by Phil Rosenthal & Bill Groneman, published by the Old Army Press, Ft. Collins, Colorado, 1985.
12. *Almanac,* 61-63.

13. Williams, *SWHQ,* 37:28.
14. Dan Kilgore, *How Did Davy Die?* (College Station: Texas A&M University, 1978), 16-17. In *A Time to Stand,* Walter Lord said, "This (the Caro account) and all other Mexican accounts are highly flavored, yet essential to the story."
15. Pena, 37.
16. Ibid, xii.
17. Ibid, 50.
18. William F. Gray, *From Virginia to Texas* (privately published, 1909), entry for March 20, 1836.
19. Williams, *SWHQ,* 37:39-40.
20. Pena, 44.
21. See "Alamo Misconceptions" elsewhere is this volume.
22. Kilgore, 34.
23. William P. Zuber, "Inventing Stories About the Alamo." J. Frank Dobie, [editor], *In the Shadow of History* (Austin: Texas Folklore Society, Number 15, 1939), 45-46.
24. Kilgore, 35.
25. See "The Crown Jewel of Texas Legends" elsewhere in this volume.
26. John S. Ford, *Origin and Fall of the Alamo: March 6, 1836* (San Antonio: Johnson Brothers Printing Co., 1901), 16-23.
27. *Almanac,* 39-40.
28. Kilgore, 39.
29. Ibid.
30. Ibid, 40.
31. J. M. Morphis, *History of Texas* (New York: United States Publishing Company, 1875), 177.
32. Richard C. King, *Susanna Dickinson: Messenger of the Alamo* (Austin: Shoal Creek Publishers, Inc., 1976), 76-77.
33. James T. DeShields, *Tall Men with Long Rifles: The Glamorous Story of the Texas Revolution, as Told by Captain Creed Taylor* (San Antonio: Naylor Co., 1935), 162-164.
34. *Fort Worth Gazette,* July 12, 1889.
35. Kilgore, 47.
36. Gray, March 20, 1836 entry.
37. *Telegraph and Texas Register,* March 24, 1836.
38. Ibid.
39. San Antonio *Daily Express,* April 28, 1881.
40. Kilgore, 41.
41. Williams, *SWHQ,* 37:39-40.
42. Santos, 76. In his notes concerning the Ruiz account, page 84, Santos says he has tried unsuccessfully for years to find the original of the Ruiz account "due to some obvious errors or omissions."
43. Pena, xi.
44. Kilgore, 27.

Other Obituaries

1. Barker and Williams, 4:17-19.
2. Apparently one of the Texas defenders did make a desperate leap to freedom holding a child in his arms. Such an incident is mentioned by Colonel Pena, Sergeant Becero, and others, although some mention Dickinson as being the Texan. All agree that the man held a boy and that both died after leaping from a considerable height. The interesting aspect of this story is that the highest point in the Alamo at the time of the siege would been roughly equivalent to a low, two-story, modern building. A leap from such a height would certainly be perilous but not necessarily fatal. It is possible the man and the boy were killed by Mexican soldiers either while falling or shortly after landing.
3. Gray, diary entry March 20, 1836.
4. *SWHQ,* 37:39-40.
5. Williams' thesis, *A Critical Study of the Siege of the Alamo and of the Personnel of Its Defenders* was reprinted in condensed form in volumes thirty-six and thirty-seven of the *Southwestern Historical Quarterly,* 1933-1934.
6. Twelve law enforcement officers with specific knowledge of suicides were questioned. The men interviewed had a total of more than 150 years experience and none had ever seen or heard of a suicide attempted with a shot through the forehead.
7. *SWHQ,* 37:35-36.
8. Hunnicut, *The Library Chronicle,* vol. 4, no. 2, 63. It should be noted that in *A Time to Stand,* Walter Lord advanced the theory that Navarro and the unknown soldier were actually the same person.
9. *SWHQ,* 37:307.
10. Barker and Williams, 4:17-19.
11. Although James Bowie did serve for a time in the regular army of Texas, he resigned long before the siege of the Alamo began. Houston sent Bowie to the Alamo as a volunteer and the rank of colonel was honorary.
12. Reuben Potter, *The Fall of the Alamo, 1860* [pamphlet].
13. Ibid, 1868.
14. Reuben Potter, "The Fall of the Alamo," *Magazine of American History,* January 1878.
15. Dr. John Sutherland, *The Fall of the Alamo* (San Antonio: The Naylor Company, 1936), 19-22. Sutherland's account of the fall of the Alamo also appeared as a feature article in the Dallas News, February 5 and 12, 1911.
16. Maurice Elfer, *Madame Candelaria, Unsung Heroine of the Alamo* (Houston: Rein Company, 1933), 8. There is also one

published report that James Bowie actually died two days before the Mexicans attacked and that Madame Candelaria, one of the most controversial figures connected with the Alamo legend, kept vigil over his body.

17. Edward G. Rohrbough, "How Jim Bowie Died," *In the Shadow of History*, J. Frank Dobie, editor, 48-53.

18. E. Alexander Powell, *The Road to Glory* (New York: Charles Scribner's Sons, 1915), 177.

19. Elfer, 16-18.

20. William Brooker, *Texas: An Epitome of Texas History* (Columbus: Nitsche Brothers, 1897), 64.

21. McCullough-Williams, "A Man and His Knife, Passages from the Life of James Bowie," *Harper's Magazine*, July 1898.

22. John J. Bowie, "Early Life in the Southwest — The Bowies," *DeBow's Review*, volume 13, October, 1852.

23. J. Frank Dobie, "James Bowie," *Heroes of Texas* (Waco: Texian Press, 1946), 45.

24. Walter W. Bowie, *The Bowies and Their Kindred* (Washington, 1899), 261-262.

25. A recent translation of the Seguin eulogy from *The Alamo Long Barrack Museum* (published by the Daughters of the Republic of Texas, 1986), 43.

26. Ibid.

27. Charles Grosvenor, in notes for a reprint of Reuben Potter's *The Fall of the Alamo* (Hillsdale, New York: The Otterden Press, 1977), 63.

The Travis Account Book Mystery

1. Ruby Mixon, *William Barret Travis, His Life and His Letters*, Masters Thesis, University of Texas, 1930. This thesis is one of the best sources of information on William B. Travis.

2. The original of the Travis diary is in the Archives of the Texas State Library in Austin. In 1966, Texian Press of Waco published a reprint of the diary edited by Robert E. Davis.

3. Robert E. Davis, *The Diary of William Barret Travis: August 30, 1833 — June 1834* (Waco, Texas: Texian Press, 1876). Reprint of the original diary with extensive endnotes. Diary entry for January 2, 1834.

4. *Houston Morning Star*, March 14, 1840.

5. Mixon, 406.

6. Binkley, 362-363.

7. Ibid, 416-417.

8. Ibid, 419-412.

9. Ibid, 425.

10. Jenkins, document number 2105.

11. Binkley, 439-440.
12. Jenkins, document number 2135.
13. Williams, *SWHQ,* 37:13-14.
14. Henry S. Foote, *Texas and the Texans,* 2 volumes (Philadelphia: Thomas, Cowperthwait & Co., 1841), 2:224.
15. Williams, *SWHQ,* 37:14.
16. Ibid, 37:28.
17. Foote, 2:219-222.
18. Jenkins, document number 2233.
19. Williams, *SWHQ,* 37:24-25.
20. The exact circumstances of the disappearance of the documents are not known. It is presumed they were stolen.
21. This is a faithful copy of the claim as found in the Ruby Mixon papers in the Barker Texas History Center at the University of Texas in Austin.
22. Williams, *SWHQ,* 37:14.
23. See the 1970 *Texas Almanac* for a complete copy of Santa Anna's report.

What Happened to Lt. Col. James C. Neill?

1. Jenkins, document number 1576.
2. Binkley, 409-410.
3. Ibid, 416-417.
4. Ibid, 419-420.
5. Louis W. Kemp, *The Signers of the Texas Declaration of Independence* (Houston: The Anson Jones Press, 1944), 5.
6. Binkley, 425.
7. Kemp, 5.
8. Binkley, 419-421.
9. Archives, Texas State Library, Austin.
10. Frank X. Tolbert, *The Day of San Jacinto* (New York: Pemberton Press, 1959), 37.
11. The original letter in is the files of the DRT Library at the Alamo in San Antonio.
12. Ibid.
13. Jenkins, document number 2254.
14. Jenkins, document number 2269.
15. Binkley, 481-482.
16. Jenkins, document number 2280.
17. Ibid, document number 2289.
18. Barker and Williams, 4:367-368.
19. Ibid, 4:364-366.
20. From a typescript of the original Zuber letter in the archives of the Texas State Library in Austin.
21. Dobie, *In the Shadow,* 42-47.

The Missing Alamo Letter That Toppled a Government

1. Barker and Williams, 4:332-333.
2. Gammel, 1:758-761.
3. Ibid, 1:761-746.
4. Ibid, 1:772.
5. Ibid, 1:773-774.
6. Binkley, 272-275.
7. Jenkins, document number 1784.

The Alamo Mystery Letter

1. There are many different spellings for the name Dimitt. Phillip spelled his name with one m and two t's, but the county named for him used two m's and one t. There is also a Dimmitt, Texas in Castro County which has nothing to do with Phillip Dimitt or Dimmit County.
2. Walter P. Webb, [Editor-in-Chief], *The Handbook of Texas*, 3 vols. (Austin: Texas State Historical Association, 1952-1976), 2:503-504.
3. *SWHQ,* 11:21.
4. The original letter is in the Austin Papers, Texas State Library Archives, Austin.
5. *SWHQ,* 11:48.
6. B. B. Paddock, *History of Texas, Fort Worth & Northwest Texas Edition,* 5 vols. (Chicago: Lewis Publishing Co., 1922), 1:246.
7. *SWHQ,* 41:228
8. Binkley, 202-203.
9. Archives, Texas State Library, Austin.
10. Gammel, 1:649.
11. *SWHQ,* 42:75.
12. Gammel, 1:191.
13. Binkley, 284-285.
14. Barker and Williams, 4:339-340.
15. Binkley, 294-295.
16. A typescript of the entries in Travis' notebook can be found among the Ruby Mixon Papers in the Barker Texas History Center, UT Austin.
17. Jenkins, document number 2194.
18. Williams, *SWHQ,* 37:28.
19. Dr. John Sutherland, *The Fall of the Alamo* (San Antonio: Naylor Co., 1936), 11-12.
20. Barker and Williams, 3:366.
21. For complete records of the convention see H. P. M. Gammel, *The Laws of Texas, 1822-1897.*
22. Webb, 1:504.

Fannin's Follies

1. Huson, 33.
2. Foote, 2:224.
3. Ibid, 2:225.
4. Barker and Williams, 4:17-19.
5. *SWHQ*, 7:320 In "Notes and Fragments" there is a letter authored by Fannin encouraging some West Point men to come to Texas. In part he says, "When the hurly burly is begun, we will be glad to see as many West Point boys as can be spared — many of whom are known to me, & by whom I am known as J. W. Walker — my maternal Grandfather's name & by whom I was raised and adopted, & whose name I then bore." The historian for West Point confirms that a J. W. Walker did attend the Point for a short time.
6. The contract between Fannin and Mimms is often said to have been in 1834. However, a copy of the partnership agreement in the DRT Library at the Alamo seems to clearly show the date as January 12, 1836.
7. In the DRT Library at the Alamo can be found the certificate appointing James W. Fannin, Jr. the rank of colonel of artillery in the Regulars.
8. Foote, 2:186.
9. Gulick, 3:309.
10. Ibid, 3:315-316.
11. Foote, 2:201-205.
12. Gulick, 3:330-331.
13. Ibid, 3:331-333.
14. Ibid.
15. Foote, 2:210-212.
16. Ibid.
17. Gray, diary entry for March 5, 1836.
18. Foote, 2:212-213.
19. In his famous letter from the Alamo, dated March 3, William Barret Travis wrote, "Col Bonham, my special messenger, arrived at LaBahia [Goliad] fourteen days ago. . . ." Fourteen days earlier than March 3 would have been February 19, two days before Fannin wrote his letter of the February 21.
20. Foote, 2:214-215.
21. Ibid, 2:215-217.
22. Ibid, 2:225.
23. Ibid, 2:226.
24. Lord, *A Time to Stand*, 140.
25. Barker and Williams, 4:367-368.
26. Ibid, 4:305.

27. Potter, *Magazine of American History*, January, 1878, 66-70. Potter measured the size of the ruins of the Alamo mission when remnants of the outer courtyard were still visible. He concluded that courtyard measured 154 yards long and 54 yards wide.
28. Binkley, 349-351.
29. From a typescript of Susanna Dickenson's testimony before the Texas State Adjutant General on September 23, 1876 in the Archives of the Texas State Library in Austin.
30. *SWHQ*, 9:190-192.
31. Ibid, 48:19. In his diary entry for February 29, Almonte said, "Gen Sesma left the camp with the calvary of Dolores and the infantry of Allende to meet the enemy coming from La Bahia."
32. Potter, *Magazine of American History*, January, 1878, 66-70. Some of the best research done on the size of the Mexican army was done by Reuben Potter, the earliest known researcher on the fall of the Alamo. Potter published many articles on the fall of the Alamo but perhaps his best, most complete work was in the *Magazine of American History*.
33. Barker and Williams, 4:364-365.

Military Malpractice

1. Foote, 2:219-222, William B. Travis to the government of Texas.
2. Gulick, 3:331-332.
3. Ibid.
4. Hunnicut, 62.
5. Pena, 42.
6. Ibid.
7. *SWHQ*, 9:190-192. It should be noted that during much of the siege of the Alamo, it was assumed by many that General Sesma was in charge. Although Santa Anna was at the Alamo all along, it was widely thought that he did not arrive until March 3, 1836.
8. Pena, 43.
9. Ibid.
10. Gulick, 3:292-293.
11. Binkley, 2:239-240.
12. Jenkins, document number 1625.
13. Binkley, 2:272-275.
14. Ibid, 2:419-420.
15. Gulick, 3:264.

16. Binkley, 2:419-420.
17. Pena, 35.
18. Ibid, 38.
19. The possibility that the men of the Alamo might have survived had they chosen another mission is fully explored in *Forget the Alamo* by Wallace O. Chariton (Wordware Publishing, Inc., Plano, Texas, 1990).

The Alamo Number Game

1. Williams, *SWHQ*, 37:13-14.
2. Ibid, 37:39-40.
3. Binkley, 267-268.
4. Ibid, 212. A list of those killed and wounded in the Texans' siege of the Alamo.
5. Ibid, 272-275.
6. Ibid, 294-295.
7. Gammel, 1:788.
8. Barker, 4:339-340.
9. De Zavala, 23-25.
10. See *Roll Call at the Alamo* by Phil Rosenthal & Bill Groneman for a discussion of the Bowie command.
11. Williams, *SWHQ*, 37:272-273.
12. Binkley, 349-351.
13. Ibid, 381-383.
14. See receipt dated February 11 and signed by Micajah Autry and Daniel Cloud in the DRT Library at the Alamo.
15. Binkley, 409-410.
16. Ibid, 416-417.
17. Jenkins, document number 2105.
18. Williams, *SWHQ*, 37:13-14.
19. Foote, 2:224.
20. Williams, *SWHQ*, 37:24-25, Travis to Grimes.
21. Pena, 54.
22. Ibid.
23. Williams, *SWHQ*, 37:35-36.
24. San Antonio *Daily Express*, April 28, 1881.
25. Archives of the Texas State Library.
26. *The Dallas Morning News*, February 12, 1911.

The Thorny Problem of Mr. Rose

1. The original Zuber story was in the form of a letter from Prairie Plains, Grimes County, Texas, dated May 7, 1871. In was first printed in the 1873 *Texas Almanac* and has subsequently been printed elsewhere. In 1895, Zuber told the story with various added details for the revised edition of Mrs. Pennybacker's *History of Texas for Schools*. A reprint of the Pennybacker version with the added parts bracketed to separate them from the original can be found in *In the Shadow of History*, edited by J. Frank Dobie.
2. *SWHQ*, 5:11.
3. Ibid, 6:68.
4. Zuber included the following statement with his story, dated May 9, 1871, and signed by his mother, Mary Ann Zuber, in Prairie Plains, Grimes County, Texas: "I have carefully examined the foregoing letter of my son, William P. Zuber, and feel that I can endorse it with the greatest propriety. The arrival of Moses Rose at our residence, his condition when he came, what transpired during his stay, and the tidings that we afterwards heard of him, are all correctly stated. The part which purports to be Rose's statement of what he saw and heard in the Alamo, of his escape, and of what befell him afterwards is precisely the substance of what Rose stated to my husband and myself."
5. *SWHQ*, 5:1-11.
6. King, 70.
7. Ibid, 75-77. Controversy continues over there being two Roses in the Alamo. Walter Lord, in *A Time to Stand* identified James M. Rose as the nephew of Ex-President James Madison (p. 46) and says he became friends with Crockett (p. 54).
8. *SWHQ*, 37:164.
9. Rosenthall, 55.
10. The complete text of Travis' letter of the third of March can be found in many places, including Foote, 2:219-222.
11. *SWHQ*, 5:1-11.
12. Ibid, 5:263.
13. Ibid.
14. Ibid, 5:1-11.
15. Ibid.
16. R. B. Blake, "A Vindication of Rose and His Story," *In the Shadow of History*. Blake did extensive research concerning the life of Louis Rose, and he presented many of his findings in "A Vindication of Rose and His Story," a chapter in *In the Shadow of History*. Blake not only discloses his findings concerning the Rose testimony in the land cases, but he also

presents details on the character of the man and even provided clues that Rose did, perhaps, talk somewhat openly about his escape from the Alamo because he was not ready to die.

17. Many of Susanna Dickenson's statements are "signed" with an x which was certified to be her mark.
18. *SWHQ,* 5:3.
19. Lord, *A Time to Stand,* 202.
20. A typescript copy of the Millsaps letter can be found in the DRT Library at the Alamo.
21. James Butler Bonham, who arrived at 11:00 a.m. on March 3, apparently carried the news that Fannin was not coming. We have no record of Bonham's words; but we know that when he visited Fannin, the decision had already been made that Fannin would defend Goliad and not march to the Alamo. It can be reasonably assumed that Bonham carried that news to Travis.

Travis and the Grand Canyon Line

1. William P. Zuber to General William Steele, September 14, 1877, from a typescript in the Archives of the Texas State Library.
2. The entire Zuber story can be found in many places but was originally published in the 1873 *Texas Almanac.*
3. Foote, 2:219-222.
4. Jenkins, document number 2233.
5. Dobie, *In the Shadow of History,* 14.
6. Ibid, 16.

Oh, Susanna

1. Morphis, 176.
2. From unidentified newspaper clipping in the DRT Library at the Alamo.
3. Walter Lord, "Myths and Realities of the Alamo," *The Republic of Texas* (Palo Alto, California: American West Publishing Company, 1968), 14.
4. King, 70, 75-77.
5. San Antonio *Express,* April 28, 1881.
6. From a typescript in Archives of the Texas State Library, Austin.
7. Lord, *A Time to Stand,* 202.

8. According to *The Handbook of Texas* (volume 1:500), Almaron Dickinson, Susanna's first husband, was a native of Tennessee.
9. Copies of the bill can be found in the Archives of the Texas State Library, Austin.
10. Ibid. It is interesting to note that in addition to her worldly goods, Susanna also notes that $150 in cash was lost to the Mexicans. From all accounts the Alamo garrison was in desperate need of money, and Lt. Col. J. C. Neill continuously asked for operating funds. In one letter, dated January 6 (Binkley, 272-275), Neill even said, "If there has ever been a dollar here I have no knowledge of it." In another letter, (Jenkins, document number 1855), one of the men even complained that the troops did not even have enough money to get their pitifully clothes washed. If Susanna did have $150, it would appear she was not willing to share with the men.
11. All of Neill's statements are in the Susanna Dickinson file in the Archives of the Texas State Library, Austin.
12. King, 55-56.
13. Susanna Dickinson file in the Archives of the Texas State Library, Austin.
14. King, 56.
15. Ibid, 58.
16. Ibid, 59.
17. Ibid, 63.
18. Ibid, 64.
19. Minutes of Courts, Harris County, vol. H, page 479, no. 3618. Peter Bellow vs Susanna Bellows, granted June 5, 1857.
20. King, 78-79.
21. Ibid, 109.
22. San Antonio *Express*, April 28, 1881.
23. King, 117.

Alamo Misconceptions

1. Lord, *A Time to Stand*, 227.
2. The *New Yorker* of April 16, 1836 contained a letter from A. Briscoe that was reprinted from the *Red River Herald*.
3. Jenkins, document number 2137.
4. Ibid, document number 2294.
5. Thomas Rees to Gerald Birch, DRT Library at the Alamo; John Cross to his family, DRT Library at the Alamo; B.H. Duval to his father, *SWHQ*, 9:49-50; John Brooks to James Hagerty, *SWHQ*, 9:190-192.
6. Binkley, 416-417.

7. Ibid, 409-410.
8. Williams, *SWHQ*, 37:14.
9. Foote, 2:219-222.
10. Jenkins, document number 2222.
11. Barker and Williams, 4:365-366.
12. Potter, *Magazine of American History*, January 1878.
13. *Almanac*, 39-40.
14. A recap of the various estimates of those killed at the Alamo, on both sides, can be found at Santos, Santa Anna's Campaign against Texas, 79.
15. Williams, *SWHQ*, 37:307.
16. Foote, 2:210-212.
17. James Bonham served as messenger twice for Travis and he returned empty handed both times. His second return, on March 3, meant he was going back to almost certain death and still he went to report the results of his mission to Travis. His action is considered one of the bravest of the entire Alamo saga.
18. Williams, *SWHQ*, 37:306.
19. Jenkins, document number 2222.
20. Williams, *SWHQ*, 37:24-25.
21. Foote, 2:219-222.
22. Ibid, 2:194-196.
23. Jenkins, document number 1762.
24. Binkley, 328.
25. Gulick, 3:307-308.
26. Binkley, 345-346.
27. Ibid, 423-424.
28. Ibid, 409-410.
29. Williams, *SWHQ*, 37:24-25.
30. Potter, *Magazine of American History*, January 1878.
31. *SWHQ*, 48:16-17.
32. Ibid, 23.
33. Foote, 2:219-222. Travis' letter of March 3 contains a description of how he felt about the local Mexicans.
34. Williams, *SWHQ*, 37:272-273.
35. Ibid, in notes.
36. De Zavala, 23-25.
37. Binkley, 272-275.
38. Ibid, 349-351.
39. Jenkins, document number 1877.
40. *Fort Worth Gazette*, July 12, 1889.
41. Foote, 2:219-222.
42. DRT Library at the Alamo.
43. *SWHQ*, 38:49-50.
44. Ibid, 9:190-192.

Sources

Articles:

Almonte, Colonel Juan Nepomuceno, "The Private Journal of Juan Nepomuceno Almonte," *Southwestern Historical Quarterly*, volume 48, July 1944.

Austin, Stephen F., "General Austin's Order Book for the Campaign of 1835," *Southwestern Historical Quarterly*, volume 2, January 1899.

Bowie, John J., "Early Life in the Southwest — The Bowies," *DeBow's Review*, volume 13, October 1852.

Connelly, Thomas L. [editor], "Did David Crockett Surrender at the Alamo? A Contemporary Letter," *Journal of Southern History*, August 1960.

Hunnicutt, Helen, "A Mexican View of the Texas War: Memoirs of a Veteran of the Two Battles of the Alamo," *The Library Chronicle*, volume IV, Austin: University of Texas, summer 1951.

McCullough-Williams, "A Man and His Knife, Passages from the Life of James Bowie," *Harper's Magazine*, July 1898.

Potter, Reuben, *The Fall of the Alamo*, 1860 [phamphlet].

Potter, Reuben, "The Fall of the Alamo," *Magazine of American History*, January 1878.

Books:

Austin, Stephen F., *The Austin Papers*, complied and edited by Eugene C. Barker, volume 1 and 2 (Washington: Government Printing Office, 1924 and 1928), volume 3 (Austin: University of Texas Press, 1927).

Baker, D. W. C., *A Texas Scrap-Book*. (New York: A. S. Barnes & Company, 1875).

Barker, E. C. and Williams, A. W. [editors], *The Writings of Sam Houston*, 7 volumes (Austin: The University of Texas Press, 1938).

Binkley, William C. [editor], *Official Correspondence of the Texas Revolution, 1835-1836.*, 2 vols. (New York: D. Appleton-Century Company, 1938).

Bowie, Walter W., *The Bowies and their Kindred* (Washington, 1899).

Brooker, William, *Texas: An Epitome of Texas History* (Columbus: Nitsche Brothers, 1897).

Burke, James Wakefield, *David Crockett: The Man Behind the Myth* (Austin: Eakin Press, 1984).

Castaneda, Carlos E., *The Mexican Side of the Revolution* (Dallas: P. L. Turner, 1928).

Davis, Robert E. [editor], *The Diary of William Barret Travis: August 30, 1833 - June 1834* (Waco: Texian Press, 1976). (Reprint of the original diary with extensive notes.)

De Zavala, Adina, *History and Legends of the Alamo and Other Missions In and Around San Antonio* (San Antonio: by the author, 1917).

DeShields, James T., *Tall Men with Long Rifles: The Glamorous Story of the Texas Revolution, as Told by Captain Creed Taylor* (San Antonio: Naylor Co., 1935).

Dixon, Sam Houston and Louis Kemp, *The Heroes of San Jacinto* (Houston: The Anson Jones Press, 1932).

Dobie, J. Frank [editor], *In the Shadow of History* (Austin: Texas Folklore Society, 1939).

Dobie, J. Frank, "James Bowie," *Heroes of Texas* (Waco: Texian Press, 1946).

Elfer, Maurice, *Madame Candelaria, Unsung Heroine of the Alamo* (Houston: Rein Company, 1933).

Fehrenbach, T. R., *Lone Star: A History of Texas and the Texans* (New York: McMillan, 1968).

Foote, Henry S., *Texas and the Texans*, 2 volumes (Philadelphia: Thomas, Cowperthwait & Co., 1841).

Ford, John S., *Origin and Fall of the Alamo: March 6, 1836* (San Antonio: Johnson Brothers Printing Co., 1901).

Gammel, H. P. M. [compiler and arranger], *The Laws of Texas, 1822-1897*, 10 volumes (Austin: The Gammel Book Company, 1898).

Houston, Andrew Jackson, *Texas Independence* (Houston: The Anson Jones Press, 1938).

Huson, Hobart [editor], *Dr. J. H. Barnard's Journal* (privately published, 1950).

Huston, Cleburne, *Deaf Smith, Incredible Texas Spy* (Waco: Texian Press, 1973).

Gray, William F., *From Virginia to Texas* (privately published, 1909).

Grosvenor, Charles, [Introduction and notes], *The Fall of the Alamo*, by Reuben Potter (Hillsdale, New York: The Otterden Press, 1977). This book is a reprint of the Potter story that appeared in the January 1878 issue of the *Magazine of American History*, with an introduction and extensive, updated notes.

Gulick, Charles A., Jr. [editor], *The Papers of Mirabeau Buonaparte Lamar*, 3 volumes (Austin, Texas State Library, 1930).

Jenkins, John H., [General Editor], *The Papers of the Texas Revolution, 1835-1836,* 10 volumes (Austin: Presidial Press, 1973).

Kemp, Louis W., *The Signers of the Texas Declaration of Independence* (Houston: The Anson Jones Press, 1944).

Kilgore, Dan, *How Did Davy Die?* (College Station: Texas A&M University, 1978).

King, Richard C., *Susanna Dickinson: Messenger of the Alamo* (Austin: Shoal Creek Publishers, Inc., 1976).

Lord, Walter, *A Time to Stand* (New York: Harper & Brothers, 1961).

Lord, Walter, "Myths and Realities of the Alamo," *The Republic of Texas* (Palo Alto, California: American West Publishing Company, 1968).

Meyers, John, *The Alamo* (New York: E. P. Dutton, 1948).

Morphis, J. M., *History of Texas* (New York: United States Publishing Company, 1875).

Muster Rolls of the Texas Revolution (Austin: Daughters of the Republic of Texas, Inc., 1986).

Paddock, B. B., *History of Texas, Fort Worth & Northwest Texas Edition,* 5 volumes (Chicago: Lewis Publishing Co., 1922).

Pena, Enrique de la, *With Santa Anna in Texas,* translated and edited by Carmen Perry (College Station: Texas A&M University, 1975).

Powell, E. Alexander, *The Road to Glory* (New York: Charles Scribner's Sons, 1915).

Rosenthal, Phil and Bill Groneman, *Roll Call at the Alamo* (Fort Collins, Colorado: Old Army Press, 1985).

Santos, Richard G., *Santa Anna's Campaign Against Texas* (Waco: Texian Press, 1968).

Shackford, James A. and Stanley Folmsbee, *A Narrative on the Life of David Crockett* (Knocksville: University of Tennessee Press, 1973).

Sutherland, Dr. John, *The Fall of the Alamo* (San Antonio: Naylor Co., 1936).

Tinkle, Lon, *Thirteen Days to Glory* (New York: McGraw-Hill, 1958).

The Alamo Long Barrack Museum, published by the Daughters of the Republic of Texas, 1986.

The Texas Almanac, 1857-1873: A Compendium of Texas History (Waco: Texian Press, 1967).

Tolbert, Frank X., *The Day of San Jacinto* (New York: Pemberton Press, 1959).

Turner, Martha Anne, *William Barret Travis: His Sword and His Pen* (Waco: Texian Press, 1978).

Wallace, Ernest [editor], *Documents of Texas History* (Austin: The Steck Company, 1960).

Webb, Walter P., [Editor-in-Chief], *The Handbook of Texas,*
    3 volumes (Austin: Texas State Historical Association,
    1952-1976).
Yoakum, Henderson, *History of Texas From Its First Settlement in
    1685 to Its Annexation to the United States in 1846,* 2 volumes
    (New York: Redfield, 1856).

Manuscripts:

Cloud, Daniel William, various letters in the Daughters of the
    Republic of Texas Library at the Alamo.
Mixon, Ruby, *William Barret Travis, His Life and His Letters.*
    Masters Thesis, University of Texas, 1930.
Williams, Amelia W., *A Critical Study of the Siege of the Alamo and
    of the Personnel of Its Defenders.* Ph.D. Thesis, University of
    Texas, 1931.

Newspapers:

Columbia, Tennessee *Observer,* April 14, 1836
Corpus Christi *Times,* July 31, 1974.
Fort Worth Gazette, July 12, 1889.
Houston *Morning Star,* March 14, 1840.
New Orleans *Post Union,* March 29, 1836.
New Yorker, April 16 and 30, 1836.
San Antonio *Daily Express,* January 5, 1878; April 28, 1881; May
    12 and 19, 1907.
Telegraph and Texas Register, March 24, 1836.
The Dallas Morning News, February 12, 1911.

Official Records:

Bexar County Archives; Daughters of the Republic of Texas Library
at the Alamo; Archives of the Texas State Library in Austin;
Records of the Barker Texas History Center, University of Texas;
Texas and Dallas Collection, Dallas Public Library.

Index

About the Author

Wallace Owen Chariton is a fifth-generation native Texan who was born in Fort Worth and raised in San Antonio — almost, as they say, in the shadow of the Alamo. He attended Texas Tech University in Lubbock and now lives with his family in Plano.

Chariton's ancestor, Harrison Owen, originally came to Texas in 1836 to join in the fight for independence. While on his way to join Travis at the Alamo, Owen learned of the fall of that mission fortress and marched off in search of what remained of the Texas army. Owen was subsequently assigned by Sam Houston to help warn settlers of the advance of the Mexican army and to urge everyone in Texas to move east of the Brazos River in what came to be called the "Runaway Scrape." Owen was off following Houston's orders on April 21, 1836 when the decisive battle of San Jacinto occurred.

Fiercely proud of his Lone Star State heritage, Chariton has had a life-long love affair with the Alamo and anything Texan. He has studied the state's history and heritage from the days of the Republic of Texas to the present. He is a dedicated collector of Texanna and his first book, *Texas Centennial: The Parade of an Empire* (self-published in 1979) chronicled the Texas centennial and established the value of many artifacts from that celebration.

Chariton is also an avid collector of sayings used in the everyday Texas language, Texas trivia, quotations by Texans, as well as Texas jokes and humor. In addition to the Alamo books, he is the author of *This Dog'll Hunt*, an entertaining Texas dictionary, *Rainy Days in Texas Workbook*, a fun book designed to entertain and educate children, and *Texas Wit and Wisdom*, a collection of anecdotes from the world of Texas and Texans.

100 DAYS
IN
TEXAS
THE ALAMO LETTERS

Wallace O. Chariton

The period between December 9, 1835, the day the Mexican army first hoisted a white flag over the Alamo, until March 17, 1836, the day Texas got a new constitution and Sam Houston first wrote that the Alamo must be avenged, is one of the most dramatic one hundred day periods in Texas history. During these one hundred days, the meager Texas army went from being undefeated to almost being annihilated. No one could predict what fate lay ahead for Texas.

The story of those dramatic days can best be told by the men who lived through and died in the adventure. To allow those participants to tell their story, Wallace O. Chariton searched for years to uncover as many documents as possible that relate, either directly or indirectly, to the Alamo saga. The documents uncovered include primary letters by participants, government proceedings, selected newspaper articles, diary and notebook entries, muster rolls, and even receipts. The material is presented in chronological order so the entire story, including the joy, optimism, pain, panic, and even the humor, unfolds exactly as it did in 1835-1836. The original documentation is supported by vintage photographs, maps, charts, and extensive endnotes to make this book an adventure in itself because it is, after all, the true story of the Alamo.

FORGET
THE
ALAMO

Wallace O. Chariton

Historians have argued for years that William B. Travis and the men in his command made a tragic mistake when they chose to face Antonio Lopez de Santa Anna's army from the huge, dilapidated mission San Antonio de Valero — the Alamo. The theory is that the 180-odd men in Travis's command might have fared much better had they chosen to make their dramatic stand against tyranny from one of the smaller, more compact missions in the San Antonio area. But does the theory have validity?

After years of intensive research, Wallace O. Chariton has addressed that question and the answer is dramatic. Much of what you read in this book is absolute historical fact. The remainder is interpolated fiction based on the actual events and on predictions of how the main characters might have reacted under slightly different circumstances.

This is a book of what ifs: What if Travis, Bowie, Crockett, Bonham, and the others had chosen Mission Concepcion as their fortress of destiny? What if James Fannin was the hero of the Texas revolution instead of the goat? What if Sam Houston had been the goat? The evidence shows it all could have so easily happened and if it had, the pages of Texas history would tell a vastly different story.